Lying and Truthfulness

Other titles from
HACKETT READINGS

Certainty
Free Will
God
The Good Life
Human Nature
The Idea of Race
Justice
Life and Death
Materialism and the Mind-Body Problem
Reality
Time

Lying and Truthfulness

Edited, with Introductions, by

Kevin DeLapp and Jeremy Henkel

Hackett Publishing Company, Inc.
Indianapolis/Cambridge

Printed in the United States of America

19 18 17 16 1 2 3 4 5 6 7

For further information, please address
Hackett Publishing Company, Inc.
P.O. Box 44937
Indianapolis, Indiana 46244-0937

www.hackettpublishing.com

Composition by Aptara, Inc.

Cataloging-in-Publication data is on file with the Library of Congress.
978-1-62466-450-2 (paperback)
978-1-62466-451-9 (cloth)

The paper used in this publication meets the minimum requirements of American National Standard for Information Sciences—Permanence of Paper for Printed Library Materials, ANSI Z39.48–1984.

∞

TABLE OF CONTENTS

INTRODUCTION

Across a wide range of philosophical curricula, the phenomena related to lying are frequently deployed in the form of thought experiments, examples, and objections. Ethics classes often rely on scenarios involving lying and honesty as means of pumping intuitions and adjudicating competing normative theories. In discussions within epistemology, the philosophy of mind, and the philosophy of language, the topic of lying helps sharpen analyses of concepts such as intention, assertion, belief, and reliable inference. The well-known Liar's Paradox (whether the sentence "This sentence is a lie" could itself be true, or even have a truth value at all) is a thriving cottage industry within philosophical logic. Indeed, we might even say that lying served as the midwife for the very birth of all modern Western philosophy, when Rene Descartes (1596–1650) framed his groundbreaking new skeptical method by wondering about the possibilities of deception. (And that statement itself raises an important question: Is exaggeration a form of lying?)

Despite the central role that lying has played within philosophy, its theoretical genealogy has been sadly neglected. While several important analyses of the definition and ethics of lying have appeared over the years, there has been very little appreciation for the rich history of what earlier philosophers have had to say on the subject. Moreover, most of the attention that has been given to the philosophy of lying has failed (like so many other areas of philosophy) to engage with the many insightful treatments that have been offered by thinkers from non-Western traditions.

This anthology brings together the most influential and sophisticated accounts of lying, deception, and truthfulness from several of the world's philosophical traditions. One advantage of including multiple traditions is that it highlights the real multiplicity and complexity of the topic. While many of the authors included in this volume are primarily addressing the questions of how lying is to be *defined* and whether (and under what conditions) it might be *ethically permitted*, many of the authors are also exploring other important corollaries such as:

- the difference (conceptual as well as ethical), if any, between overtly lying to someone versus passively allowing them to persist in believing something false;

- the diverse constellation of subsidiary phenomena, such as the breaking of promises, treaties, and contracts; the swearing of oaths; and speaking with exaggeration, secrecy, flattery, ambiguity, or subtle insinuation;
- the different status of lies within the fields of politics, religion, education, and war;
- how lying and truthfulness stand in relation to human nature and psychology;
- and even the aesthetics of deception, i.e., whether we take pleasure in deceiving and being deceived, and whether art essentially lies about reality.

A common orientation for presenting philosophical topics of this sort is to proceed chronologically. We have not followed this convention for two reasons. First, the philosophical debates about lying have not received linear or cumulative attention—such that a purely historical progression of selections would give the misleading appearance that later thinkers were in all cases responding explicitly to their predecessors. Given the inclusion of non-Western materials in this volume, such an approach would be particularly problematic for our purposes. Second, in many cases it seems plausible to find within certain selections entirely new ways of framing an issue or using terminology, and a chronological arrangement might project more commensurability between authors and traditions than is warranted.

Despite the inclusion of non-Western sources, we have also not elected to organize this book by philosophical tradition, and this for the same reasons we have chosen not to organize it chronologically. Instead of either a purely historical or a tradition-based arrangement, we have opted for an organization that integrates voices from different traditions; voices who might nonetheless be addressing similar questions either in similar ways or in ways that differ from one another in an informative way. Specifically, we have divided the selections into the following broad categories: (1) What is a lie?, (2) Is it morally permissible to lie?, and (3) What is the value of truthfulness?

Of course, many of our selections range in their analyses over more than one of these questions, and we resist subdividing each excerpt on the grounds that it would hamper critical engagement with any single voice. We hope, though, that this topical arrangement might stimulate more fruitful juxtapositions and encourage readers to think through their own comparisons. Furthermore, in ordering the three sections as we have, we also do not mean to suggest any logical priority of one over the other. Although we have placed the conceptual question *What is a lie?* prior to the evaluative question *Is it morally permissible to lie?*, we leave it as an open question whether definitions must, or indeed *can*, be settled without first investigating or appealing to ethical intuitions concerning lying and truthfulness. As is apparent from the final chapter (chapter 20, "The State of the Art"), a majority of contemporary analytic philosophy prioritizes the conceptual over the evaluative in precisely this way. One of the advantages of taking a culturally and historically comparative perspective on lying and truthfulness is that it illustrates the contingency of this default methodology. The composers of the *Mahābhārata*, those in the Confucian tradition, and certain classical Christian authors might find it inconceivable that the question of how a lie is to be defined could be bracketed from normative notions of the human good, moral exemplars, or God's benevolence.

It is not the purpose of this book to articulate or defend any specific answer to the three questions posed in the section titles: many of the selections disagree with one another about lying and truthfulness, and we leave it to the reader to reflect on which accounts she finds most compelling and how different authors' terminologies and ways of framing the issues might be made consistent. Nevertheless, certain conceptual trajectories can be discerned within each section.

First, with respect to the question *What is a lie?*, we begin with Augustine's analysis of a liar as one "who has one thing in his mind and utters another in words." Augustine disambiguates lies proper from mere falsehoods and jokes, actively deceiving versus passively going along with a deception, and the role of intention and harm in defining and condemning genuine lies. He also draws from the Bible to provide examples, evidence, and test cases, and he extrapolates at length about how his philosophical definition of lying can jibe with specific topics in Christian casuistry (namely, circumcision, rape, bearing false witness, and apostasy). Augustine in many ways is responsible for bequeathing to the subsequent history of Western philosophy a particular way of framing the topic of lying, and the selection by Hugo Grotius, writing over a thousand years later, shows the extent and influence of the former's thought. In Grotius, additionally, we begin to see the association of lying and truthfulness with Enlightenment conceptions of individual rights and liberties, as well as with particular applications to the question of strategic deception in military contexts. The selections from Aristotle offer an alternative way of framing the definition of lying: instead of appealing to what is in the mind of the liar or to putative claims which others might have on our truth-telling, Aristotle grounds the notion of lying in personal habits and traits of honesty. His analysis of the way deception operates in different rhetorical contexts also helps remind us of the real breadth of the topic, insofar as actual embodied human discourse is rarely solely a matter of exchanging direct assertions and declarative sentences. The section concludes with an excerpt from the *Mahābhārata* which reflects on the dangers of a myopic or legalistic fixation on truth-telling, and explores the ways in which equivocation and conversational context can affect whether something is genuinely a lie or not.

In the second section, *Is it morally permissible to lie?*, the authors of the selections are still engaged in trying to define lying and its various subcategories, but the analyses focus more on the rightness or wrongness of those practices. We begin this discussion with excerpts from classical Confucian thinkers who paint a portrait of the ethically ideal person who is trustworthy and eschews ingratiation, without being naive concerning dissimulation and when it might be appropriate. Immanuel Kant offers a radically different approach, looking less at how trustworthiness is embodied in trustworthy people, but instead formulating a universal rational principle that can adjudicate the permissibility of lying. Kant's analysis is one of the most famous in the philosophy of lying, but we have here included multiple selections from his various writings in order to highlight the actual diversity of his thought on the subject. We then return to the *Mahābhārata* to explore cases in which overly literal or obsessive honesty can become ethically worse than lying. In light of the subtle approach that the *Mahābhārata* urges, we consider Plato's condemnation of rhetorical abuses of truth as well as his influential defense of so-called "noble falsehoods" told by enlightened rulers for the sake of the good of a community. Chapter 10 returns to ancient China and presents the views of Sunzi and Han Feizi, who defend the ethical permissibility of deception and secrecy in certain extreme cases of martial and political strife. In the selection from Thomas Aquinas, we revisit the Christian casuistical project initiated by Augustine and the conceptual landscape is broadened to include perjury, oaths, jokes, and the question of what particular type of sin is involved in lying. The Buddhist selections that follow present an interesting contrast to Aquinas' Christian framework. In the "Discourse to Prince Abhaya," the Buddha suggests that the beneficial outcomes of a lie ought to be factored into its ethical evaluation, and also notes the difference between something being true and being worth communicating. The excerpt from the *Lotus Sutra* expands upon both these points by offering a concrete example of an instance of permissible deception, with implications for how to interpret seemingly contradictory or "deceptive" texts more generally. The final selections for this section are from the Enlightenment thinkers Thomas Hobbes and David Hume, who connect the ethics of lying with conceptions of human nature and the social necessity of mutual trust.

The third section of the book considers the question *What is the value of truthfulness?* The issue of "value" here is in many ways broader than the specific ethical focus of the preceding section. There, the primary focus was on whether lies and other forms of deception or misdirection are permissible, but the authors in this section ask even more fundamental questions concerning the role of truth in human life generally. Francis Bacon examines the connection between truthfulness, pleasure, and the good life, and John Locke draws our attention to some of the aesthetic dimensions of truthfulness and deception. In the *Mahābhārata* excerpt, truthfulness is analyzed as the root of all values and duties, even trans-moral ones. And the Buddhist "Discourse on the Parable of the Water Snake" situates truth and truthfulness in the context of skepticism, motivation, and cognition more broadly. The final selection, by Friedrich Nietzsche, highlights the many (not always gentle) historical and institutional forces operative in shaping the way we think and speak about truth and lies.

A concluding chapter provides an overview of how the debate has evolved within some areas of twentieth- and twenty-first-century philosophy.

Each selection is prefaced with an introduction designed to provide historical, cultural, and methodological context. Open-ended questions are included for each reading, which can help stimulate reflection and discussion, draw attention to specific distinctions and assumptions in the text, and suggest possible points of contact between different traditions.

Several additional editorial choices need to be acknowledged. First, the reader will notice that there are no selections from women philosophers. Women have made numerous contributions within the history of world philosophy, but a majority of them have sadly been neglected or marginalized by various canonizing powers. Although contemporary historiography of philosophy continues to make vital progress in recovering women's voices (or else more explicitly critiquing their exclusion), what exists thus far does not deal directly with the subjects of lying or truthfulness. This presents something of a historical irony insofar as many male theorists across cultures casually either associated women with trickery and deceit, or else treated deceptions made toward women differently than those made toward men. Note, for example, in this volume, Confucius' condemnation of "feminine wiles," or the differential way in which Plato applies his noble falsehood to women (and old men) as opposed to other citizens, or the special attention Augustine lavishes on whether women can lie to escape rape or sexual blandishment, etc. We hope that this volume will help make these biases and the historical exclusion of women more apparent, and in the final chapter we note the ways in which certain contemporary women philosophers (such as Sissela Bok, Jennifer Saul, and Jennifer Lackey) have challenged, expanded, and advanced the subject.

Other editorial minutiae: our selections are drawn from very different eras and languages, and we have elected to preserve original spellings, typographies, and formatting styles where possible. Thus, for example, older editions or translations may use B.C. as a dating nomenclature whereas later ones opt for BCE, or may use single quotations instead of double quotes. In an effort to help facilitate further reading and research, we have specified any chapter, section, or sub-section numbering from primary sources—although formatting may differ from selection to selection in accordance with the original author's, translator's, or editor's style. British spelling conventions have been retained according to respective copyright. We have also made the choice to insert diacritical marks for the Indian selections in an attempt to more accurately render proper names and technical terms. A short pronunciation guide for the Indian and Chinese selections is included as an appendix. Finally, several of our selections feature original footnotes from the author or translator, and we have distinguished these from additional notes that we have supplied by placing the latter in brackets.

Throughout the process of putting this volume together, we have received enormous help and support from the staff at Hackett Publishing Company, and we would like especially to thank Deborah Wilkes, Christina Kowalewski, Laura Clark, and Jennifer McBride for their editorial stewardship. We are also grateful to Cambridge University Press for the rights to reprint the selections from Kant's *Metaphysics of Morals* and *Lectures on Ethics* and from Nietzsche, as well as to Columbia University Press for the rights to reprint all selections from the *Lotus Sutra* and *Han Feizi* (see the Sources & Permissions listing at the end of this volume). Lastly, we would like to thank our students at Converse College (in a first-year course on "Truth and Lying" in fall 2010) and Wofford College (during an upper-level course on "Language, Truth, and Ethics" in spring 2015) who served as critical and enthusiastic guinea pigs for this material as it was in development. Their insights, questions, and suggestions helped to clarify our focus and appreciate connections between different selections.

PART ONE

WHAT IS A LIE?

1

AUGUSTINE

Saint Augustine (354–430) was bishop of Hippo, a Roman province in northern Africa, and was an important voice in the developing systematic theology of early Christianity. He explored the philosophy of lying in several of his works (something he alludes to in the opening of the first selection), but these excerpts from his *Enchiridion* ("Handbook") and *De Mendacio* ("Of Lying") are the most sustained and substantive analyses.

Stylistically, as a theologian, Augustine takes pains to ground his ethical claims in a way that is consistent with his reading of Christian scripture and the other inherited teachings of his tradition. Frequently, religious examples are used to illustrate a point, whereas at other times, biblical passages are taken as data that must be accommodated in an acceptable analysis. It is worth reflecting on whether any of Augustine's analyses might be nonstarters for those who do not share his particular religious commitments, such as whether circumcision or idolatry can constitute forms of lying, or whether interpreting the Bible in figurative terms involves viewing the text as somehow deceitful at the literal level.

Augustine's line of reasoning can be difficult to follow at times. He often introduces a new viewpoint by first laying out what "some" versus "others" think about it, which sometimes makes his own commitments harder to discern. In this regard, it may be worth keeping in mind the metaphor which Augustine himself suggests at the beginning of the *De Mendacio* selection: the philosophy of lying can be "full of dark corners, and has many cavern-like windings," and he is intent on taking his reader down each path and blind alley in this maze in an effort to fully map out the conceptual terrain. His accomplishment in doing so is evident in the fact that his positions and even many of his examples have continued to serve as jumping-off points for later philosophers, such as the scenario of being deceived into a roadside ambush, or of lying to protect an innocent person one might be harboring.

Augustine consistently affirms the sinfulness of lying. The specific definition of "lying," however, receives far subtler treatment, and Augustine also disambiguates *degrees* of sin when it comes to lying. Lies proper are differentiated from both jokes (where there is no expectation of truthfulness) and falsehoods, since sometimes even knowingly telling the truth can be a way of trying to deceive someone—for instance, if you think that the person will not believe you. By invoking a distinction between the motivation or cause of a deception and its effects (harmful or beneficial), Augustine thereby makes possible several new dimensions of complication, such as whether one can lie to oneself, whether one can mime a lie outwardly while eschewing it inwardly, and whether something with elusive or purely figurative meaning (as Augustine thinks parts of the Bible can be) can serve truth in other ways. Intentionality (which he sometimes refers to poetically as speaking with the "mouth of the heart") also helps Augustine differentiate lying as an action from the state of being a liar.

Although the selections for this first section focus more on the definition of lying, for Augustine that question is inseparable from the issue of whether lying is ethically permissible. He offers several reasons for viewing all lies as sinful, and certain lies as more or less sinful than others. The potential for harm is an important part of what makes lies morally wrong, he claims, but he understands "harm" as involving primarily spiritual rather than physical damage. That is, being lied to (especially about vital doctrinal matters pertaining to salvation) or telling lies taints one's soul in a way that has both theological ramifications (jeopardizing one's status in the afterlife) and aesthetic dimensions (lying "pollutes" the liar in an ugly way). In addition, lying abuses not only the trust of others (and for this reason, Augustine thinks it is wrong to lie for the pedagogical purpose of helping the deceived appreciate higher truths) but also what Augustine sees as the teleological function of language, namely, to match words to reality.

As you assess Augustine's arguments, reflect on the following questions as well:

1. How much of Augustine's ethics of lying hinges on his particular metaphysical commitments? Would his arguments fare differently to someone who had different beliefs concerning God, the soul, or the afterlife?

2. In the opening discussion of the *Enchiridion,* Augustine states that rashly believing and promulgating something that is actually false is not technically the same as lying, though it might be ethically wrong for other reasons. To what extent do we have a responsibility to diligently investigate the truth before consenting to believe it? Can you give examples (or counterexamples) of the difference between deliberate lying and negligent truth-holding?
3. In *De Mendacio,* Augustine argues that biblical episodes, which might otherwise appear to condone lying, can instead be interpreted as merely figurative. Are there other examples (literary or otherwise) that you can think of which might involve a similar figurative distortion? In general, by what criteria can we decide whether or not a given text is to be read as deceptive rather than figurative?

Enchiridion

18. But here arises a very difficult and very intricate question, about which I once wrote a large book, finding it necessary to give it an answer. The question is this: whether at any time it can become the duty of a good man to tell a lie? For some go so far as to contend that there are occasions on which it is a good and pious work to commit perjury even, and to say what is false about matters that relate to the worship of God, and about the very nature of God Himself. To me, however, it seems certain that every lie is a sin, though it makes a great difference with what intention and on what subject one lies. For the sin of the man who tells a lie to help another is not so heinous as that of the man who tells a lie to injure another; and the man who by his lying puts a traveler on the wrong road, does not do so much harm as the man who by false or misleading representations distorts the whole course of a life. No one, of course, is to be condemned as a liar who says what is false, believing it to be true, because such a one does not consciously deceive but rather is himself deceived. And, on the same principle, a man is not to be accused of lying, though he may sometimes be open to the charge of rashness, if through carelessness he takes up what is false and holds it as true; but, on the other hand, the man who says what is true, believing it to be false, is, so far as his own consciousness is concerned, a liar. For in saying what he does not believe, he says what to his own conscience is false, even though it should in fact be true; nor is the man in any sense free from lying who with his mouth speaks the truth without knowing it, but in his heart wills to tell a lie. And therefore not looking at the matter spoken of, but solely at the intention of the speaker, the man who unwittingly says what is false, thinking all the time that it is true, is a better man than the one who unwittingly says what is true but in his conscience intends to deceive. For the former does not think one thing and say another, but the latter, though his statements may be true in fact, has one thought in his heart and another on his lips; and that is the very essence of lying. But when we come to consider truth and falsehood in respect to the subjects spoken of, the point on which one deceives or is deceived becomes a matter of the utmost importance. For although, as far as a man's own conscience is concerned, it is a greater evil to deceive than to be deceived, nevertheless it is far less evil to tell a lie in regard to matters that do not relate to religion, than to be led into error in regard to matters the knowledge and belief of which are essential to the right worship of God. To illustrate this by example: suppose that one man should say of some one who is dead that he is

still alive, knowing this to be untrue; and that another man should, being deceived, believe that Christ shall at the end of some time (make the time as long as you please) die; would it not be incomparably better to lie like the former than to be deceived like the latter? and would it not be a much less evil to lead some man into the former error, than to be led by any man into the latter?

19. In some things, then, it is a great evil to be deceived; in some it is a small evil, in some no evil at all, and in some it is an actual advantage. It is to his grievous injury that a man is deceived when he does not believe what leads to eternal life, or believes what leads to eternal death. It is a small evil for a man to be deceived, when, by taking falsehood for truth, he brings upon himself temporal annoyances; for the patience of the believer will turn even these to a good use, as when, for example, taking a bad man for a good, he receives injury from him. But one who believes a bad man to be good, and yet suffers no injury, is nothing the worse for being deceived, nor does he fall under the prophetic denunciation: "Woe to those who call evil good!"[1] For we are to understand that this is spoken not about evil men, but about the things that make men evil. Hence the man who calls adultery good, falls justly under that prophetic denunciation. But the man who calls the adulterer good, thinking him to be chaste, and not knowing him to be an adulterer, falls into no error in regard to the nature of good and evil, but only makes a mistake as to the secrets of human conduct. He calls the man good on the ground of believing him to be what is undoubtedly good; he calls the adulterer evil, and the pure man good; and he calls this man good, not knowing him to be an adulterer, but believing him to be pure. Further, if by making a mistake one escapes death, as I have said above once happened to me, one even derives some advantage from one's mistake. But when I assert that in certain cases a man may be deceived without any injury to himself, or even with some advantage to himself, I do not mean that the mistake in itself is no evil, or is in any sense a good; I refer only to the evil that is avoided, or the advantage that is gained, through making the mistake. For the mistake, considered in itself, is an evil: a great evil if it concern a great matter, a small evil if it concern a small matter, but yet always an evil. For who that is of sound mind can deny that it is an evil to receive what is false as if it were true, and to reject what is true as if it were false, or to hold what is uncertain as certain, and what is certain as uncertain? But it is one thing to think a man good when he is really bad, which is a mistake; it is another thing to suffer no ulterior

1. [Isaiah 5:20.]

injury in consequences of the mistake, supposing that the bad man whom we think good inflicts no damage upon us. In the same way, it is one thing to think that we are on the right road when we are not; it is another thing when this mistake of ours, which is an evil, leads to some good, such as saving us from an ambush of wicked men.

22. But every lie must be called a sin, because not only when a man knows the truth and even when, as a man may be, he is mistaken and deceived, it is his duty to say what he thinks in his heart, whether it be true or whether he only think it to be true. But every liar says the opposite of what he thinks in his heart, with purpose to deceive. Now it is evident that speech was given to man, not that men might therewith deceive one another, but that one man might make known his thoughts to another. To use speech, then, for the purpose of deception, and not for its appointed end, is a sin, because it is sometimes possible, by telling a lie, to do service to another. For it is possible to do this by theft also, as when we steal from a rich man, who never feels the loss, to give to a poor man, who is sensibly benefited by what he gets. And the same can be said of adultery also, when, for instance, some woman appears likely to die of love unless we consent to her wishes, while if she lived she might purify herself by repentance; but yet no one will assert that on this account such an adultery is not a sin. And if we justly place so high a value upon chastity, what offense have we taken at truth, that, while no prospect of advantage to another will lead us to violate the former by adultery, we should be ready to violate the latter by lying? It cannot be denied that they have attained a very high standard of goodness who never lie except to save a man from injury; but in the case of men who have reached this standard, it is not the deceit, but their good intention, that is justly praised, and sometimes even rewarded.

De Mendacio

1. There is a great question about Lying, which often arises in the midst of our every day business, and gives us much trouble, that we may not either rashly call that a lie which is not such, or decide that it is sometimes right to tell a lie, that is, a kind of honest, well-meant, charitable lie. This question we will painfully discuss by seeking with them that seek: whether to any good purpose, we need not take upon ourselves to affirm, for the attentive reader will sufficiently gather from the course of the discussion. It is, indeed, very full of dark corners, and has many cavern-like windings, whereby it oft eludes the eagerness of the seeker; so that at one moment what was found seems to slip out of

one's hands, and anon comes to light again, and then is once more lost to sight. At last, however, the chase will bear down more surely, and will overtake our sentence. Wherein if there is any error, yet as Truth is that which sets free from all error, and Falsehood that which entangles in all error, one never errs more safely, methinks, than when one errs by too much loving the truth, and too much rejecting of falsehood. For they who find great fault say it is too much, whereas perhaps Truth would say after all, it is not yet enough. But whoever reads this, you will do well to find no fault until you have read the whole; so will you have less fault to find. Eloquence you must not look for: we have been intent upon things, and upon dispatch in putting out of hand a matter which nearly concerns our every day life, and therefore have had small pains, or almost none, to bestow upon words.

2. Setting aside, therefore, jokes, which have never been accounted lies, seeing they bear with them in the tone of voice, and in the very mood of the joker a most evident indication that he means no deceit, although the thing he utters be not true: touching which kind of discourse, whether it be meet to be used by perfect minds,[1] is another question which we have not at this time taken in hand to clear; but setting jokes apart, the first point to be attended to, is, that a person should not be thought to lie, who lies not.

3. For which purpose we must see what a lie is. For not every one who says a false thing lies, if he believes or opines that to be true which he says. Now between believing and opining there is this difference, that sometimes he who believes feels that he does not know that which he believes (although he may know himself to be ignorant of a thing, and yet have no doubt at all concerning it, if he most firmly believes it): whereas he who opines, thinks he knows that which he does not know. Now whoever utters that which he holds in his mind either as belief or as opinion, even though it be false, he lies not. For this he owes to the faith of his utterance, that he thereby produce that which he holds in his mind, and has in that way in which he produces it. Not that he is without fault, although he lie not, if either he believes what he ought not to believe, or thinks he knows what he knows not, even though it should be true: for he accounts an unknown thing for a known. Wherefore, that man lies, who has one thing in his mind and utters another in words, or by signs of whatever kind. Whence also the heart of him who lies is said to be double; that is, there is a double thought: the one, of that thing which he either knows or thinks to be

1. [The Latin word translated throughout this selection as "mind" is *animus*, better understood as "soul."]

true and does not produce; the other, of that thing which he produces instead thereof, knowing or thinking it to be false. Whence it comes to pass, that he may say a false thing and yet not lie, if he thinks it to be so as he says although it be not so; and, that he may say a true thing, and yet lie, if he thinks it to be false and utters it for true, although in reality it be so as he utters it. For from the sense of his own mind, not from the verity or falsity of the things themselves, is he to be judged to lie or not to lie. Therefore he who utters a false thing for a true, which however he opines to be true, may be called erring and rash: but he is not rightly said to lie; because he has not a double heart when he utters it, neither does he wish to deceive, but is deceived. But the fault of him who lies, is, the desire of deceiving in the uttering of his mind; whether he do deceive, in that he is believed when uttering the false thing; or whether he do not deceive, either in that he is not believed, or in that he utters a true thing with will to deceive, which he does not think to be true: wherein being believed, he does not deceive though it was his will to deceive: except that he deceives in so far as he is thought to know or think as he utters.

4. But it may be a very nice question whether in the absence of all will to deceive, lying is altogether absent. Thus, put the case that a person shall speak a false thing, which he esteems to be false, on the ground that he thinks he is not believed, to the intent, that in that way falsifying his faith he may deter the person to whom he speaks, which person he perceives does not choose to believe him. For here is a person who tells a lie with studied purpose of not deceiving, if to tell a lie is to utter any thing otherwise than you know or think it to be. But if it be no lie, unless when something is uttered with wish to deceive, that person lies not, who says a false thing, knowing or thinking it to be false, but says it on purpose that the person to whom he speaks by not believing him may not be deceived, because the speaker either knows or thinks the other will not believe him. Whence if it appear to be possible that a person should say a false thing on purpose that he to whom it is said may not be deceived, on the other hand there is this opposite case, the case of a person saying the truth on purpose that he may deceive. For if a man determines to say a true thing because he perceives he is not believed, that man speaks truth on purpose that he may deceive: for he knows or thinks that what is said may be accounted false, just because it is spoken by him. Wherefore in saying a true thing on purpose that it may be thought false, he says a true thing on purpose to deceive. So that it may be inquired, which rather lies: he who says a false thing that he may not deceive, or he who says a true thing that he may deceive? The one knowing or thinking that

he says a false thing, and the other knowing or thinking that he says a true thing? For we have already said that the person who does not know the thing to be false which he utters, does not lie if he thinks it to be true; and that that person rather lies who utters even a true thing when he thinks it false: because it is by the sense of their mind that they are to be judged. Concerning these persons therefore, whom we have set forth, there is no small question. The one, who knows or thinks he says a false thing, and says it on purpose that he may not deceive: as, if he knows a certain road to be beset by robbers, and fearing lest some person for whose safety he is anxious should go by that road, which person he knows does not trust him, should tell him that that road has no robbers, on purpose that he may not go by it, as he will think there are robbers there precisely because the other has told him there are none, and he is resolved not to believe him, accounting him a liar. The other, who knowing or thinking that to be true which he says, says it on purpose that he may deceive: for instance, if he tells a person who does not believe him, that there are robbers in that road where he really knows them to be, that he to whom he tells it may then rather go by that road and so fall among robbers, because he thinks that to be false, which the other told him. Which then of these lies? The one who has chosen to say a false thing that he may not deceive? Or the other who has chosen to say a true thing that he may deceive? That one, who in saying a false thing aimed that he to whom he spoke should follow the truth? Or this one, who in saying a true thing aimed that he to whom he spoke should follow a falsehood? Or perhaps have both lied? The one, because he wished to say a false thing: the other, because he wished to deceive? Or rather, has neither lied? Not the one, because he had the will not to deceive: not the other, because he had the will to speak the truth? For the question is not now which of them sinned, but which of them lied: as indeed it is presently seen that the latter sinned, because by speaking a truth he brought it about that a person should fall among robbers, and that the former has not sinned, or even has done good, because by speaking a false thing he has been the means of a person's avoiding destruction. But then these instances may be turned the other way, so that the one should be supposed to wish some more grievous suffering to the person whom he wishes not to be deceived; for there are many cases of persons who through knowing certain things to be true, have brought destruction upon themselves, if the things were such as ought to have continued unknown to them: and the other may be supposed to wish some convenience to result to the person whom he wishes to be deceived; for there have been instances of persons who would have destroyed themselves had they known some evil that had really befallen those who were dear to them, and through deeming it false have spared themselves: and so to be deceived has been a benefit to them, as to others it has been a hurt to know the truth. The question therefore is not with what purpose of doing a kindness or a hurt, either the one said a false thing that he might not deceive, or the other a true thing that he might deceive: but, setting apart the convenience or inconvenience of the persons spoken to, in so far as relates to the very truth and falsehood, the question is, whether both of them or neither has lied. For if a lie is an utterance with will of uttering a false thing, that man has rather lied who willed to say a false thing, and said what he willed, albeit he said it of set purpose not to deceive. But if a lie is any utterance whatever with will to deceive; then not the former has lied, but the latter, who even in speaking truth willed to deceive. And if a lie is an utterance with will of any falsity, both have lied; because both the former willed his utterance to be false, and the latter willed a false thing to be believed concerning his utterance which was true. Further, if a lie is an utterance of a person wishing to utter a false thing that he may deceive, neither has lied; because both the former in saying a false thing had the will to make a true thing believed, and the latter to say a true thing in order that he might make a false thing believed. We shall be clear then of all rashness and all lying, if, what we know to be true or right to be believed, we utter when need is, and wish to make that thing believed which we utter. If, however, either thinking that to be true which is false, or accounting as known that which is to us unknown, or believing what we ought not to believe, or uttering it when need is not, we yet have no other aim than to make that believed which we utter; we do not stand clear indeed of the error of temerity, but we do stand clear of all lying. For there is no need to be afraid of any of those definitions, when the mind has a good conscience, that it utters that which to be true it either knows, or opines, or believes, and that it has no wish to make any thing believed but that which it utters.

5. But whether a lie be at some times useful, is a much greater and more concerning question. Whether, as above, it be a lie, when a person has no will to deceive, or even makes it his business that the person to whom he says a thing shall not be deceived although he did wish the thing itself which he uttered to be false, but this on purpose that he might cause a truth to be believed; whether, again, it be a lie when a person willingly utters even a truth for the purpose of deceiving; this may be doubted. But none doubts that it is a lie when a person willingly utters a falsehood for the purpose of deceiving: wherefore a false utterance put forth with will to deceive is manifestly a lie. But

whether this alone be a lie, is another question. Meanwhile, taking this kind of lie, in which all agree, let us inquire, whether it be sometimes useful to utter a falsehood with will to deceive. They who think it is, advance testimonies to their opinion, by alleging the case of Sarah, who, when she had laughed, denied to the Angels that she laughed: of Jacob questioned by his father, and answering that he was the elder son Esau: likewise that of the Egyptian midwives, who to save the Hebrew infants from being slain at their birth, told a lie, and that with God's approbation and reward: and many such like instances they pick out, of lies told by persons whom you would not dare to blame, and so must own that it may sometimes be not only not blameworthy, but even praiseworthy to tell a lie.[2] They add also a case with which to urge not only those who are devoted to the Divine Books, but all men and common sense, saying, "Suppose a man should take refuge with you, who by your lie might be saved from death, would you not tell it? If a sick man should ask a question which it is not expedient that he should know, and might be more grievously afflicted even by your returning him no answer, will you venture either to tell the truth to the destruction of the man's life, or rather to hold your peace, than by a virtuous and merciful lie to be serviceable to his weak health?" By these sort of arguments they think they most plentifully prove, that if occasion of doing good require, we may sometimes tell a lie.

6. On the other hand, those who say that we must never lie, plead much more strongly, using first the Divine authority, because in the very Decalogue[3] it is written "You shall not bear false witness"; under which general term it comprises all lying: for whoso utters any thing bears witness to his own mind. But lest any should contend that not every lie is to be called false witness, what will he say to that which is written, "The mouth that lies slays the soul":[4] and lest any should

2. [The allusions are from the Hebrew Bible (Christian Old Testament): Sarah, the wife of Abraham, had laughed when she was informed that she would bear a child despite her old age (Genesis 18:12–15); Jacob and Esau are the grandchildren of Sarah and Abraham, and Jacob disguises himself as his elder brother Esau in order to receive the latter's birthright from their father (Genesis 27:18–24); the Egyptian midwives had been commanded by Pharaoh to kill any male Hebrew babies, but they disobeyed this order, thereby delivering Moses (Exodus 1:16–19).]

3. [The Ten Commandments, handed down from God to Moses (Exodus 20: 3–17). The prohibition against bearing false witness is traditionally understood as the ninth commandment.]

4. [Wisdom 1:11.]

suppose that this may be understood with the exception of some liars, let him read in another place, "You will destroy all that speak lies."[5] Whence with His own lips the Lord says, "Let your communication be yea, yea; nay, nay; for whatsoever is more than these comes of evil."[6] Hence the Apostle also in giving precept for the putting off of the old man, under which name all sins are understood, says straightway, "Wherefore putting away lying, speak ye truth."[7]

7. Neither do they confess that they are awed by those citations from the Old Testament which are alleged as examples of lies: for there, every incident may possibly be taken figuratively, although it really did take place: and when a thing is either done or said figuratively, it is no lie. For every utterance is to be referred to that which it utters. But when any thing is either done or said figuratively, it utters that which it signifies to those for whose understanding it was put forth. Whence we may believe in regard of those persons of the prophetical times who are set forth as authoritative, that in all that is written of them they acted and spoke prophetically; and no less, that there is a prophetical meaning in all those incidents of their lives which by the same prophetic Spirit have been accounted worthy of being recorded in writing. As to the midwives, indeed, they cannot say that these women did through the prophetic Spirit, with purpose of signifying a future truth, tell Pharaoh one thing instead of another (albeit that Spirit did signify something, without their knowing what was happening inside them), but they say that these women were according to their degree approved and rewarded of God. For if a person who is used to tell lies for harm's sake comes to tell them for the sake of doing good, that person has made great progress. But it is one thing that is set forth as laudable in itself, another that in comparison with something worse is preferred. It is one sort of congratulation that we express when a man is in sound health, another when a sick man is getting better. In the Scripture, even Sodom is said to be justified in comparison with the crimes of the people Israel.[8] And to this rule they apply all the instances of lying which are produced from the Old Books, and are found not reprehended, or cannot be reprehended:

5. [Psalms 5:6.]

6. [Matthew 5:37.]

7. ["The Apostle" is Saint Paul, born Saul of Tarsus (c. 5–67 CE). The quotation about speaking truth is from Paul's letter to the Ephesians (4:25).]

8. [Sodom was an ancient Canaanite city famously destroyed by God as punishment for the wickedness of its inhabitants (Genesis 19:1–29). Israel is compared unfavorably to Sodom in Ezekiel 16:47–48.]

either they are approved on the score of a progress towards improvement and hope of better things, or in virtue of some hidden signification they are not altogether lies.

8. For this reason, from the books of the New Testament, except the figurative pre-significations used by our Lord, if you consider the life and manners of the Saints, their actions and sayings, nothing of the kind can be produced which should provoke to imitation of lying. For the simulation of Peter and Barnabas is not only recorded, but also reproved and corrected.[9] For it was not, as some suppose, out of the same simulation that even Paul the Apostle either circumcised Timothy, or himself celebrated certain ceremonies according to the Jewish rite; but he did so, out of that liberty of his mind whereby he preached that neither are the Gentiles the better for circumcision, nor the Jews the worse.[10] Wherefore he judged that neither the former should be tied to the custom of the Jews, nor the Jews deterred from the custom of their fathers. Whence are those words of his: "Is any man called being circumcised let him not become uncircumcised. Is any called to be non-circumcised? Let him not be circumcised. Circumcision is nothing, and non-circumcision is nothing, but the keeping of the commandments of God. Let every man abide in the same calling wherein he was called."[11] How can a man become uncircumcised after circumcision? But let him not do so, says he: let him not so live as if he had become uncircumcised, that is, as if he had covered again with flesh the part that was bared, and ceased to be a Jew.

9. But if no authority for lying can be alleged, neither from the ancient Books, be it because that is not a lie which is received to have been done or said in a figurative sense, or be it because good men are not challenged to imitate that which in bad men, beginning to amend, is praised in comparison with the worse; nor yet from the books of the

9. [Peter and Barnabas were early Christian apostles who, while evangelizing in the city of Antioch, committed hypocrisy regarding the observance of Jewish dietary and circumcision customs (Galatians 2:11–13).]

10. [Male circumcision was a long-standing Jewish rite (Leviticus 12:3), as part of a covenant with God dating back to Abraham (Genesis 17:13). "Gentiles" were uncircumcised non-Jews. One of the controversies of early Christianity was whether or not Gentiles who wished to convert would therefore have to undergo circumcision. In this context, there were worries about potential converts lying about being uncircumcised, or about circumcised Christians who were victims of persecution lying about their religious affiliation in order to escape martyrdom. Paul preached a path of accommodation, whereby circumcision became merely optional (Galatians 2:10).]

11. [1 Corinthians 7:18–20.]

New Testament, because Peter's correction rather than his simulation, even as his tears rather than his denial, is what we must imitate: then, as to those examples which are fetched from common life, they assert much more confidently that there is no trust to be given to these. For first they teach, that a lie is iniquity, by many proofs of holy writ, especially by that which is written, You, Lord, hate all workers of iniquity, you shall destroy them that speak lies. For either as the Scripture is wont, in the following clause it expounds the former; so that, as iniquity is a term of a wider meaning, lying is named as the particular sort of iniquity intended: or if they think there is any difference between the two, lying is worse than iniquity in the same degree as destroying is worse than hating. For it may be that God hates a person to that degree more mildly, as not to destroy him, but whom He destroys He hates the more exceedingly, by how much He punishes more severely. Now He hates all who work iniquity: but all who speak lies He also destroys. For those who are moved only by examples: What about a man should seek shelter with you who by your lie may be saved from death? For that death which men are foolishly afraid of who are not afraid to sin, kills not the soul but the body, as the Lord teaches in the Gospel; whence He charges us not to fear that death: but the mouth which lies kills not the body but the soul.[12] For in these words it is most plainly written, "The mouth that lies slays the soul." How then can it be said without the greatest perverseness, that to the end one man may have life of the body, it is another man's duty to incur death of the soul? The love of our neighbor has its bounds in each man's love of himself. "You shall love," says He, "your neighbor as yourself."[13] How can a man be said to love as himself that man, for whom that he may secure a temporal life, himself loses life eternal? Since if for his temporal life he lose but his own temporal life, that is not to love as himself, but more than himself: which exceeds the rule of sound doctrine. Much less then is he by telling a lie to lose his own eternal for another's temporal life. His own temporal life, of course, for his neighbor's eternal life a Christian man will not hesitate to lose: for this example has gone before, that the Lord died for us. To this point He also says, "This is my commandment, that you love one another as I have loved you. Greater love has no man than this, that

12. [In making this point about bodily death being something not worth fearing and something distinct from spiritual well-being, Augustine is not only drawing from the Bible, but also from Plato, upon whose works he was a prominent commentator.]

13. [Matthew 22:39; Mark 12:31; Luke 10:27.]

a man lay down his life for his friends."[14] For none is so foolish as to say that the Lord did other than consult for the eternal salvation of men, whether in doing what He has charged us to do, or in charging us to do what Himself has done. Since then by lying eternal life is lost, never for any man's temporal life must a lie be told. And as to those who take it ill and are indignant that one should refuse to tell a lie, and thereby slay his own soul in order that another may grow old in the flesh; what if by our committing theft, what if by committing adultery, a person might be delivered from death: are we therefore to steal, to commit whoredom? They cannot prevail with themselves in a case of this kind: namely, if a person should bring a noose and demand that one should yield to his carnal lust, declaring that he will hang himself unless his request be granted: they cannot prevail with themselves to comply for the sake of, as they say, saving a life. If this is absurd and wicked, why should a man corrupt his own soul with a lie in order that another may live in the body, when, if he were to give his body to be corrupted with such an object, he would in the judgment of all men be held guilty of nefarious turpitude? Therefore the only point to be attended to in this question is, whether a lie be iniquity. And since this is asserted by the texts above rehearsed, we must see that to ask, whether a man ought to tell a lie for the safety of another, is just the same as asking whether for another's safety a man ought to commit iniquity. But if the salvation of the soul rejects this, seeing it cannot be secured but by equity, and would have us prefer it not only to another's, but even to our own temporal safety: what remains, say they, that should make us doubt that a lie ought not to be told under any circumstances whatsoever? For it cannot be said that there is anything among temporal goods greater or dearer than the safety and life of the body. Wherefore if not even that is to be preferred to truth, what can be put in our way for the sake of which they who think it is sometimes right to lie, can urge that a lie ought to be told?

10. As concerning purity of body; here indeed a very honorable regard seems to come in the way, and to demand a lie in its behalf; to wit, that if the assault of the ravisher may be escaped by means of a lie, it is indubitably right to tell it: but to this it may easily be answered, that there is no purity of body except as it depends on integrity of mind; this being broken, the other must needs fall, even though it seem intact; and for this reason it is not to be reckoned among temporal things, as a thing that might be taken away from people against their will. By no means therefore must the mind corrupt itself by a lie

14. [John 15:13.]

for the sake of its body, which it knows remains incorrupt if from the mind itself incorruptness depart not. For that which by violence, with no lust foregoing, the body suffers, is rather to be called vexation than corruption.[15] Or if all vexation is corruption, then not every corruption has turpitude, but only that which lust has procured, or to which lust has consented. Now by how much the mind is more excellent than the body, so much the more heinous is the wickedness if that [the mind] be corrupted. There, then, purity can be preserved, because there none but a voluntary corruption can have place. For assuredly if the ravisher assault the body, and there is no escaping him either by contrary force, or by any contrivance or lie, we must needs allow that purity cannot be violated by another's lust. Wherefore, since no man doubts that the mind is better than the body, to integrity of body we ought to prefer integrity of mind, which can be preserved for ever. Now who will say that the mind of him who tells a lie has its integrity? Indeed lust itself is rightly defined, "An appetite of the mind by which to eternal goods any temporal goods whatever are preferred." Therefore no man can prove that it is at any time right to tell a lie, unless he be able to show that any eternal good can be obtained by a lie. But since each man departs from eternity just in so far as he departs from truth, it is most absurd to say, that by departing therefrom it is possible for any man to attain to any good. Else if there be any eternal good which truth comprises not, it will not be a true good, therefore neither will it be good, because it will be false. But as the mind to the body, so must also truth be preferred to the mind itself, so that the mind should desire it not only more than the body, but even more than its own self. So will the mind be more entire and chaste, when it shall enjoy the immutability of truth rather than its own mutability. Now if Lot, being so righteous a man that he was meet to entertain even Angels, offered his daughters to the lust of the Sodomites, to the intent, that the bodies of women rather than of men might be corrupted by them;[16] how much more diligently and constantly ought the mind's chasteness in

15. [The translator of this selection (H. Browne, 1887) uses the archaic word "deforcement," meaning to withhold something by means of force. We have substituted the word "vexation" as a more literal translation of Augustine's *vexatio*. Augustine's point, terminology aside, is that it is still morally impermissible to lie even if the lie would save one's body from "ravishing," and that the victim of ravishing who has preserved his or her honesty may be corrupted in body, but not in soul/mind—a situation he acknowledges to be "vexing" but sinless.]

16. [See note 8 above for more on this allusion to the wickedness of Sodom.]

the truth to be preserved, seeing it is more truly preferable to its body, than the body of a man to the body of a woman?

11. But if any man supposes that the reason why it is right for a person to tell a lie for another is, that he may live the while, or not be offended in those things which he much loves, to the end he may attain unto eternal truth by being taught: that man does not understand, in the first place, that there is no villainous thing which he may not upon the same ground be compelled to commit, as has been above demonstrated; and in the next place, that the authority of the doctrine itself is cut off and altogether undone if those whom we attempt to bring thereunto, are by our lie made to think that it is sometimes right to lie. For seeing the doctrine which brings salvation consists partly in things to be believed, partly in things to be understood; and there is no attaining unto those things which are to be understood, unless first those things are believed, which are to be believed; how can there be any believing one who thinks it is sometimes right to lie, unless perhaps he lie at the moment when he teaches us to believe?[17] For how can it be known whether he have at that moment some cause, as he thinks, for a well-meant lie, deeming that by a false story a man may be frightened and kept from lust, and in this way account that by telling a lie he is doing good even in spiritual things? Which kind of lie once admitted and approved, all discipline of faith is subverted altogether; and this being subverted, neither is there any attaining to understanding, for the receiving of which that discipline nurtures the babes: and so all the doctrine of truth is done away, giving place to most licentious falsehood, if a lie, even well-meant, may from any quarter have place opened for it to enter in. For either whoso tells a lie prefers temporal advantages, his own or another's, to truth; than which what can be more perverse? Or when by aid of a lie he wishes to make a person fit for gaining the truth, he bars the approach to truth, for by wishing when he lies to be accommodating, it comes to pass that when he speaks the truth, he cannot be depended upon. Wherefore, either we must not believe good men, or we must believe those whom we think obliged sometimes to tell a lie, or we must not believe that good men sometimes tell lies: of these three the first is pernicious, the second foolish; it remains therefore that good men should never tell lies.

12. Thus has the question been on both sides considered and treated; and still it is not easy to pass sentence: but we must further

17. [Augustine is worried here that, since salvation depends upon faith—which depends upon the beliefs one holds—lies can endanger salvation since they can cause us to form erroneous beliefs.]

lend diligent hearing to those who say, that no deed is so evil, but that in avoidance of a worse it ought to be done; moreover that the deeds of men include not only what they do, but whatever they consent to be done unto them. Wherefore, if cause have arisen that a Christian man should choose to burn incense to idols,[18] that he might not consent to bodily defilement which the persecutor threatened him withal, unless he should do so, they think they have a right to ask why he should not also tell a lie to escape so foul a disgrace. For the consent itself to endure violation of the person rather than to burn incense to idols, this, they say, is not a passive thing, but a deed; which rather than do, he chose to burn incense. How much more readily then would he have chosen a lie, if by a lie he might ward off from a holy body so shocking a disgrace?

15. The whole stress, then, of this question comes to this; whether it be true universally that no sin of another, committed upon you, is to be imputed to you, if, being able to avoid it by a lighter sin of your own, you do it not; or whether there be an exception of all bodily defilement. No man says that a person is defiled by being murdered, or cast into prison, or bound in chains, or scourged, or afflicted with other tortures and pains, or proscribed and made to suffer most grievous losses even to utter nakedness, or stripped of honors, and subjected to great disgrace by reproaches of whatsoever kind; whatever of all these a man may have unjustly suffered, no man is so senseless as to say that he is thereby defiled. But if he have filth poured all over him, or poured into his mouth, or crammed into him, or if he be carnally used like a woman; then almost all men regard him with a feeling of horror, and they call him defiled and unclean. One must conclude then that the sins of others, be they what they may, those always excepted which defile him on whom they are committed, a man must not seek to avoid by sin of his own, either for himself or for any other, but rather he must put up with them, and suffer bravely; and if by no sins of his own he ought to avoid them, therefore not by a lie: but those which by being committed upon a man do make him unclean, these we are bound to avoid even by sinning ourselves; and for this reason those things are not to be called sins, which are done for the purpose of avoiding that uncleanness. For whatever is done, in consideration that the not doing it were just cause of blame, that thing is not sin. Upon the same principle, neither is that to be called uncleanness when there is no way of avoiding it; for even in that extremity he who suffers

18. [Idolatry is forbidden in Christianity, as per the second commandment (Exodus 20:4).]

it has what he may do aright, namely, patiently bear what he cannot avoid. Now no man while acting aright can be defiled by any corporal contagion. For the unclean in the sight of God is every one who is unrighteous; clean therefore is every one who is righteous; if not in the sight of men, yet in the sight of God, Who judges without error. Nay, even in the act of suffering that defilement with power given of avoiding it, it is not by the mere contact that the man is defiled; but by the sin of refusing to avoid it when he might. For that would be no sin, whatever might be done for the avoiding of it. Whoever therefore, for the avoiding of it, shall tell a lie, sins not.

16. Or, are some lies, also, to be excepted, so that it were better to suffer something else than to tell such lies? If so, then not everything that is done in order to avoid defilement ceases to be sin; since certain lies can be worse than suffering foul violence. For, consider someone who might be sexually defiled[19] by another, but that it be possible to screen him by a lie; who dares to say that even in such a case a lie ought not be told?[20] But, if the lie by which he may be concealed be one which may hurt the fair fame of another, by bringing upon him a false accusation of that very uncleanness, to suffer which the other is sought after; as, if it should be said to the inquirer, "Go see so-and-so (naming some chaste man who is a stranger to vices of this kind), and he will procure for you one whom you will find a more willing subject, for he knows and loves such"; and thereby the person might be diverted from him whom he sought. I know not whether one man's fair fame ought to be violated by a lie, in order that another's body may not be violated by lust to which he is a stranger. And in general, it is never right to tell a lie for any man, such as may hurt another, even if the hurt be slighter than would be the hurt to him unless such a lie were told. Because neither must another man's bread be taken from him against his will, though he be in good health, and it is to feed one who is weak; nor must an innocent man, against his will, be beaten

19. [Browne instead has "deflowered."]

20. [Note the potential contrast here with Augustine's earlier conclusions in section 10, where he sharply condemned the telling of lies in order to escape bodily ravishing. Here, he considers a slight variation in which one person might tell a lie to protect a second person, but thereby harm the reputation of a third person. Augustine seems to recognize that this is a murkier case morally, but his comments in the rest of the section can help clarify his stance: just as it would be wrong to steal bread from someone in order to feed a hungry third party, so too would it be wrong to lie to someone in order to protect a defiled third party.]

with rods, that another may not be killed. Of course, if they are willing, let it be done, because they are not hurt if they be willing that so it should be: but whether, even with his own consent, a man's fair fame ought to be hurt with a false charge of foul lusts, in order that lust may be averted from another's body, is a great question. And I know not whether it be easy to find in what way it can be just that a man's fair fame, even with his consent, should be stained with a false charge of lust, any more than a man's body should be polluted by the lust itself against his will.

17. But yet if the option were proposed to the man who chose to burn incense to idols rather than yield his body to abominable lust, that, if he wished to avoid that, he should violate the fame of Christ by some lie; he would be most mad to do it. I say more: that he would be mad, if, to avoid another man's lust, and not to have that done upon his person which he would suffer with no lust of his own, he should falsify Christ's Gospel with false praises of Christ; more eschewing that another man should corrupt his body, than himself to corrupt the doctrine of sanctification of souls and bodies. Wherefore, from the doctrine of religion, and from those utterances universally, which are uttered on behalf of the doctrine of religion, in the teaching and learning of the same, all lies must be utterly kept aloof. Nor can any cause whatever be found, one should think, why a lie should be told in matters of this kind, when in this doctrine it is not right to tell a lie for the very purpose of bringing a person to it the more easily. For, once break or but slightly diminish the authority of truth, and all things will remain doubtful: which unless they be believed true, cannot be held as certain. It is lawful then either to him that discourses, disputes, and preaches of things eternal, or to him that narrates or speaks of things temporal pertaining to edification of religion and piety, to conceal at fitting time whatever seems fit to be concealed: but to tell a lie is never lawful, therefore neither to conceal by telling a lie.

18. This being from the very first and most firmly established, touching other lies the question proceeds more securely. But by consequence we must also see that all lies must be kept aloof which hurt any man unjustly: because no man is to be wronged, even if a lighter one is done to him, that another may have a heavier kept from him. Nor are those lies to be allowed, which, though they hurt not another, yet do nobody any good, and are hurtful to the persons themselves who gratuitously tell them. Indeed, these are the persons who are properly to be called liars. For there is a difference between lying and being a liar. A man may tell a lie unwillingly; but a liar loves to lie, and inhabits in his mind in the delight of lying. Next to such are those to be

placed who by a lie wish to please men, not that they may do wrong or bring reproach upon any man; for we have already before put away that kind; but that they may be pleasant in conversation. These, differ from the class in which we have placed liars in this respect, that liars delight in lying, rejoicing in deceit for its own sake: but these lust to please by agreeable talk, and yet would rather please by saying things that were true, but when they do not easily find true things to say that are pleasant to the hearers, they choose rather to tell lies than to hold their tongues. Yet it is difficult for these sometimes to undertake a story which is the whole of it false; but most commonly they interweave falsehood with truth, where they are at a loss for something sweet. Now these two sorts of lies do no harm to those who believe them, because they are not deceived concerning any matter of religion and truth, or concerning any profit or advantage of their own. It suffices them, to judge the thing possible which is told, and to have faith in a man of whom they ought not rashly to think that he is telling a lie. For where is the harm of believing that such an one's father or grandfather was a good man, when he was not? Or that he has served with the army even in Persia, though he never set foot out of Rome? But to the persons who tell these lies, they do much harm: to the former sort, because they so desert truth as to rejoice in deceit: to the latter, because they want to please people better than the truth.

19. These sorts of lies having been without any hesitation condemned, next follows a sort, as it were by steps rising to something better, which is commonly attributed to well-meaning and good people, when the person who lies not only does no harm to another, but even benefits somebody. Now it is on this sort of lies that the whole dispute turns, whether that person does harm to himself, who benefits another in such sort as to act contrary to the truth. Or, if that alone may be called truth which illustrates the very minds of men with an intimate and constant light, at least he acts contrary to some true thing, because although the bodily senses are deceived, yet he acts contrary to a true thing who says that a thing is so or not so, whereof neither his mind nor senses nor his opinion or belief gives him any report. Whether therefore he does not hurt himself in so profiting another, or in that compensation not hurt himself in which he profits the other, is a great question. If it be so, it should follow that he ought to profit himself by a lie which damages no man. But these things hang together, and if you concede that point, it necessarily draws in its train some very embarrassing consequences. For should it be asked, what harm it does to a person rolling in superfluous wealth, if from countless thousands of bushels of wheat he lose one bushel, which

bushel may be profitable as necessary food to the person stealing it; it will follow that theft also may be committed without blame, and false witness borne without sin. Than which, what can be mentioned more perverse? Or truly, if another had stolen the bushel, and you saw it done, and were questioned, would you tell a lie with honesty for the poor man, and if you do it for your own poverty will you be blamed? As if it were your duty to love another more than yourself. Both then are disgraceful, and must be avoided.

20. But perhaps some may think that there is an exception to be added; that there be some honest lies which not only hurt no man, but profit some man, excepting those by which crimes are screened and defended: so that the reason why the aforesaid lie is disgraceful, is that, although it hurt no man, and profit the poor, it screens a theft; but if it should in such sort hurt nobody and profit somebody as not to screen and defend any sin, it would not be morally wrong. As, put the case that some one should in your sight hide his money that he might not lose it by theft or violence, and thereupon being questioned you should tell a lie; you would hurt no man, and would serve him who had need that his money were hidden, and would not have covered a sin by telling a lie. For it is no sin if a man hide his property which he fears to lose. But, if we therefore sin not in telling a lie, for that, while covering no man's sin, we hurt nobody and do good to somebody, what are we about as concerning the sin itself of a lie? For where it is laid down, "You shall not steal," there is also this, "You shall not bear false witness."[21] Since then each is severally prohibited, why is false witness culpable if it cover a theft or any other sin, but if without any screening of sin it be done by itself, then not culpable, whereas stealing is culpable in and by itself, and so other sins? Or is it so that to hide a sin is not lawful; to do it, lawful?

21. If this be absurd, what shall we say? Is it so, that there is no false witness, but when one tells a lie either to invent a crime against some man, or to hide some man's crime, or in any way to oppress any man in judgment? For a witness seems to be necessary to the judge for cognizance of the cause. But if the Scripture named a witness only so far as that goes, the Apostle would not say, "Yea, and we are found false witnesses of God; because we have testified of God that He raised up Christ: whom He raised not up."[22] For so he shows that it is false witness to tell a lie, yea, in falsely praising a person. Or perhaps, does

21. [Augustine is here again referring to the Ten Commandments of Exodus 20:3–17.]

22. [1 Corinthians 15:15.]

the person who lies then utter false witness he either invents or hides any man's sin, or hurts any man in whatever way? For, if a lie spoken against a man's temporal life is detestable, how much more one against eternal life? As is every lie, if it take place in doctrine of religion. And it is for this reason that the Apostle calls it false witness, if a man tell a lie about Christ, yea, one which may seem to pertain to His praise. Now if it be a lie that neither invents or hides any man's sin, nor is answered to a question of the judge, and hurts no man, and profits some man, are we to say that it is neither false witness, nor a reprehensible lie?

22. What then, if a murderer seek refuge with a Christian, or if he see where the murderer has taken refuge, and be questioned of this matter by him who seeks, in order to bring to punishment a man, the slayer of man? Is he to tell a lie? For how does he not hide a sin by lying, when he for whom he lies has been guilty of a heinous sin? Or is it because he is not questioned concerning his sin, but about the place where he is concealed? So then to lie in order to hide a person's sin is evil; but to lie in order to hide the sinner is not evil? Yea, surely: says some one: for a man sins not in avoiding punishment, but in doing something worthy of punishment. Moreover, it pertains to Christian discipline neither to despair of any man's amendment, nor to bar against any man the way of repentance. What if you be led to the judge, and then questioned concerning the very place where the other is in hiding? Are you prepared to say, either, "He is not there," when you know him to be there; or, "I know not, and have not seen," what you know and hast seen? Are you then prepared to bear false witness, and to slay your soul that a manslayer may not be slain? Or, up to the presence of the judge will you lie, but when the judge questions you, then speak truth that you be not a false witness? So then you are going to slay a man yourself by betraying him. Surely the betrayer too is one whom the divine Scripture detests. Or perhaps is he no betrayer, who in answer to the judge's interrogation gives true information; but would be a betrayer, if, unasked, he should denounce a man to his destruction? Put the case with respect to a just and innocent man, that you know where he is in hiding, and be questioned by the judge; which man, however, has been ordered to be taken to execution by a higher power, so that he who interrogates is charged with the execution of the law, not the author of the sentence? Will it be no false witness that you shall lie for an innocent man, because the interrogator is not a judge, but only charged with the execution? What if the author of the law interrogate you, or any unjust judge, making quest of an innocent man to bring him to punishment? What will you

do? Will you be false witness, or betrayer? Or will he be a betrayer, who to a just judge shall voluntarily report a lurking murderer; and he not so, who to an unjust judge, interrogating him of the hiding-place of an innocent man whom he seeks to slay, shall inform against the person who has thrown himself upon his honor?[23] Or between the crime of false witness and that of betrayal, will you remain doubtful and unable to make up your mind? Or by holding your peace or professing that you will not tell, will you make up your mind to avoid both? Then why not do this before you come to the judge, that you may shun the lie also? For, having kept clear of a lie, you will escape all false witness; whether every lie be false witness, or not every: but by keeping clear of all false witness in your sense of the word, you will not escape all lying. How much braver then, how much more excellent, to say, "I will neither betray nor lie?"

23. This did a former Bishop of the Church of Thagasta, Firmus by name, and even more firm in will.[24] For, when he was asked by command of the emperor, through officers sent by him, for a man who was taking refuge with him, and whom he kept in hiding with all possible care, he made answer to their questions, that he could neither tell a lie, nor betray a man; and when he had suffered so many torments of body (for as yet emperors were not Christian), he stood firm in his purpose. Thereupon being brought before the emperor, his conduct appeared so admirable, that he without any difficulty obtained a pardon for the man whom he was trying to save. What conduct could be more brave and constant? But perhaps some more timid person may say, "I can be prepared to bear any torments, or even to submit to death, that I may not sin"; but, since it is no sin to tell a lie such that you neither hurt any man, nor bear false witness, and benefit some man, it is foolish and a great sin, voluntarily and to no purpose to submit to torments, and, when one's health and life may perhaps be useful, to fling them away for nothing to people in a rage. Of whom I ask; Why he fears that which is written, "You shall not bear false witness," and fears *not* that which is said unto God, "You will destroy all those who speak lies?" Says he, "It is not written, *Every* lie": but I understand it as if it were written, "You will destroy *all* that speak false witness." But neither there is it said, "*All* false witness." "Yes, but

23. [Compare this hypothetical to the one Kant considers at the start of "On a Supposed Right to Lie because of Philanthropic Concerns," in chapter 6 of this volume.]

24. [Augustine himself was born in Thagasta (alternate spelling "Tagaste"). Saint Firmus was bishop there during the end of the third century CE.]

it is set there," says he, "where the other things are set down which are in every sort evil." What, is this the case with what is set down there, "You shall not kill?" If this be in every sort evil, how shall one clear of this crime even just men, who, upon a law given, have killed many? But, it is rejoined, that man does not himself kill, who is the minister of some just command. These men's fear, then, I do accept, that I still think that laudable man who would neither lie, nor betray a man, did both better understand that which is written, and what he understood did bravely put into practice.

24. But one sometimes comes to a case of this kind, that we are not interrogated about the location of the person who is sought, nor forced to betray him, if he is hidden in such a way that he cannot easily be found unless betrayed: but we are asked, whether he be in such a place or not. If we know him to be there, by holding our peace we betray him, or even by saying that we will in no wise tell whether he be there or not: for from this the questioner gathers that he is there, as, if he were not, nothing else would be answered by him who would not lie nor betray a man, but only, that he is not there. So, by our either holding our peace, or saying such words, a man is betrayed, and he who seeks him has but to enter in, if he have the power, and find him: whereas he might have been turned aside from finding him by our telling a lie. Wherefore if you know not where he is, there is no cause for hiding the truth, but you must confess that you know not. But, if you know where he is, whether he be in the place which is named in the question or elsewhere; you must not say, when it is asked whether he be there or not, "I will not tell you what you ask," but you must say, "I know where he is, but I will never show." For if, touching one place in particular you answer not and profess that you will not betray, it is just as if you should point to that same place with your finger: for a sure suspicion is thereby excited. But if at the first you confess that you know where he is, but will not tell, perhaps the inquisitor may be diverted from that place, and begin now to ply you that the place where he is may be betrayed. For which good faith and humanity whatever you shall bravely bear, is judged to be not only not culpable, but even laudable; save only these things which if a man suffer he is said to suffer not bravely, but immodestly and foully. For this is the last description of lie, concerning which we must treat more diligently.

25. For first to be eschewed is that capital lie and far to be fled from, which is done in doctrine of religion; to which lie a man ought by no consideration to be induced. The second, that he should hurt some man unjustly: which is such that it profits no man and hurts some man. The third, which so profits one as to hurt another, but not in corporal

defilement. The fourth, that which is done through only lust of lying and deceiving, which is an unmixed lie. The fifth, what is done with desire of pleasing by agreeableness in talk. All these being utterly eschewed and rejected, there follows a sixth sort which at once hurts nobody and helps somebody; as when, if a person's money is to be unjustly taken from him, one who knows where the money is, should say that he does not know, by whomsoever the question be put. The seventh, which hurts none and profits some: except if a judge interrogate: as when, not wishing to betray a man who is sought for to be put to death, one should lie; not only a just and innocent, but also a culprit; because it belongs to Christian discipline neither to despair of any man's amendment, nor to bar the way of repentance against any. Of which two sorts, which are wont to be attended with great controversy, we have sufficiently treated, and have shown what was our judgment; that by taking the consequences, which are honorably and bravely borne, these kinds also should be eschewed by brave and faithful and truthful men and women. The eighth sort of lie is that which hurts no man, and does good in the preserving somebody from corporal defilement, at least that defilement which we have mentioned above. For the Jews thought even to eat with unwashed hands was defilement. Or if a person think this also a defilement, yet not such that a lie ought to be told to avoid it. But if the lie be such as to do an injury to any man, even though it screen a man from that uncleanness which all men abhor and detest; whether a lie of this kind may be told provided the injury done by the lie be such as consists not in that sort of uncleanness with which we are now concerned, is another question: for here the question is no longer about lying, but it is asked whether an injury ought to be done to any man, even otherwise than by a lie, that the said defilement may be warded off from another. Which I should by no means think: though the case proposed be the slightest wrongs, as that which I mentioned above, about a single measure of wheat; and though it be very embarrassing whether it be our duty not to do even such an injury to any man, if thereby another may be defended or screened from a lustful outrage upon his person. But, as I said, this is another question: at present let us go on with what we have taken in hand: whether a lie ought to be told, if even the inevitable condition be proposed that we either do this, or suffer the deed of lust or some execrable pollution; even though by lying we do no man harm.

31. Thus then what is written, "The mouth that lies, slays the soul";[25] of *which* mouth it speaks, is the question. For in general when

25. [Wisdom 1:11.]

the Scripture speaks of the mouth, it signifies the very seat of our conception in the heart, where is approved and decreed whatever also by the voice, when we speak the truth, is uttered: so that he lies with the heart who approves a lie; yet that man may possibly not lie with the heart, who utters other than is in his mind, in such sort that he knows it to be for the sake of avoiding a greater evil that he admits an evil, disapproving withal both the one and the other. And they who assert this, say that thus also is to be understood that which is written, "He that speaks the truth in his heart":[26] because always in the heart truth must be spoken; but not always in the mouth of the body, if any cause of avoiding a greater evil require that other than is in the mind be uttered with the voice. And that there is indeed a mouth of the heart, may be understood even from this, that where there is speech, there a mouth is with no absurdity understood: nor would it be right to say, "Who speaks in his heart, unless it were right to understand that there is also a mouth in the heart." Though in that very place where it is written, "The mouth that lies, slays the soul," if the context of the lesson be considered, it may perhaps be taken for no other than the mouth of the heart. For there is an obscure response there, where it is hidden from men, to whom the mouth of the heart, unless the mouth of the body sound therewith, is not audible. But that mouth, the Scripture in that place says, does reach to the hearing of the Spirit of the Lord, Who has filled the whole earth; at the same time mentioning lips and voice and tongue in that place; yet all these the sense permits not to be taken, but concerning the heart, because it says of the Lord, that what is spoken is not hidden from Him: now that which is spoken with that sound which reaches to our ears, is not hidden from men either. Thus, namely, is it written: "The Spirit of wisdom is loving, and will not acquit an evil-speaker of his lips: for of his reins God is witness, and of his heart a true searcher, and of his tongue a hearer. For the Spirit of the Lord has filled the whole earth, and that which contains all things has knowledge of the voice. Therefore he that speaks unrighteous things cannot be hid: but neither shall the judgment when it punishes pass by him. For in the thoughts of the ungodly shall there be interrogation; and the hearing of his words shall come from the Lord, to the punishment of his iniquities. For the ear of jealousy hears all things, and the tumult of murmurings will not be hid. Therefore keep yourselves from murmuring, which profits nothing, and from backbiting refrain your tongue: because an obscure response will not go into the void. But the mouth that lies, slays the

26. [Psalms 15:2.]

soul."[27] It seems then to threaten them who think that to be obscure and secret, which they agitate and turn over in their heart. And this, it would show, is so clear to the ears of God, that it even calls it tumult.

32. Manifestly also in the Gospel we find the mouth of the heart: so that in one place the Lord is found to have mentioned the mouth both of the body and of the heart, where he says, "Are ye also yet without understanding? Do ye not yet understand, that whatsoever enters in at the mouth, goes into the belly, and is cast out into the draught? But those things which proceed out of the mouth come forth from the heart, and they defile the man. For out of the heart proceed evil thoughts, murders, adulteries, fornications, thefts, false witness, blasphemies: these are the things which defile a man."[28] Here if you understand but one mouth, that of the body, how will you understand, "Those things which proceed out of the mouth, come forth from the heart"; since spitting also and vomiting proceed out of the mouth? Unless perhaps a man is but then defiled when he eats anything unclean, but is defiled when he vomits it up. But if this be most absurd, it remains that we understand the mouth of the heart to have been expounded by the Lord, when He says, "The things which proceed out of the mouth, come forth from the heart." For being that theft also can be, and often is, perpetrated with silence of the bodily voice and mouth; one must be out of his mind so to understand it as then to account a person to be contaminated by the sin of theft, when he confesses or makes it known, but when he commits it and holds his peace, then to think him undefiled. But, in truth, if we refer what is said to the mouth of the heart, no sin whatever can be committed tacitly: for it is not committed unless it proceed from that mouth which is within.

33. But, like as it is asked of what mouth the Scripture says, "The mouth that lies, slays the soul," so it may be asked, "of what *lie*?" For it seems to speak of that lie in particular, which consists in detraction. It says, "Keep yourselves from murmuring, which profits nothing, and from detraction refrain your tongue." Now this detraction takes place through malevolence, when any man not only with mouth and voice of the body does utter what he forges against any, but even without speaking wishes him to be thought such; which is in truth to detract with the mouth of the heart; which thing, it says, cannot be obscure and hidden from God.

27. [Wisdom 1:6–11.]

28. [Matthew 15:16–20.]

34. For what is written in another place, "Wish not to use every lie,"[29] some people claim does not actually mean that a person is *never* to lie in *any* form.[30] Therefore, when one man shall say, "that according to this testimony of Scripture we must to that degree hold every sort and kind of lie in detestation, that even if a man wish to lie, yea, though he lie not, the very wish is to be condemned"; and to this sense interprets, that it is not said, "Do not use every lie," but, "Do not *wish* to use every lie"; that one must not dare not only to tell, but not even to wish to tell, any lie whatever: says another man, "Nay, in that it says, "Do not wish to use every lie," it wills that from the mouth of the heart we exterminate and estrange lying: so that while from some lies we must abstain with the mouth of the body, as are those chiefly which pertain to doctrine of religion; from some, we are not to abstain with the mouth of the body, if reason of avoiding a greater evil require; but with the mouth of the heart we must abstain utterly from every lie. Where it behooves to be understood what is said, "Do not wish": namely, the will itself is taken as it were the mouth of the heart, so that it concerns not the mouth of the heart when in shunning a greater evil we lie unwillingly. There is also a third sense in which you may so take this word, "not every", that, except some lies, it gives you leave to lie. Like as if he should say, "wish not to believe every man": he would not mean to advise that none should be believed; but that not all, some however, should be believed. And that which follows, "For assiduity thereof will not profit for good," sounds as if, not lying, but *assiduous* lying, that is, the custom and love of lying, should seem to be that which he would prohibit. To which that person will assuredly slide down, who either shall think that every lie may be boldly used (for so he will shun not that even which is committed in the doctrine of piety and religion; than which what more abominably wicked thing can you easily find, not among all lies, but among all sins?) or to some lie (no matter how easy, how harmless) shall accommodate the inclination of the will; so as to lie, not unwillingly for the sake of escaping a greater evil, but willingly and with liking. So, seeing there be three things which may be understood in this sentence, either "Every lie, not only tell not, but do not even wish to tell": or, "Do not wish, but even unwillingly tell a lie when anything worse is to be avoided": or, "Not every, to wit, that except some lies, the rest are admitted": one

29. [Sirach 7:13.]

30. [In this section, Augustine worries about the slippery slope of self-serving justifications that might occur once we start nitpicking the language of prohibitions against lying as a way of searching for loopholes.]

of these is found to make for those who hold that one is never to lie, two for those who think that sometimes one may tell a lie. But yet what follows, "For assiduity thereof will not profit to good," I know not whether it can countenance the first sentence of these three; except perhaps so, that while it is a precept for the perfect not only not to lie, but not even to wish; assiduity of lying is not permitted even to beginners. As if, namely, on laying down the rule at no time whatever not merely to lie but so much as to have a wish to lie, and this being gainsaid by examples, in regard that there are some lies which have been even approved by great authority, it should be rejoined that those indeed are lies of beginners, which have, in regard of this life, some kind of duty of mercy; and yet to that degree is every lie evil, and by perfect and spiritual minds in every way to be eschewed, that not even beginners are permitted to have assiduous custom thereof. For we have already spoken concerning the Egyptian midwives, that it is in respect of the promise of growth and proficiency to better things that they while lying are spoken of with approval: because it is some step towards loving the true and eternal saving of the soul, when a person does mercifully for the saving of any man's albeit mortal life even tell a lie.

35. Moreover what is written "You will destroy all that speak lies":[31] one says that no lie is here excepted, but all condemned. Another says: Yea verily: but they who speak lies from the heart, as we disputed above; for that man speaks truth in his heart, who hates the necessity of lying, which he understands as a penalty of the moral life. Another says: All indeed will God destroy who speak lies, but not all lying: for there is some lying which the Prophet was at that time insinuating, in which none is spared; that is, if refusing to confess each one his sins, he defend them rather, and will not do penance, so that not content to work iniquity, he must needs wish to be thought just, and succumb not to the medicine of confession: as the very distinction of the words may seem to intimate no other, "You hate all that work iniquity; but will not destroy them if upon repenting they speak the truth in confession, that by doing that truth they may come to the light," as is said in the Gospel according to John, "But he that does truth comes unto the light."[32] You will destroy all who not only work what You hate, but also speak lies; in holding out before them false righteousness, and not confessing their sins in penitence.

31. [Psalms 5:6.]
32. [John 3:21.]

38. Certain it is, albeit all this disputation go from side to side, some asserting that it is never right to lie, and to this effect reciting divine testimonies: others gainsaying, and even in the midst of the very words of the divine testimonies seeking place for a lie; yet no man can say, that he finds this either in example or in word of the Scriptures, that any lie should seem a thing to be loved, or not had in hatred; however sometimes by telling a lie you must do that you hate, that what is more greatly to be detested may be avoided. But then here it is that people err; they put the precious beneath the vile. For when you have granted that some evil is to be admitted, that another and more grievous may not be admitted; not by the rule of truth, but by his own cupidity and custom does each measure the evil, accounting that to be the more grievous, which himself more greatly dreads, not which is in reality more greatly to be fled from. All this fault is engendered by perversity of loving. For being there are two lives of ours; the one eternal, which is promised of God; the other temporal, in which we now are: when a man shall have begun to love this temporal more than that eternal, for the sake of this which he loves he thinks all things right to be done; and there are not any, in his estimation, more grievous sins than those which do injury to this life, and either take away from it any commodity unjustly and unlawfully, or by inflicting of death take it utterly away. And so thieves, and robbers, and ruffians, and torturers, and slayers, are more hated of them than lascivious, drunken, luxurious men, if these molest no man. For they do not understand or at all care, that these do wrong to God; not indeed to any inconvenience of Him, but to their own pernicious hurt; seeing they corrupt His gifts bestowed upon them, even His temporal gifts, and by their very corruptions turn away from eternal gifts: above all, if they have already begun to be the Temple of God; which to all Christians the Apostle says thus: "Do you not know that you are the temple of God, and that the Spirit of God dwells in you? Whoso shall corrupt God's temple, God will corrupt him. For the temple of God is holy: which temple are you."[33]

40. Now the things which are to be kept safe for sanctity's sake are these: chastity of body, and chastity of soul, and verity of doctrine. Chastity of body, without consent and permission of the soul, does no man violate.[34] For, whatever against our will and without our

33. [1 Corinthians 3:16–17.]

34. [Throughout this section, although we have modified the translation to refer to "chastity" of both body and soul, Augustine himself uses different words for each: *castitas* in relation to the mind, *pudicitia* in relation to the body. H. Browne retains the English "pudicity" for the latter, and reserves "chastity" solely for the former.]

empowering the same is by greater force done upon our body, is no lewdness. However, of permitting there may be some reason, but of consenting, none. For we consent, when we approve and wish: but we permit even not willing, because of some greater turpitude to be eschewed. Consent, truly, to corporal lewdness violates also chastity of mind. For the mind's chastity consists in a good will and sincere love, which is not corrupted, unless when we love and desire that which Truth teaches ought not to be loved and desired. We have therefore to guard the sincerity of love toward God and our neighbor; for in this is chastity of mind sanctified: and we must endeavor with all the strength in our power, and with pious supplication, that, when the chastity of our body is sought to be violated, not even that outermost sense of the soul, which is entangled with the flesh, may be touched with any delight; but if it cannot this, at least the mind and thought in not consenting may have its chastity preserved entire. Now what we have to guard in chastity of mind, is, as pertaining to the love of our neighbor, innocence and benevolence; as pertaining to the love of God, piety. Innocence is that we hurt no man; benevolence, that we also do good to whom we can; piety, that we worship God. But as for verity of doctrine, of religion and piety, that is not violated unless by a lie; whereas the highest and inmost Verity Itself, Whose that doctrine is, can in no way be violated: which Truth to attain unto, and in It on every wise to remain, and to It thoroughly to cleave, will not be permitted, but when this corruptible shall have put on incorruption, and this mortal shall have put on immortality. But, because all piety in this life is practice by which we tend to that life, which practice has a guidance afforded unto it from that doctrine, which in human words and signs of corporal sacraments does insinuate and intimate Truth herself: for this cause this also, which by lying is possible to be corrupted, is most of all to be kept incorrupt; that so, if anything in that chastity of mind be violated, it may have that wherefrom it may be repaired. For once corrupt authority of doctrine, and there can be none either course or recourse to chastity of mind.

41. There results then from all these this sentence, that a lie which does not violate the doctrine of piety, nor piety itself, nor innocence, nor benevolence, may on behalf of chastity of body be admitted. And yet if any man should propose to himself so to love truth, not only that which consists in contemplation, but also in uttering the true thing, which each in its own kind of things is true, and no otherwise to bring forth with the mouth of the body his thought than in the mind it is conceived and beheld; so that he should prize the beauty of truth-telling

honesty, not only above gold and silver and jewels and pleasant lands, but above this temporal life itself altogether and every good thing of the body, I know not whether any could wisely say that that man errs. And if he should prefer this and prize it more than all that himself has of such things; rightly also would he prefer it to the temporal things of other men, whom by his innocence and benevolence he was bound to keep and to help. For he would love perfect faith, not only of believing aright those things which by an excellent authority and worthy of faith should to himself be spoken, but also of faithfully uttering what himself should judge right to be spoken, and should speak. For faith has its name in the Latin tongue, from that the thing is done which is said:[35] and thus it is manifest that one does not exhibit when telling a lie. And even if this faith be less violated, when one lies in such sort that he is believed to no inconvenience and no pernicious hurt, with added intention moreover of guarding either one's life or corporal purity; yet violated it is, and a thing is violated which ought to be kept safe in chastity and sanctity of mind. Whence we are constrained, not by opinion of men, which for the most part is in error, but by truth itself, truth which is eminent above all, and alone is most invincible, to prefer even to purity of body, perfect faith. For chastity of mind is, love well ordered, which does not place the greater below the smaller. Now it is less, whatever in the body than whatever in the mind can be violated. For assuredly when for corporal chasteness a man tells a lie, he sees indeed that his body is threatened with corruption, not from his own, but from another's lust, but is cautious lest by permitting at least, he be a party. That permission, however, where is it but in the mind? So then, even corporal chasteness cannot be corrupted but in the mind; which not consenting nor permitting, it can by no means be rightly said that corporal chasteness is violated whatever in the body be perpetrated by another's lust. Whence it is gathered, that much more must the chastity of the mind be preserved in the mind, in which is the guardianship of the chastity of the body. Wherefore, what in us lies, both the one and the other must by holy manners and conversation be walled and hedged round, lest from another quarter it be violated. But when both cannot be, which is to be slighted in comparison of which, who does not see? When he sees which to which is to be preferred, the mind to the body, or the body to the mind; and which is more to be shunned among sins, the permitting of another's deed, or the committing of the deed yourself.

35. ["Faith" in Latin is *fides,* which Augustine links with action and speaking—as in "giving one's word."]

42. It clearly appears then, all being discussed, that those testimonies of Scripture have none other meaning than that we must never at all tell a lie: seeing that not any examples of lies, worthy of imitation, are found in the manners and actions of the Saints, as regards those Scriptures which are referred to no figurative signification, such as is the history in the Acts of the Apostles. For all those sayings of our Lord in the Gospel, which to more ignorant minds seem lies, are figurative significations. And as to what the Apostle says, "I am made all things to all men, that I might gain all,"[36] the right understanding is, that he did this not by lying, but by sympathy; so that he dealt with them in liberating them with so great charity, as if he were himself in that evil from which he wished to make them whole. There must therefore be no lying in the doctrine of piety: it is a heinous wickedness, and the first sort of detestable lie. There must be no lying of the second sort; because no man must have a wrong done to him. There must be no lying of the third sort; because we are not to consult any man's good to the injury of another. There must be no lying of the fourth sort, that is, for the lust of lying, which of itself is vicious. There must be no lying of the fifth sort, because not even the truth itself is to be uttered with the aim of men-pleasing, how much less a lie, which of itself, as a lie, is a foul thing? There must be no lying of the sixth sort; for it is not right that even the truth of testimony be corrupted for any man's temporal convenience and safety. But unto eternal salvation none is to be led by aid of a lie. For not by the ill manners of them that convert him is he to be converted to good manners: because if it is meet to be done towards him, himself also ought when converted to do it toward others; and so is he converted not to good, but to ill manners, seeing that is held out to be imitated by him when converted, which was done unto him in converting him. Neither in the seventh sort must there be any lying; for it is meet that not any man's commodity or temporal welfare be preferred to the perfecting of faith. Not even if any man is so ill moved by our right deeds as to become worse in his mind, and far more remote from piety, are right deeds therefore to be foregone: since what we are chiefly to hold is that whereunto we ought to call and invite them whom as our own selves we love; and with most courageous mind we must drink in that apostolic sentence: To some we are a savor of life unto life, to others a savor of death unto death; and who is sufficient for these things? Nor in the eighth sort must there be lying: because both among good things chastity of mind is greater than chastity of body; and among evil things, that which ourselves do,

36. [1 Corinthians 9:22.]

than that which we suffer to be done. In these eight kinds, however, a man sins less when he tells a lie, in proportion as he emerges to the eighth: more, in proportion as he diverges to the first. But whoso shall think there is any sort of lie that is not sin, will deceive himself foully, while he deems himself honest as a deceiver of other men.

43. So great blindness, moreover, has occupied men's minds, that to them it is too little if we pronounce some lies not to be sins; but they must needs pronounce it to be sin in some things if we refuse to lie: and to such a pass have they been brought by defending lying, that even that first kind which is of all the most abominably wicked they pronounce to have been used by the Apostle Paul. For in the Epistle to the Galatians, written as it was, like the rest, for doctrine of religion and piety, they say that he has told a lie, in the passage where he says concerning Peter and Barnabas, "When I saw that they walked not uprightly according to the truth of the Gospel."[37] For, while they wish to defend Peter from error, and from that depravity into which he had fallen; the very way of religion in which is salvation for all men, they by breaking and mincing the authority of the Scriptures do endeavor themselves to overthrow. In which they do not see that it is not only lying, but perjury that they lay to the charge of the Apostle in the very doctrine of piety, that is, in an Epistle in which he preaches the Gospel; seeing that he there says, before he relates that matter, "What I write unto you, behold, before God, I lie not."[38] But it is time that we set bounds to this disputation: in the consideration and treatment whereof altogether there is nothing more meet to be, before all else, borne in mind and made our prayer, than that which the same Apostle says: "God is faithful, Who will not suffer you to be tempted above that you are able to bear, but will with the temptation make also a way to escape, that you may be able to bear it."[39]

37. [Galatians 2:14. Cf. note 9 above.]

38. [Galatians 1:20.]

39. [1 Corinthians 10:13.]

2
GROTIUS

The early Enlightenment thinker Hugo Grotius (1583–1645) was a Dutch philosopher, theologian, and legal theorist. He is a seminal figure in the fields of international law and just war theory, in part because of the secular nature of many of his arguments. Though he was a Christian, one of the goals Grotius set himself was to articulate a theory of international law and justice that would hold even in the absence of a deity. Published in 1625, *The Law of War and Peace,* from which the present selection is taken, is thus one of the earliest European legal treatises that seeks to ground its claims through the use of reason and not merely in scripture. In it Grotius sets out to delineate the conditions under which it is legitimate to go to war, as well as what constitutes appropriate conduct in times of war. It is worth keeping in mind that Grotius' discussion of lying and deception occurs under this final heading: he is interested in whether, and when, it is permissible to deceive one's opponent in an explicitly adversarial setting. At the same time, his discussion considers a wide variety of possible cases and has implications beyond just what we may do in the midst of conflict.

Grotius' approach to lying borrows much from Augustine's (presented in chapter 1 of this volume), in that he considers views from a broad range of thinkers, providing arguments on both sides of an issue before presenting his own view. Also like Augustine, Grotius draws many subtle distinctions between different sorts of deception. It is worth taking care to keep these distinctions straight, in order to follow the thread of his argument.

Grotius seems to subscribe to the view that there is something presumptively wrong with lying. The principle behind Grotius' account is that lying is bad because it violates another's right—specifically, the right to "liberty of judgment." In this, his reasoning both echoes Augustine and anticipates in many ways what Kant will say nearly 200 years later (see the selections from Kant in chapter 6 of this volume). But Grotius breaks from Augustine in holding that warfare, at least, engenders many exceptions to this presumptive prohibition. Just as the exercise of physical violence can be legitimate in cases of self-defense, so too can various forms of deception that would otherwise be objectionable. For instance, he indicates that it is okay to deceive by speaking the truth but leaving out potentially relevant details—what he refers to as deceit "in a negative action." He allows for even more blatant forms of deception as well, including not just deceptive behaviors (pretense) but also, in certain circumstances, explicitly uttered falsehoods.

His discussion of the circumstances in which the presumptive right to liberty of judgment can be curtailed reveals the extent to which the surface similarity to Augustine breaks down. There are, it turns out, many circumstances under which this right ceases to exist. These include instances in which deception is necessary in order to save another's life and in which the speaker is allowed to presume that the audience would waive the right to truthfulness—a "tacit consent" to being deceived, which, of course, would work only if it remains tacit.

Despite all these exceptions to the general rule not to deceive, Grotius concludes by pointing out that even if deception is not unjust, it is nonetheless unbecoming to lie, and is a sign of weakness to have no better alternative than to extricate oneself from a difficult situation by lying.

As you read the selection, consider the following questions:

1. Is the analogy between wartime deception and violence in self-defense a good one? Is Grotius overlooking any important disanalogies?
2. Grotius acknowledges several exceptions to the general rule not to deceive, but has he allowed too much? Does the presumption that one should tell the truth have any bite left after Grotius has defanged it so?
3. Grotius insists that deceptive promises and oaths cannot be permissible. Is this consistent with the rest of his account? Is there a philosophically defensible difference between insincerely telling a person that I will do something and insincerely promising that I will do it, such that the former is permissible but the latter is blameworthy?

The Law of War and Peace

Book 3, Chapter 1

GENERAL RULES FROM THE LAW OF NATURE REGARDING WHAT IS PERMISSIBLE IN WAR; WITH A CONSIDERATION OF RUSES AND FALSEHOOD[1]

VI. Whether it is permissible to use a ruse in war

1. So far as the manner of conducting operations is concerned, violence and frightfulness are particularly suited to wars. The question is often raised, however, whether one may resort to ruses also. Homer, at any rate, said that one must harm his foe, "By ruse or violence, by open ways or hidden." In Pindar we find, "And every means must be employed, to bring the foeman low." In Virgil there is also this: "Whether craft or valour, who would ask in war?"

2. In Homer, Ulysses, the typical man of wisdom, is at all times full of wiles against the enemy; whence Lucian deduced the rule that those who deceive the foe deserve praise. Xenophon asserted that in war nothing is more useful than deceptions. In Thucydides, Brasidas says that the renown won by the stratagems of war is particularly conspicuous; and in Plutarch, Agesilaus declares that to deceive an enemy is both just and permissible.

Polybius thinks that what is accomplished by main force in war is to be considered of less importance than what is done by taking advantage of opportunities and by the use of deception. Hence Silius represents Corvinus as saying, "War must be waged with guile;[2] force brings less fame to the leader." Similar, according to Plutarch, was the view even of the stern Spartans: he observes that a larger victim was sacrificed by the one who had gained a victory through a ruse than by him who had won by open fighting. The same writer thinks highly

1. [Grotius quotes liberally from classical Greek and Roman sources, and peppers his discussion with remarks by biblical commentators. Many of his original footnotes have been excised in an effort to enhance readability. Classical and biblical allusions in the main text have been retained and are annotated only when some context is necessary for his argument or where the allusion is especially obscure.]

2. There is a similar saying of Mohammed, *el-harbu hud'atun*, that is, "battles require deceit."

of Lysander[3] for "varying with ruses most of the operations of war." Plutarch counts it among the merits of Philopoemen that, having been trained in the Cretan system, he combined the straightforward and honourable method of fighting with craft and ruses. It is a saying of Ammianus that "All successful issues of war are to be praised without distinction of valour or guile."

3. The Roman jurists call it a good ruse "whenever any one lays a plot against the enemy"; and again, they say that it makes no difference whether any one escapes from the power of the enemy by force or by trickery. This is "deception which cannot be censured, such as that of a general," as Eustathius notes in his commentary on the fifteenth book of the *Iliad*. Among the theologians, Augustine declares: "When one undertakes a righteous war, it makes no difference, in respect to justness, whether he fights openly or by ambuscades." Chrysostom says that generals who have won a victory by a ruse receive the highest praise.

4. However, there is no lack of opinions which seem to advocate the opposite view, and some of these we shall present below. The final conclusion will depend upon the answer to the question whether deceit belongs to the class of things that are always evil, in regard to which the saying is true that one must not do evil that good may come; or whether it is in the category of things which from their very nature are not at all times vicious but which may even happen to be good.

VII. In a negative action, deceit is not in itself impermissible

It must be observed, then, that deceit is of one sort in a negative action, of another sort in a positive action. The word deceit I extend, on the authority of Labeo, even to those things which occur in a negative action; he classes it as deceit, but not harmful deceit, when any one "protects his own or another's possessions through dissimulation." It cannot be doubted that Cicero spoke too sweepingly when he said: "Pretence and dissimulation must be removed from every phase of life." For since you are not required to reveal to others all that you know or desire, it follows that it is right to dissimulate, that is to conceal and hide some things from some persons. "One may," said Augustine, "conceal the truth wisely, by the use of dissimulation in some degree." Cicero himself in more than one place admits that such

3. Plutarch compares him to Sulla, in whose soul Carbo used to say there were a lion and a fox.

dissimulation is absolutely necessary and unavoidable, especially for those to whom the care of the state is entrusted.

The narrative of Jeremiah (chapter 38) offers a notable example touching this point. The prophet had been questioned by the king as to the outcome of the siege, but in the presence of the princes, at the king's request, he wisely concealed that fact, assigning another and yet not untrue reason for the conference. With this, again, we may class the action of Abraham in concealing his marriage and calling Sarah his sister, that is, according to the usage of the time, a near relative.

VIII. Deceit in a positive action falls under two heads: deceit exhibited in actions not limited in significance, and that exhibited in actions the significance of which is, as it were, fixed by agreement; it is shown that deceit of the former sort is permissible

1. Deceit which consists in a positive action, if it is exhibited in acts, is called pretence; if in words, falsehood. Some persons establish this distinction between the two terms, because they say that words are naturally the signs of thoughts, while acts are not. But the contrary is true, that words by their very nature and apart from the human will have no significance, unless perchance a word is confused and "inarticulate," such as is uttered by a person in grief, when it comes rather under the term act than speech.

If now the assertion is made that the nature of man possesses superiority over that of other living creatures in this, that it can convey to others the ideas of the mind and that words were invented for this purpose, that is true. But it must be added that such conveying of thought is accomplished not by means of words alone but also by signs, as among dumb persons, whether these signs naturally have something in common with the thing signified or whether they possess significance merely by agreement.

Similar to these signs are those characters which, as Paul the jurist says, do not express words formed by the tongue but objects themselves, either from some resemblance, as in the case of hieroglyphic signs, or by mere arbitrary convention, as among the Chinese.

2. At this point then we must introduce another distinction, such as we employed to remove the ambiguity in the term law of nations. For we said that the term law of nations includes both what is approved by separate nations without mutual obligation and what contains a mutual obligation in itself. Words, then, and signs, and the written characters we have mentioned, were invented as a means of expression under a mutual obligation; as Aristotle called it, "by convention."

This is not the case with other things. Hence it comes about that we may avail ourselves of other things, even if we foresee that another person will derive therefrom a false impression. I am speaking of what is intrinsic, not of what is incidental. And so we must give an example, in which no harm follows as a consequence, or in which the harm itself, without consideration of the deceit, is permissible.

3. An example of the former case is found in Christ, who in the presence of His companions on the way to Emmaus "made as though He would" go further, that is, gave the impression of intending to go further; unless we prefer truly to believe that He wished to go further, on condition, nevertheless, that He should not be detained by a great effort. Thus God is said to will many things which do not come to pass, and in another place Christ is said to have intended to pass by the Apostles who were in a ship, that is had He not been urgently entreated to embark.

Another example may be found in Paul's circumcision of Timothy, when he was well aware that the Jews would interpret this as though the injunction of circumcision, which had in fact already been done away with, was still binding upon the children of Israel, and as though Paul and Timothy themselves thought so.[4] However, Paul did not have this in view, but merely sought to obtain for himself and Timothy the opportunity of associating with the Jews on more intimate terms. After the removal of the divine law circumcision no longer implied such an obligation by agreement; and the evil arising from the error, which followed for the time being, and was later to be corrected, was not of so great importance as the good which Paul sought, that is the introduction of the truth of the Gospel.

This sort of pretence the Greek fathers often call "management." In regard to it there is a notable opinion of Clement of Alexandria, who in a discussion of the good man speaks thus: "For the benefit of his neighbour he will do things which otherwise he would not do of his own accord and original purpose." Of this nature was the act of the Romans who threw bread from the Capitol into the posts of the enemy that they might not be believed to be distressed by famine.

4. An example illustrating the latter case is found in a pretended flight, such as Joshua ordered his men to make so as to take Ai by storm, and such as other commanders have frequently ordered. For in this instance we regard the injury which follows as legitimate according to the justice of war. Moreover, flight itself has no

4. [For more details about the context of this biblical allusion, see the notes to section 8 of Augustine's *De Mendacio* (chapter 1 of this volume).]

significance by agreement, although an enemy may interpret it as a sign of fear; such interpretation the other party is not obliged to guard against in his use of his freedom to go hither and thither, more or less rapidly, and with this or that gesture or outward appearance. In the same category we may class the actions of those of whom we read that they made use of the weapons, standards, uniforms, and tents of their enemies.

5. All these things are in fact of such a sort that they may be employed by any one at his discretion, even contrary to custom; for the custom itself was introduced by the choice of individuals, not as it were by universal consent, and such a custom constrains no one.

IX. The difficulty of the inquiry in respect to the second sort of deceit is indicated

1. Of greater difficulty is the discussion with respect to those types of deceit which, if I may so say, are in common use among men in commerce and in which falsehood in the true sense is found.

There are many injunctions against falsehood in Holy Writ: "A righteous man," that is the good man, "hateth lying" (Proverbs 8:5); "Remove far from me falsehood and lies" (Proverbs 30:8); "Thou wilt destroy them that speak lies" (Psalms 5:6); "Lie not one to another" (Colossians 3:9).

This point of view is rigidly maintained by Augustine; and even among the philosophers and poets there are those who are seen to be in sympathy with it. Well known is this saying of Homer: "To me as hateful as the jaws of Hell is he, whose mind thinks other than his tongue reveals." Sophocles says, "What is foreign to truth it is never fitting to utter. Yet, if the telling of truth will bring sure doom to another, pardon to him must be granted who does that which is not fitting." Cleobulus has this line: "Falsehood is hateful to him who in his heart is wise." Aristotle said: "Falsehood in itself is base and worthy of censure, but truth is noble and deserving of praise."

2. Nevertheless authority is not lacking in support of the opposite view also. In the first place in Holy Writ there are examples of men cited without a mark of censure; and, in the second place, there are the declarations of the early Christians, Origen, Clement, Tertullian, Lactantius, Chrysostom, Jerome, and Cassian, indeed of nearly all, as Augustine himself acknowledges. Although disagreeing with them, he nevertheless recognizes that it is "a great problem," "a discussion full of dark places," "a dispute in which the learned are at variance," to use words that are all his own.

3. Among the philosophers there stand openly on this side Socrates and his pupils Plato and Xenophon; at times, Cicero; if we may trust Plutarch and Quintilian, also the Stoics, who among the endowments of the wise man include ability to lie in the proper place and manner. In some places Aristotle too seems to agree with them, for his phrase "in itself," which we have quoted, may be interpreted generally, that is, considering the thing without regard to attendant circumstances. The commentator upon Aristotle, Andronicus of Rhodes, thus speaks of the physician who lies to a sick man: "He deceives indeed, but he is not a deceiver," adding the reason: "for his aim is not the deception of the sick man, but his cure."

4. Quintilian, whom I have mentioned, in defending this same view says that there are many things which are made honourable or base, not so much by the nature of the facts as by their causes. Says Diphilus: "The falsehood told for safety's sake, if I may judge, can cause no detriment." In Sophocles, when Neoptolemus asks: "Do you not think a lie is base?", Ulysses answers: "If safety from the lie arise, I do not."

X. *Not every use of an expression, which is known to be taken in another sense, is impermissible*

1. Perhaps we may find some way of reconciling such divergent views in a wider or more strict interpretation of the meaning of falsehood.

Adopting the point of view of Gellius when he distinguishes between telling an untruth and lying, we do not understand as a falsehood what an ignorant person happens to say; but we are concerned with that which is consciously uttered with a meaning that is at variance with the idea in the mind, whether in understanding or in an act of will. For ideas of the mind are what are primarily "and immediately" indicated by words and similar signs; so he does not lie who says something untrue which he believes to be true, but he lies who says that which is indeed true but which he believes to be false. Falsity of meaning, therefore, is that which we need to exemplify the general nature of falsehood.

From this it follows that, when any term or phrase has "several meanings," that is, may be understood in more than one way, either from common usage, or the practice of an art, or some figure of speech easily understood, then, if the idea in mind fits one of these meanings, it is not held to be a lie, even if it is thought that he who hears it will understand it in another way.

2. It is indeed true that the rash employment of such a mode of speech is not to be approved. It may nevertheless be justified by incidental causes, as, for instance, if thereby aid is rendered in the instruction of one who has been entrusted to our care, or in avoiding an unfair question.

Christ Himself gave an example of the former sort, when He said: "Lazarus our friend is fallen asleep," which the Apostles understood as though it were said of the sleep of the living. Again, what He had said about rebuilding the Temple, meaning it in regard to His own body, He knew the Jews took with reference to the actual Temple. Similarly when He promised to the Apostles twelve exalted seats next to the King, like judges of the tribes among the Jews, and elsewhere that they should drink of a new wine in His Father's kingdom, He seems to have been fully aware that they took this to refer to none other than some kingdom in this life, with the expectation of which they were filled until the very moment when Christ was about to ascend up into heaven. On another occasion also He spoke to the people through the indirectness of parables, that those who heard Him might not understand, unless, that is, they should bring thereto such earnestness of mind and readiness to be taught as were required.

An example of the latter use may be given from profane history in the case of Lucius Vitellius, whom Narcissus pressed to explain his ambiguities and reveal the truth fully, but whom he could not force to refrain from giving replies that were dubious and capable of varied interpretation.[5] Here applies a saying of the Jews: "If any one knows how to use ambiguous language, it is well: but if not, let him remain silent."

3. On the other hand, a case may arise when it is not only not praiseworthy but even wicked to employ such a mode of speech; as when the glory of God, or the love due to our neighbour, or reverence toward a superior, or the nature of the thing in question requires that everything which is thought in the mind shall be completely revealed. Just so in the case of contracts, we said that that must be made known which the nature of the contract is understood to demand; and in this sense we may not inaptly interpret the rule of Cicero, "All falsehood must be removed from matters of contract," which is taken from the ancient Athenian law prohibiting "the uttering of falsehoods in the market-place." In these passages apparently the word falsehood receives so broad a meaning that it covers even an obscure statement.

5. The same Tacitus, *Histories*, says: "He spoke obscurely, with the intention of interpreting his words in such a way as might be advantageous."

But this, strictly speaking, we have already excluded from the idea of a falsehood.

XI. The character of falsehood, in so far as it is impermissible, consists in its conflict with the right of another; this is explained

1. In order to exemplify the general idea of falsehood, it is necessary that what is spoken, or written, or indicated by signs or gestures, cannot be understood otherwise than in a sense which differs from the thought of him who uses the means of expression.

Upon this broader signification, however, a stricter meaning of falsehood must be imposed, carrying some characteristic distinction. This distinction, if we regard the matter aright, at least according to the common view of nations, can be described, we think, as nothing else than a conflict with the existing and continuing right of him to whom the speech or sign is addressed; for it is sufficiently clear that no one lies to himself, however false his statement may be.

By right in this connexion I do not mean every right without relation to the matter in question, but that which is peculiar to it and connected with it. Now that right is nothing else than the liberty of judgement which, as if by some tacit agreement, men who speak are understood to owe to those with whom they converse. For this is merely that mutual obligation which men had willed to introduce at the time when they determined to make use of speech and similar signs; for without such an obligation the invention of speech would have been void of result.

2. We require, moreover, that this right be valid and continuing at the time the statement is made; for it may happen that the right has indeed existed, but has been taken away, or will be annulled by another right which supervenes, just as a debt is cancelled by an acceptance or by the cessation of the condition. Then, further, it is required that the right which is infringed belong to him with whom we converse, and not to another, just as in the case of contracts also injustice arises only from the infringement of a right of the contracting parties.

3. Moreover, the right of which we have spoken may be abrogated by the express consent of him with whom we are dealing, as when one says that he will speak falsely and the other permits it. In like manner it may be cancelled by tacit consent, or consent assumed on reasonable grounds, or by the opposition of another right which, in the common judgement of all men, is much more cogent.

The right understanding of these points will supply to us many inferences, which will be of no small help in reconciling the differences in the views which have been cited above.

XII. The view is maintained that it is permissible to say what is false before infants and insane persons

The first inference is that even if something which has a false significance is said to an infant or insane person no blame for falsehood attaches thereto. For it seems to be permitted by the common opinion of mankind that, "The unsuspecting age of childhood may be mocked." Quintilian, speaking of boys, said: "For their profit we employ many fictions." The reason is by no means far to seek; since infants and insane persons do not have liberty of judgement, it is impossible for wrong to be done them in respect to such liberty.

XIII. It is permissible to say what is false when he to whom the conversation is not addressed is deceived, and when it would be permissible to deceive him if not sharing in it

1. The second inference is that, so long as the person to whom the talk is addressed is not deceived, if a third party draws a false impression therefrom there is no falsehood.

There is no falsehood in relation to him to whom the utterance is directed because his liberty remains unimpaired. His case is like that of persons to whom a fable is told when they are aware of its character, or those to whom figurative language is used in "irony," or in "hyperbole," a figure which, as Seneca says, reaches the truth by means of falsehood, while Quintilian calls it a lying exaggeration. There is no falsehood, again, in respect to him who chances to hear what is said; the conversation is not being held with him, consequently there is no obligation toward him. Indeed if he forms for himself an opinion from what is said not to him, but to another, he has something which he can credit to himself, not to another. In fine, if, so far as he is concerned, we wish to form a correct judgement, the conversation is not a conversation, but something that may mean anything at all.

2. Cato the censor therefore committed no wrong in falsely promising aid to his allies, nor did Flaccus, who said to others that a city of the enemy had been stormed by Aemilius, although in both cases the enemy was deceived. A similar ruse is told of Agesilaus by Plutarch. Nothing in fact was said to the enemy; the harm, moreover, which

followed was something foreign to the statement, and of itself not impermissible to desire or to accomplish.

To this category Chrysostom and Jerome refer Paul's speech, in which at Antioch he rebuked Peter for being too zealous a Jew. They think that Peter was well aware that this was not done in earnest; at the same time the weakness of those present was humoured.

XIV. It is permissible to say what is false when the conversation is directed to him who wishes to be deceived in this way

1. The third inference is that, whenever it is certain that he to whom the conversation is addressed will not be annoyed at the infringement of his liberty in judging, or rather will be grateful therefor, because of some advantage which will follow, in this case also a falsehood in the strict sense, that is a harmful falsehood, is not perpetrated; just so a man does not commit theft who with the presumed consent of the owner uses up some trifling thing in order that he may thereby secure for the owner a great advantage.

In these matters which are so certain, a presumed wish is taken as one that is expressed. Besides, in such cases it is evident that no wrong is done to one who desires it. It seems, therefore, that he does not do wrong who comforts a sick friend by persuading him of what is not true, as Arria did by saying what was not true to Paetus after the death of their son; the story is told in the Letters of Pliny. Similar is the case of the man who brings courage by a false report to one who is wavering in battle, so that, encouraged thereby, he wins victory and safety for himself, and is thus "beguiled but not betrayed," as Lucretius says.

2. Democritus says: "We must speak the truth, wherever that is the better course." Xenophon writes: "It is right to deceive our friends, if it is for their good." Clement of Alexandria concedes "the use of lying as a curative measure." Maximus of Tyre says: "A physician deceives a sick man, a general deceives his army, and a pilot the sailors; and in such deception there is no wrong." The reason is given by Proclus in commenting on Plato: "For that which is good is better than the truth."

To this class of untruths belong the statement reported by Xenophon,[6] that the allies would presently arrive; that of Tullus Hostilius, that the

6. "And when Agesilaus had come into Boeotia and had learned that Pisander had been beaten in a naval battle by Pharnabazus and Conon he gave orders that the opposite should be told to his troops; and he came forth wearing a wreath, and he offered sacrifice as if in gratitude for a victory" —Plutarch, *Agesilaus*.

army from Alba was making a flank movement by his order; what histories term the "salutary lie" of the consul Quinctius, that the enemy were in flight on the other wing; and similar incidents found in abundance in the writings of the historians. However, it is to be observed that in this sort of falsehood the infringement upon the judgement is of less account because it is usually confined to the moment, and the truth is revealed a little later.

XV. It is permissible to say what is false when the speaker makes use of a superior right over one subject to himself

1. A fourth inference, akin to the foregoing, applies to the case when one who has a right that is superior to all the rights of another makes use of this right either for his own or for the public good. This especially Plato seems to have had in mind when he conceded the right of saying what is false to those having authority. Since the same author seems now to grant this privilege to physicians, and again to deny it to them, apparently we ought to make the distinction that in the former passage he means physicians publicly appointed to this responsibility, and in the latter those who privately claim it for themselves. Yet Plato also rightly recognizes that falsehood is not becoming to deity, although deity has a supreme right over men, because it is a mark of weakness to take refuge in such devices.

2. An instance of blameless mendacity, of which even Philo approves, may perhaps be found in Joseph, who, when ruling in the king's stead, accused his brothers first of being spies, and then of being thieves, pretending, but not really believing, that they were such. Another instance is that of Solomon, who gave an example of wisdom inspired by God, when to the women who were disputing over the child he uttered the words which indicated his purpose to slay it, although his real intent was the furthest possible from such a course, and his desire was to assign to the true mother her own offspring. There is a saying of Quintilian: "Sometimes the common good requires that even falsehoods should be upheld."

XVI. It is perhaps permissible to say what is false when we are unable in any other way to save the life of an innocent person, or something else of equal importance

A fifth inference may be applicable to cases where the life of an innocent person, or something else of equal importance, cannot be saved without falsehood, and another person can in no other way be diverted from the accomplishment of a wicked crime.[7] Such was the deed of Hypermnestra, who is often lauded for this reason: "Nobly false, and for all time a maiden famed."[8]

XVII. The authors who have judged that falsehood spoken in the presence of enemies is permissible

3. In almost all matters, [recent authors] have chosen to follow Augustine alone of the teachers of antiquity. But the same school admits of unspoken interpretations, which are so repugnant to all practice that one may question whether it would not be more satisfactory to admit to certain persons the use of falsehoods in the cases we have mentioned, or in some of them (for I assume that nothing has been settled here), than so indiscriminately to exempt such interpretations from the definition of falsehood. Thus when they say "I do not know," it may be understood as "I do not know so as to tell you"; and when they say "I have not," it may be understood as "so as to give you"; and other things of this sort which the common sense of mankind repudiates, and which, if admitted, will offer no obstacle to our saying that whoever affirms anything denies it himself, and whoever denies affirms.

4. It is assuredly quite true that in general there is no word which may not have a doubtful meaning; for all words, in addition to the significance which is called that of the first notion, have another of a second notion, and this significance varies in the different arts; moreover, words have different meanings also in metaphor and other figures of speech.

Again, I do not approve of the view of those who apply the term jokes to falsehoods which are uttered with a particularly serious expression and tone, as if they shrank from the word rather than the thing.

7. Augustine, *On Psalm V* says, "There are, however, two sorts of lies in which there is no great fault, yet which are not entirely free from fault. The one sort is told when we are joking, the other when we lie for the benefit of our neighbour. Now the first sort, which consists in a joke, is not so dangerous, because it does not deceive. For he to whom it is told knows that it has been told in jest. But the second sort of lie is still less dangerous, because it contains some element of kindness." Tertullian, *On Modesty*, classes among the sins of daily occurrence, to which we are all subject, the necessity of lying.

8. [Hypermnestra was a princess from Greek mythology. When she and her sisters were coerced into marrying the princes of a rival kingdom, they made a pact to murder their new husbands on their wedding nights. Hypermnestra was the only princess to break this promise, allowing her husband Lynceus to live because he honored her virginity.]

XVIII. The use of falsehood is not to be extended to statements containing a promise

We must, however, bear in mind that what we have said regarding falsehood is to be applied to assertions, and such indeed as injure no one but a public enemy, but not to promises.[9] For by a promise, as we have just begun to say, a new and particular right is conferred upon him to whom the promise is made.

This holds true even among enemies, without any exception arising from the hostility existing at the time. It holds true not only in the case of promises actually expressed, but also in the case of those that are implied, as we shall show in discussing the demand for a parley when we come to the part that deals with the observing of good faith in warfare.

XIX. The use of falsehood is not to be extended to oaths

This also must be repeated from the portion of our foregoing discussion which dealt with the subject of oaths, that whether the oath is assertive or promissory it has the force to exclude all exceptions which might be sought in the person of him with whom we are dealing. The reason is that an oath establishes a relation not only with a man, but also with God, to whom we are bound by the oath, even if no right arises for the man.

In the same place we have furthermore stated that in an oath we do not, as we do in other speech, admit that interpretations not wholly without warrant may be put upon words, in order to absolve us from falsehood; but we do require that the truth be spoken with the meaning which a man listening is supposed to understand in perfect good faith. Obviously, then, we must abhor the impiety of those who did not hesitate to assert that it is proper to deceive men by oaths just as boys do by means of dice.

XX. Nevertheless it is more noble, and more becoming to Christian simplicity, to refrain from falsehood even toward an enemy; this view is illustrated by comparisons

1. We know, too, that certain types of fraud, which we have said were naturally permitted, have been rejected by some peoples and persons.

9. Agesilaus, and with him Plutarch, make this distinction: "To violate sworn agreements is to despise the gods. Otherwise, to deceive the enemy with words is not only just but glorious, and brings glory and satisfaction together with gain."

But this does not happen because they view such means of deception as unjust, but because of a remarkable loftiness of mind, and, in some cases, because of confidence in their strength. There is in Aelian a saying of Pythagoras, that in two things man comes very close to God, in speaking the truth at all times and in doing good to others; and in Iamblichus veracity is called a guide to all good things, divine and human. For Aristotle "the magnanimous man is a lover of free speech and of the truth." For Plutarch, "To lie is worthy of a slave."

Arrian says of Ptolemy: "And for him, who was a king, it was more disgraceful to lie than for another." In the same author, Alexander declares: "The king must speak nothing but the truth to his subjects." Mamertinus says of Julian: "In our emperor there is a marvellous agreement between mind and tongue. He knows that lying is not only a mark of a low and mean spirit, but also a slavish vice; and in truth, since want or fear makes men liars, the emperor who lies is ignorant of the greatness of his fortune." In Plutarch, praise is given to Aristides' "character rooted in firm morality and tenacious of justice, not even resorting to falsehood in any kind of sport." Of Epaminondas, Probus says that he was "so devoted to truth that he did not lie even in jest."

2. This point of view assuredly is all the more to be insisted on by Christians; for not only is simplicity enjoined upon them (Matthew 10:16), but vain speaking is forbidden (Matthew 12:36); and He is set for their example in whose mouth no guile was found. Lactantius says: "And so the true and upright traveller will not quote that saying of Lucilius: 'I lie not to a man who is my friend and intimate,' but he will think that he should not lie even to an enemy and a stranger; nor will he ever consent that his tongue, the interpreter of his mind, shall disagree with his meaning and thought."

3. Thus Alexander declared that he would not steal a victory. Polybius relates that the Achaeans shrank from all deceit against the enemy, because they considered that the only sure victory which, if I may express his meaning in the words of Claudian, "Conquers foes whose minds have been subdued." Such was the attitude of the Romans almost to the close of the second Punic War. Aelian records that "The Romans know that they are brave, and that they have not overcome their foes by artifice . . . and trickery." Hence when Perseus, king of Macedon, was deceived by hopes of peace, the elder senators declared that they did not recognize the methods of the Romans, that the ancestors of these never boasted that they had waged war more by craft than by courage; that it had been the Roman method to wage war not by the ruses of the Carthaginians, nor by the subtlety of the Greeks, who would esteem it more glorious to outwit an enemy than

to overcome him by force. Then they added the following: "In some cases, for the moment, more is accomplished by deceit than by valour, but only his mind is forever conquered from whom the confession has been extorted that he has been conquered not by artifice, nor by chance, but after joining forces in battle in a just and righteous war."

Later we read also in Tacitus: "The Roman people takes vengeance on its enemies, not by fraud, nor in secret, but openly with arms in hand." Such men were the Tibareans also, who even agreed upon the place and time of battle. In Herodotus Mardonius makes a similar assertion regarding the Greeks of his time.

3
ARISTOTLE

Aristotle (384–322 BCE) was a student of Plato and one of history's most influential philosophers as well as a foundational figure in the sciences. The first selection is from his *Nicomachean Ethics* (titled after a possible dedication to either his father or his son, both of whom were named Nicomachus), in which Aristotle attempts to articulate a comprehensive theory of the good life that connects moral virtue with human nature. In earlier portions of the *Nicomachean Ethics*, Aristotle defines a human being as essentially a rational and social animal. Since this is our nature and since the highest good for anything is to come as close as possible to fulfilling its nature, ethics for Aristotle becomes the study of how to live rationally and socially—how to, in other words, become truly *happy*. Virtues such as honesty are character traits which not only aid us in pursuing ultimate happiness and flourishing, but which themselves constitute the good life: being honest is both a way of being happy and an expression of our rational and social natures. For this reason, we are at our most human when we are virtuous, and the liar is less happy in the end because dishonesty compromises our rationality (by obscuring truth and communicability) as well as our sociability (by eroding trust).

The initial portions of the selection do not deal with honesty itself, but they present Aristotle's understanding of the structure of moral virtue generally. The specific examples he deploys in this preliminary discussion are the virtues of justice and temperance; but insofar as all moral virtues are given the same analysis, the reader is encouraged to substitute honesty for these other virtues. Aristotle describes all virtues as requiring the following:

- Virtues are perfect moderations or "means" with respect to possible pleasures and pains. For example, as a virtue, honesty will involve neither too much fear (cowardice) nor too little fear (recklessness), and the virtuously honest person will reliably be able to resist the temptation to lie even when the truth would be too painful or the deception too sweet. For this reason, it is also conceptually impossible on Aristotle's account to be *too honest*. As a virtue, honesty is already by definition a perfect mean between extremes, and so it cannot itself ever permit of extremity.

- Virtues are dispositions to both feel and act in certain ways at certain times. This means that one is not virtuously honest unless one both *wants* to be truthful and *does* in fact speak truthfully. And the honest person must also express these things at the right moment. (Think, for example, of the difference between speaking up about the truth too late after the fact or bluntly blurting out the truth at an inopportune moment.) This also means that the honest person is not defined by a single, isolated act of truth-telling, but rather by a habitual pattern of truthfulness. Furthermore, the virtuously honest person will tell the truth with pleasure and never grudgingly. Grudging truthfulness is still better than lying, of course, but it falls short of the kind of stable, perfected disposition that Aristotle reserves for proper virtue. The grudgingly honest person must exert effort to be truthful, which is part of a process of habituation that can ultimately result in the effortlessness of true virtue.
- Virtues are partially defined in terms of community role models who provide the standards for ideal rationality and sociability. Thus, to be honest means, among other things, to act in ways that emulate one's cultural paradigms of honesty.

Some commentators also occasionally make much of the so-called *unity of virtues* thesis, according to which Aristotle is understood to be saying that the possession of any one virtue requires the possession of all the other virtues, which are allegedly needed to balance one another. For example, the unity claim would involve construing bravery and temperance as necessary for one another: one cannot face a danger with courage if one cannot control one's bodily appetites and conversely one needs to be able to stand up with conviction against peer pressure to overindulge in one's bodily appetites. Thus, applied to the case of honesty, the unity requirement would imply that the truly honest person is also necessarily wise, courageous, just, etc. Of course, not only would this make genuine honesty that much more difficult to attain (since one would also have to attain all the other virtues), it also has the implication that, by definition, there cannot be any honest fools, honest cowards, honest criminals, etc.

Although honesty shares all these characteristics with moral virtues more generally, it is in certain other ways somewhat special. For one thing, honesty permits of several specific subspecies, many of which Aristotle claims we recognize but do not have names for. So rather than reducing the ethical domain to simply honesty versus dishonesty, Aristotle disambiguates different types of dishonesty, distinguished by their context, their motivation, and whether they permit of certain "qualifications." For example, in addition to the bald-faced lie, Aristotle also sees boasts, self-deprecations, and even understatements as varieties of insincerity. Dishonesty in business affairs is given a slightly different treatment than dishonesty in other walks of life. And although no form of dishonesty is ever virtuous, Aristotle concludes that some dishonesties are less morally egregious than others.

In addition to the selection from the *Nicomachean Ethics*, also included is an excerpt from Aristotle's *Rhetoric*, in which Aristotle analyzes the form, goals, and technique of effective persuasion. According to this analysis, the rhetorician is allowed certain flexibility with respect to truth-telling. In particular, the rhetorician may make tactical use of "enthymemes" in argument; that is, hidden or implicit assumptions upon which an argument's validity might hinge, but which often go unnoticed. Aristotle's justification for such rhetorical misdirection and manipulation is twofold. First, there is a utilitarian or pedagogical justification: the rhetorician may mislead an audience if that thereby brings them closer to a greater truth. A second justification is epistemological: by familiarizing oneself with deceptive language, the rhetorician becomes better equipped to recognize and combat it. Finally, the doctrine of virtue existing as a mean between excesses is given concrete application when Aristotle argues that neither the young nor the elderly, but only the middle-aged, possess proper credulity in the face of deceptive rhetoric.

As you read Aristotle's account of honesty and truthfulness, ask yourself these questions:

1. Whom do you look up to as a paragon of honesty? Can you formulate a general rule of thumb from this person's behavior about when to lie and when not to lie? In a world of cultural pluralism, where there may be multiple or conflicting paragons of honesty, can such a general rule exist? What if others do not regard your role model as honest?
2. Aristotle defines virtue as a fixed disposition, which means that one single act of honesty does not thereby make someone an honest person. At what point, then, does someone become honest? And does this also mean that an honest person can retain their honesty even if they commit a single act of dishonesty? How many dishonest acts are sufficient to conclude that someone is in fact a dishonest person?
3. Imagine that the "unity thesis" described above is correct, and that being truly honest requires also possessing other virtues. List your own examples of specific traits you regard as virtuous and theorize how these might be prerequisites for honesty.

Nicomachean Ethics

Book II

First of all then we have to observe, that moral qualities are so constituted as to be destroyed by excess and by deficiency—as we see is the case with bodily strength and health (for one is forced to explain what is invisible by means of visible illustrations). Strength is destroyed both by excessive and by deficient exercises, and similarly health is destroyed both by too much and by too little food and drink; while they are produced, increased and preserved by suitable quantities. The same therefore is true of temperance, courage, and the other virtues. The man who runs away from everything in fear and never endures anything becomes a coward; the man who fears nothing whatsoever but encounters everything becomes rash. Similarly he that indulges in every pleasure and refrains from none turns out a profligate, and he that shuns all pleasure, as boorish persons do, becomes what may be called insensible. Thus temperance and courage are destroyed by excess and deficiency, and preserved by the observance of the mean.[1]

But not only are the virtues both generated and fostered on the one hand, and destroyed on the other, from and by the same actions, but they will also find their full exercise in the same actions. This is clearly the case with the other more visible qualities, such as bodily strength: for strength is produced by taking much food and undergoing much exertion, while also it is the strong man who will be able to eat most food and endure most exertion. The same holds good with the virtues. We become temperate by abstaining from pleasures, and at the same time we are best able to abstain from pleasures when we have become temperate. And so with courage: we become brave by training ourselves to despise and endure terrors, and we shall be best able to endure terrors when we have become brave.

An index of our dispositions is afforded by the pleasure or pain that accompanies our actions. A man is temperate if he abstains from bodily pleasures and finds this abstinence itself enjoyable, profligate if he feels it irksome: he is brave if he faces danger with pleasure or at all events without pain, cowardly if he does so with pain.

1. [By "mean," Aristotle has in mind the notion of a midpoint between the two extremes of too-much and too-little of something; as in the mathematical sense of "mean." The Greek word here is *mesotetos*, whence the English prefix meso-, meaning "middle."]

In fact pleasures and pains are the things with which virtue is concerned. For pleasure causes us to do base actions and pain causes us to abstain from doing noble actions. Hence the importance, as Plato points out, of having been definitely trained from childhood to like and dislike things; this is what good education means.[2] Again, if the virtues have to do with actions and feelings, and every feeling and every action is attended with pleasure or pain, this too shows that virtue has to do with pleasure and pain. . . .

. . . There are three things that are the motives of choice and three that are motives of avoidance; namely, the noble, the expedient, and the pleasant, and their opposites, the base, the harmful, and the painful. Now in respect of all these the good man is likely to go right and the bad to go wrong, but especially in respect of pleasure; for pleasure is common to man with the lower animals, and also it is a concomitant of all the objects of choice, since both the noble and the expedient appear to us pleasant. . . .

. . . We may then take it as established that virtue has to do with pleasures and pains, that the actions which produce it are those which increase it, and also, if differently performed, destroy it, and that the actions from which it was produced are also those in which it is exercised.

A difficulty may however be raised as to what we mean by saying that in order to become just men must do just actions, and in order to become temperate they must do temperate actions. For if they do just and temperate actions, they are just and temperate already, just as, if they spell correctly or play in tune, they are scholars or musicians.

But perhaps this is not the case even with the arts. It is possible to spell a word correctly by chance, or because someone else prompts you; hence you will be a scholar only if you spell correctly in the scholar's way, that is, in virtue of the scholarly knowledge which you yourself possess.

Moreover the case of the arts is not really analogous to that of the virtues. Works of art have their merit in themselves, so that it is enough if they are produced having a certain quality of their own; but acts done in conformity with the virtues are not done justly or temperately if they themselves are of a certain sort, but only if the agent also is in a certain state of mind when he does them: first he must act with

2. [Plato's *Republic* articulates an ideal political system in which select children are specially reared in a way that exposes them to the good, the true, and the beautiful. See the *Republic* selection (chapter 9) for his attempt to justify this program.]

knowledge; secondly he must deliberately choose the act, and choose it for its own sake; and thirdly the act must spring from a fixed and permanent disposition of character.

. . . In respect of truth then, the middle [moderate] character may be called truthful, and the observance of the mean truthfulness;[3] pretense in the form of exaggeration is boastfulness, and its possessor is a boaster; in the form of understatement, self-depreciation, and its possessor the self-depreciator.

Book IV

The observance of the mean in relation to boastfulness has to do with almost the same things [namely, flattery and obsequiousness]. It also is without a name, but it will be as well to discuss these unnamed excellences with the rest, since we shall the better understand the nature of moral character if we examine its qualities one by one, and we shall also confirm our belief that the virtues are modes of observing the mean, if we notice how this holds good in every instance. Now we have treated of behavior in society with relation to giving pleasure and pain. Let us now discuss truthfulness and falsehood[4] similarly displayed in word and deed, and in one's personal pretensions.

As generally understood then, the boaster is a man who pretends to creditable qualities that he does not possess, or possesses in a lesser degree than he makes out, while conversely the self-depreciator disclaims or disparages good qualities that he does possess. Midway between them is the straightforward sort of man who is sincere both in behavior and in speech, and admits the truth about his own qualifications without either exaggeration or understatement.[5] Each of these things may be done with or without an ulterior motive; but when a man is acting without ulterior motive, his words, actions, and conduct always represent his true character. Falsehood is in itself base and reprehensible, and the truth noble and praiseworthy; and similarly the sincere man who stands between the two extremes is praised, and the insincere of both kinds are blamed, more especially the boaster. Let us discuss each of the two, beginning with the truthful man.

We are speaking not of truthfulness in business relations, nor in matters where honesty and dishonesty are concerned, for these

3. [For "truthfulness," Aristotle uses the Greek word *aletheia*, which has the etymology of "not forgetting."]

4. ["Falsehood" here translates *pseudomenon*.]

5. ["Sincerity" translates *alatheutikos*, which is cognate with *aletheia*, Aristotle's term for honesty.]

matters would come under a different virtue, but of cases where a man is truthful both in speech and conduct when no considerations of honesty come in, from a habitual sincerity of disposition.[6] Such sincerity may be esteemed a moral excellence, for the lover of truth,[7] who is truthful even when nothing depends on it, will be even more truthful when some interest is at stake, since having all along avoided falsehood for its own sake, he will assuredly avoid it when it is morally base; and this is a disposition that we praise. The sincere man will diverge from the truth, if at all, in the direction of understatement rather than exaggeration, since this appears in better taste, as all excess is offensive.

The man who pretends to more merit than he possesses for no ulterior object seems, it is true, to be a person of inferior character, since otherwise he would not take pleasure in falsehood; but he appears to be more foolish than vicious. When, on the other hand, a man exaggerates his own merits to gain some object, if that object is glory or honor he is not very much to be blamed [as is the boaster], but if he boasts to get money or things that fetch money, this is more unseemly. Boastfulness is not a matter of potential capacity but of deliberate purpose; a man is a boaster if he has a fixed disposition to boast—a boastful character. Similarly liars are divided into those who like lying for its own sake and those who lie to get reputation or profit. Those then who boast for the sake of reputation pretend to possess such qualities as are praised and admired; those who do so for profit pretend to accomplishments that are useful to their fellows and also can be counterfeited without detection; for instance, proficiency in prophecy, philosophy, or medicine. Because these arts have the two qualities specified they are the commonest fields of pretense and bragging.

Self-depreciators, who understate their own merits, seem of a more refined character, for we feel that the motive underlying this form of insincerity is not gain but dislike of ostentation. These also mostly disown qualities held in high esteem, as Socrates used to do. Those who disclaim merely trifling or obvious distinctions are called affected

6. [Aristotle means that truthfulness in the context of business transactions is more within the domain of justice, rather than honesty per se. The word being translated as "honesty" here is not *aletheia*, but *dikaiosune* ("justice"). Of course, justice and honesty are not disconnected: for Aristotle, the former is a broader concept that encompasses the latter. See the introduction to this selection for discussion of the idea that Aristotle sees all of the virtues as interdependent.]

7. [A "lover of truth" is a *philolethes*.]

humbugs, and are decidedly contemptible, and sometimes such mock humility seems to be really boastfulness, like the dress of the Spartans, for extreme negligence in dress, as well as excessive attention to it, has a touch of ostentation. But a moderate use of self-depreciation in matters not too commonplace and obvious has a more graceful air.

The boaster seems to be the opposite of the sincere man, because boastfulness is worse than self-depreciation.

Rhetoric

Book 1, Chapter 1

It is clear, then, that rhetorical study, in its strict sense, is concerned with the modes of persuasion.[1] Persuasion is clearly a sort of demonstration,[2] since we are most fully persuaded when we consider a thing to have been demonstrated. The orator's demonstration is an enthymeme, and this is, in general, the most effective of the modes of persuasion. The enthymeme is a sort of syllogism, and the consideration of syllogisms of all kinds, without distinction, is the business of dialectic, either of dialectic as a whole or of one of its branches.[3] It follows plainly, therefore, that he who is best able to see how and from what elements a syllogism is produced will also be best skilled in the enthymeme, when he has further learnt what its subject-matter is and in what respects it differs from the syllogism of strict logic.[4] The true and the approximately true are apprehended by the same faculty; it may also be noted that men have a sufficient natural instinct for what

1. ["Persuasion" here translates *pistis*, which carries a sense of trustworthiness, assurance, and warrant, and when applied to arguments, as Aristotle does here, it involves persuasion in terms of *proof*. Compare this with Plato's term for "persuasion" in the *Gorgias* selection (chapter 8); the Greek words used by Plato and Aristotle are cognate, but given quite different connotations.]

2. ["Demonstration" is *apodeiksis*, meaning a showing-forth or a display.]

3. ["Syllogism" and "enthymeme" are technical terms in Aristotle's logic. A syllogism refers to a specific pattern of reasoning and logical inference; an enthymeme is a syllogistic argument in which the probability of a premise or the plausibility of an inference is affected by its rhetorical appeal.]

4. ["Strict logic" would involve deductions that deal with necessary inferences, whereas enthymemes (rhetorical syllogisms) utilize probability and extra-deductive modes of persuasion.]

is true, and usually do arrive at the truth. Hence the man who makes a good guess at truth is likely to make a good guess at probabilities.

It has now been shown that the ordinary writers on rhetoric treat of non-essentials; it has also been shown why they have inclined more towards the forensic branch of oratory.[5]

Rhetoric is useful (1) because things that are true and things that are just have a natural tendency to prevail over their opposites, so that if the decisions of judges are not what they ought to be, the defeat must be due to the speakers themselves, and they must be blamed accordingly. Moreover, (2) before some audiences not even the possession of the exactest knowledge will make it easy for what we say to produce conviction. For argument based on knowledge implies instruction, and there are people whom one cannot instruct. Here, then, we must use, as our modes of persuasion and argument, notions possessed by everybody, as we observed in the Topics when dealing with the way to handle a popular audience. Further, (3) we must be able to employ persuasion, just as strict reasoning can be employed, on opposite sides of a question, not in order that we may in practice employ it in both ways (for we must not make people believe what is wrong), but in order that we may see clearly what the facts are, and that, if another man argues unfairly, we on our part may be able to confute him. No other of the arts draws opposite conclusions: dialectic and rhetoric alone do this. Both these arts draw opposite conclusions impartially. Nevertheless, the underlying facts do not lend themselves equally well to the contrary views. No; things that are true and things that are better are, by their nature, practically always easier to prove and easier to believe in. Again, (4) it is absurd to hold that a man ought to be ashamed of being unable to defend himself with his limbs, but not of being unable to defend himself with speech and reason, when the use of rational speech is more distinctive of a human being than the use of his limbs. And if it be objected that one who uses such power of speech unjustly might do great harm, that is a charge which may be made in common against all good things except virtue, and above all against the things that are most useful, as strength, health, wealth, generalship. A man can confer the greatest of benefits by a right use of these, and inflict the greatest of injuries by using them wrongly . . .

5. [By "ordinary writers," Aristotle is referring to earlier authors who tended to use terms such as "enthymeme" in looser sense or else as referring to overly specialized domains of rhetorical argument, e.g., legal ("forensic") dispute. He wants to treat rhetoric both more analytically and more universally.]

What makes a man a "sophist" is not his faculty, but his moral purpose.[6] In rhetoric, however, the term "rhetorician" may describe either the speaker's knowledge of the art, or his moral purpose. In dialectic it is different: a man is a "sophist" because he has a certain kind of moral purpose, a "dialectician" in respect, not of his moral purpose, but of his faculty. . . .

Book 2, Chapters 12–14

Let us now consider the various types of human character, in relation to the emotions and moral qualities, showing how they correspond to our various ages and fortunes. . . .

Young men have strong passions, and tend to gratify them indiscriminately. . . . Their lives are mainly spent not in memory but in expectation; for expectation refers to the future, memory to the past, and youth has a long future before it and a short past behind it: on the first day of one's life one has nothing at all to remember, and can only look forward. They are easily cheated, owing to the sanguine disposition just mentioned. . . .

The character of Elderly Men—men who are past their prime—may be said to be formed for the most part of elements that are the contrary of all these. They have lived many years; they have often been taken in, and often made mistakes; and life on the whole is a bad business. The result is that they are sure about nothing and under-do everything. They "think", but they never "know"; and because of their hesitation they always add a "possibly" or a "perhaps", putting everything this way and nothing positively. They are cynical; that is, they tend to put the worse construction on everything. Further, their experience makes them distrustful and therefore suspicious of evil. . . .

As for Men in their Prime, clearly we shall find that they have a character between that of the young and that of the old, free from the extremes of either. They have neither that excess of confidence which amounts to rashness, nor too much timidity, but the right amount of each. They neither trust everybody nor distrust everybody, but judge people correctly. Their lives will be guided not by the sole consideration either of what is noble or of what is useful, but by both; neither by parsimony nor by prodigality, but by what is fit and proper.

6. [A sophist is a proclaimed "wise person" who can speak cleverly, convincingly, and usually dazzlingly. The term took on a largely pejorative association in classical Greece, where sophists were characterized as con artists.]

4
MAHĀBHĀRATA, DROṆA PARVAN

One of the two great epics of Indian literature (the other is the *Rāmāyaṇa*), the *Mahābhārata* is a vast tome—comprising more than 100,000 two-line verses in some editions. The composition of the text began probably in the fifth century BCE, based on orally transmitted stories that have their origin much earlier. The version that we receive today probably took final shape sometime around the fourth century CE. The *Mahābhārata* tells the story of the descendants of the great king and mythical founder of India, Bharata. The focus of the epic is the struggle between two families for the throne of Hastinapura: the five sons of Pāṇḍu (the Pāṇḍavas), the eldest of whom, Yudhiṣṭhira, is the rightful heir to the throne, and the one hundred sons of Dhṛtarāṣṭra (the Kauravas), who want to usurp power from the Pāṇḍavas. This struggle culminates in the war at Kurukṣetra that is the central event of the *Mahābhārata*, the depiction of which occupies a third of the text. After eighteen days of brutal fighting the Pāṇḍavas emerge victorious, but each side has seen so many casualties that it is in many ways a pyrrhic victory. In order to win, the Pāṇḍavas have had to kill not just their cousins who were trying to usurp their right to the kingdom, but also their most beloved teachers and friends, as well as many others, who were fighting alongside the Kauravas.

The war presents many moral dilemmas for those fighting on both sides. The most famous of these is depicted in the section of the *Mahābhārata* that has become famous in its own right as the *Bhagavad Gītā*. In the *Gītā*, the warrior hero Arjuna faces a dilemma about whether to fight in a just war when doing so would involve killing friends and family. Krishna, Arjuna's charioteer who is also the god Vishnu incarnate, advises Arjuna on how to act in the face of what appear to be contradictory duties. While the dilemma that Arjuna faces in the *Bhagavad Gītā* is not explicitly about truthfulness, it nevertheless helps to illuminate those dilemmas that are about truthfulness, which we've included in this reader. Like Arjuna's dilemma, these dilemmas arise when one duty (in this case, the duty to truth) appears to be in conflict with another, equally important, duty.

Our first selection, from the seventh book (the *Droṇa Parvan*) of the *Mahābhārata*, occurs during the fifteenth day of the war at Kurukṣetra. After the first commander's defeat, Droṇa has taken over as leader of the Kaurava army. Droṇa's fighting skill is so great that nobody can overcome him in combat, and the Pāṇḍavas know this. The Pāṇḍavas experience repeated defeats when facing the Droṇa-led Kauravas and begin to despair. In the midst of the carnage, Krishna comes up with a strategy for defeating Droṇa through subterfuge and deception: all they need to do is to convince Droṇa that his son has been killed, at which time he will lose the will to fight and lay down his weapons. The Pāṇḍavas go through with Krishna's plan, but it does not have the desired effect: knowing that his son cannot be killed in battle, Droṇa suspects that it is a ruse and unleashes great fury, killing thousands of the Pāṇḍava troops. Droṇa's wrath is so great that the gods themselves come down and criticize him for conduct unbecoming a brahmin. He begins to wonder whether his suspicion is misplaced and turns to Yudhiṣṭhira to resolve his doubt. From anyone else he would suspect deceit; but Yudhiṣṭhira is well known to be perfectly pious, unflagging in his adherence to dharma (in fact he is the son of the God *Dharma*, from whom the notion of dharma as moral law is derived). Yudhiṣṭhira does not want to mislead his beloved teacher, but he succumbs to pressure from his brother Bhīma and from Krishna: in order to avert catastrophe and win the war, he says, "Lord, he is killed." But, in order to avoid uttering a falsehood, he then mutters under his breath that he is referring not to Droṇa's son, Aśvatthaman, but to an elephant of the same name. Convinced by this act of deception, Droṇa lays aside his weapons and begins to meditate, which enables him to be killed.

As you read the selection, consider the following questions:

1. Is Yudhiṣṭhira's indirect deception of Droṇa any more or less blameworthy than Bhīma's more straightforward attempt at deception? Would it be better, worse, or no different if Yudhiṣṭhira were to say, "Your son is dead"?
2. Droṇa decides to ask Yudhiṣṭhira whether Aśvatthaman is dead precisely because of Yudhiṣṭhira's reputation for being perfectly truthful. Is it fair for Droṇa to exploit Yudhiṣṭhira's truthfulness in this manner? Is Droṇa at all blameworthy for putting Yudhiṣṭhira in the position wherein he will feel compelled to deceive?
3. Krishna tells Yudhiṣṭhira that no sin will accrue to one who tells a lie in such a situation as he is in. But, as soon as Yudhiṣṭhira utters the falsehood, his chariot drops to the ground. Further, near the end of the *Mahābhārata*, Yudhiṣṭhira is made to visit hell, as a way of atoning for his deception of Droṇa, before he can ascend to heaven. What are we to make of Krishna's advice to Yudhiṣṭhira? Is Krishna lying? If yes, is his lie justified?

Mahābhārata

Droṇa Chapter, Sections 191–193

Beholding the sons of Kunti,[1] afflicted with the shafts of Droṇa and filled with fear, Keśava,[2] endued with great intelligence and, devoted to their welfare, addressed Arjuna and said, "This foremost of all bowmen is incapable of being ever vanquished by force in battle, by the very gods with Vasava at their head. When, however, he lays aside his weapons, he becomes capable of being slain on the field even by human beings. Casting aside virtue, sons of Pāṇḍu, adopt now some contrivance for gaining victory, so that Droṇa of the golden chariot may not slay us all in battle. Upon the fall of (his son) Aśvatthaman he will cease to fight, I think. Let someone, therefore, tell him that Aśvatthaman has been killed in battle." This advice, however, was not approved by Kunti's son, Dhananjaya.[3] Others approved of it. But Yudhiṣṭhira accepted it with great difficulty. Then the mighty-armed Bhīma slew with a mace a foe-crushing, terrible and huge elephant named Aśvatthaman, of his own army, belonging to Indravarman, the chief of the Malavas. Approaching Droṇa then in that battle with some bashfulness Bhīmasena[4] began to exclaim aloud, "Aśvatthaman has been killed!" That elephant named Aśvatthaman having been thus slain, Bhīma spoke of Aśvatthaman's slaughter. Keeping the true fact within his mind, he said what was untrue.

Hearing those highly disagreeable words of Bhīma and reflecting upon them, Droṇa's limbs seemed to dissolve like sands in water. Recollecting, however, the prowess of his son, he soon came to regard that report as false. Hearing, therefore, of his slaughter, Droṇa did not become demoralized. Indeed, soon recovering his senses, he became comforted, remembering that his son was incapable of being resisted by foes. Rushing towards the son of Pṛṣata[5] and desirous of slaying that hero who had been ordained as his slayer, he covered him with a thousand keen shafts, equipped with heron feathers. Then twenty

1. [Kunti is the wife of Pāṇḍu and mother of the Pāṇḍavas. "Sons of Kunti" is a common epithet to refer to the Pāṇḍavas.]
2. ["Keśava" is another name for Krishna.]
3. ["Dhananjaya" is another name for Arjuna.]
4. ["Bhīmasena" is another name for Bhīma.]
5. [The son of Pṛṣata is Dhṛṣṭadyumna, commander of the Pāṇḍava army and brother-in-law of the Pāṇḍavas.]

thousand Pancala warriors[6] of great energy covered him, while he was thus careering in battle, with their shafts. Completely shrouded with those shafts, we could not any longer see that great warrior who then resembled the sun covered with clouds in the season of rains. Filled with wrath and desirous of compassing the destruction of those brave Pancalas, that mighty warrior, that scorcher of foes, Droṇa, dispelling all those shafts of the Pancalas, then invoked into existence the *Brahma* weapon.[7] At that time, Droṇa looked resplendent like a smokeless, blazing fire. Once more filled with rage, the valiant son of Bhāradvāja[8] slaughtering all the Somakas, seemed to be invested with great splendor. In that dreadful battle, he felled the heads of the Pancalas and cut off their massive arms, looking like spiked maces and decked with golden ornaments. Indeed, those Kṣatriyas, slaughtered in battle by Bhāradvāja's son fell down on the earth and lay scattered like trees uprooted by the tempest. In consequence of fallen elephants and steeds, the earth, mired with flesh and blood, became impassable. Having slain twenty thousand Pancala warriors, Droṇa, in that battle, shone resplendent like a smokeless, blazing fire. Once more filled with rage, the valiant son of Bhāradvāja cut off, with a broad-headed arrow, the head of Vasudana from his trunk. Once more slaying five hundred Matsyas, and six thousand elephants, he slew ten thousand steeds.

Beholding Droṇa stationed on the field for the extermination of the Kṣatriya race, the Ṛṣis[9] Viśvāmitra, Jamadagni, Bhāradvāja, Gautama, Vasiṣṭha, Kaśyapa, Atri, the Sikatas, the Pṛṣṇis, Garga, the Bālakhilyas, the Marīcis, the descendants of Bhṛgu and Aṅgiras, and diverse other sages of subtle forms quickly arrived, with the bearer of sacrificial libations at their head, and, desiring to take Droṇa unto the region of Brahman, addressed Droṇa, that ornament of battle, and said, "You are fighting unrighteously. The hour of your death is come. Laying aside your weapons in battle, O Droṇa, behold us stationed here. After this, it does not behoove you to perpetrate such exceedingly cruel deeds. You are versed in the *Vedas* and their branches. You are devoted to the duties enjoined by truth, you are a Brahmin. Such acts do not become you. Lay aside your weapons. Drive away the

6. [The warriors from Pancala are allied with the Pāṇḍavas in the war. They are also referred to as the Somakas.]

7. [The Brahma weapon is a supernatural weapon that is said to be invincible and capable of destroying one's foes with a single use. It could only be used once per day.]

8. [The son of Bhāradvāja is Droṇa.]

9. [The names that follow are various gods and other divine beings.]

film of error that shrouds you. Adhere now to the eternal path. The period for which you are to dwell in the world of men is now complete. You have, with the *Brahma* weapon, burnt men on earth who are unacquainted with weapons. This act that you have perpetrated is not righteous. Lay aside your weapons in battle without delay, O Droṇa, do not wait longer on earth. Do not, perpetrate such a sinful act."

Hearing these words of theirs, as well as those spoken by Bhīmasena, and beholding Dhṛṣṭadyumna before him, Droṇa became exceedingly cheerless in battle. Burning with grief and exceedingly afflicted, he inquired of Kunti's son Yudhiṣṭhira as to whether his son had been slain or not. Droṇa firmly believed that Yudhiṣṭhira would never speak an untruth even for the sake of the sovereignty of the three worlds. For this reason, that bull among Brahmins asked Yudhiṣṭhira and not anyone else. He had counted on truth from Yudhiṣṭhira from the latter's infancy.

Meanwhile, Govinda,[10] knowing that Droṇa, that foremost of warriors, was capable of sweeping all the Pāṇḍavas off the face of the earth, became much distressed. Addressing Yudhiṣṭhira he said, "If Droṇa fights, filled with rage, for even half a day, I tell you truly, your army will then be annihilated. Save us, then, from Droṇa. Under such circumstances, falsehood is better than truth. By telling an untruth to save a life, one is not touched by sin. There is no sin in untruth spoken unto women, or in marriages, or for saving a king, or for rescuing a Brahmin." While Govinda and Yudhiṣṭhira were thus talking with each other, Bhīmasena said to Yudhiṣṭhira, "As soon, O monarch, as I heard of the means by which the high-souled Droṇa might be slain, putting forth my prowess in battle, I immediately slew a mighty elephant, like unto the elephant of Sakra himself, belonging to Indravarman, the chief of the Malavas, who was standing within your army. I then went to Droṇa and told him, 'Aśvatthaman has been slain, O Brahmin! Cease, then, to fight.' Verily, O bull among men, the preceptor did not believe in the truth of my words. Desirous of victory as you are, accept the advice of Govinda. Tell Droṇa, O King, that the son of Saradwat's daughter is no more. Told by you, that bull among Brahmins will never fight. You, O ruler of men, are reputed to be truthful in the three worlds."

Hearing those words of Bhīma and induced by the counsels of Krishna, and owing also to the inevitability of destiny, Yudhiṣṭhira made up his mind to say what he desired. Fearing to utter an untruth, but earnestly desirous of victory, Yudhiṣṭhira distinctly said that

10. ["Govinda" is another name for Krishna.]

Aśvatthaman was dead, adding indistinctly the word *elephant*. Before this, Yudhiṣṭhira's chariot had stayed at a height of four fingers' breadth from the surface of the earth; after, however, he had said that untruth, his vehicle and animals touched the earth. Hearing those words from Yudhiṣṭhira, the mighty warrior Droṇa, afflicted with grief, for the death of his son, yielded to the influence of despair. Considering the words of the Ṛṣis, he regarded himself a great offender against the high-souled Pāṇḍavas. Hearing now about the death of his son, he became perfectly cheerless and filled with anxiety; upon beholding Dhṛṣṭadyumna, that chastiser of foes could not fight as before.

Then Bhīma, of great wrath, holding the chariot of Droṇa, slowly said these words to him: "If wretches amongst Brahmins, discontented with the avocations of their own order, but well-versed in arms, did not fight, the Kṣatriya order then would not have been thus exterminated. Abstention from injury to all creatures has been said to be the highest of all virtues. The Brahmin is the root of that virtue. As regards thyself, again, you are the foremost of all persons acquainted with *Brahma*. Slaying all those Mleccas and other warriors, who, however, are all engaged in the proper avocations of their order, moved thereto by ignorance and folly, O Brahmin, and by the desire of wealth for benefiting sons and wives; indeed, for the sake of an only son, why do you not feel ashamed? He for whom you have taken up weapons, and for whom you live, he, deprived of life, lies today on the field of battle, unknown to you and behind your back. King Yudhiṣṭhira the Just has told you this. It does not behoove you to doubt this fact." Thus addressed by Bhīma, Droṇa laid aside his bow. Desiring to lay aside all his weapons also, Bhāradvāja's son of virtuous soul said aloud, "O Karṇa, Karṇa, O great bowman, O Kṛpa, O Duryodhana, I tell you repeatedly, exert yourselves carefully in battle. Let no injury happen to you from the Pāṇḍavas. As regards myself, I lay aside my weapons." Saying these words, he began loudly to chant the name of Aśvatthaman. Laying aside his weapons then in that battle, and sitting down in his chariot, he devoted himself to yoga and assured all creatures, dispelling their fears.

Beholding that opportunity, Dhṛṣṭadyumna mustered all his energy. Laying down on the chariot his formidable bow, with arrow fixed on the bow-string, he took up a sword, and jumping down from his vehicle, rushed quickly against Droṇa. All creatures, human beings and others, uttered exclamation of woe, beholding Droṇa thus subject to Dhṛṣṭadyumna's power. Loud cries were uttered. As regards Droṇa himself, abandoning his weapons, he was then in a supremely tranquil state. Having said those words, he had devoted himself to yoga.

Endowed with great radiance and possessed of high ascetic merit, he had fixed his heart on that supreme and ancient being, Vishnu. Bending his face slightly down, and heaving his breast forward, and closing his eyes, and focusing on the quality of goodness, and disposing his heart to contemplation, and thinking on the syllable Om, representing Brahma, and remembering the powerful, supreme, and indestructible God of gods, the radiant Droṇa of high ascetic merit, the preceptor retired to heaven that is so difficult to attain even by the pious. Indeed, when Droṇa thus proceeded to heaven it seemed to us that there were then two suns in the sky. The whole firmament was ablaze and seemed to be one vast expanse of equal light when the sun-like Bhāradvāja, of solar radiance, disappeared. Confused sounds of joy were heard, uttered by the delighted celestials. When Droṇa thus retired to the region of Brahman, Dhṛṣṭadyumna stood, unconscious of it all, beside him. . . . As regards Pṛṣata's son, though everybody called on him to desist, yet casting his eyes on the lifeless Droṇa's head, he began to drag it. With his sword, then, he lopped off from his foe's trunk that head. His foe remained speechless the while. Having slain Bhāradvāja's son, Dhṛṣṭadyumna was filled with great joy and roared like a lion, whirling his sword. Of a dark complexion, with white locks hanging down to his ears, that old man of eighty-five years of age, used to tear about on the field of battle with the activity of a youth of sixteen.

The mighty-armed Dhananjaya, the son of Kunti, had said, "O son of Drupada, bring the preceptor alive, do not slay him. He should not be slain." Even thus all the troops also had cried out. Arjuna in particular, melted with pity, cried out repeatedly. Disregarding, however, the cries of Arjuna as well as those of all the kings, Dhṛṣṭadyumna slew Droṇa, that bull among men, in his chariot. Covered with Droṇa's blood, Dhṛṣṭadyumna then jumped from the chariot down upon the ground. Looking red like the sun, he then seemed to be exceedingly fierce. The troops beheld Droṇa slain even thus in that battle. Then Dhṛṣṭadyumna, that great bowman, threw down that large head of Bhāradvāja's son before the warriors of the army. The soldiers, beholding the head of Bhāradvāja's son, set their hearts on flight and ran away in all directions.

Part Two

Is It Morally Permissible to Lie?

5

CONFUCIANISM

Confucianism is a moral and political system developed in China during the first centuries CE, but grounded in the earlier teachings of Confucius (the Latinized form of Kongzi, or "Master Kong"). Confucius himself lived between 551–479 BCE, during an epoch of Chinese history referred to as the Spring and Autumn Period in which what little stability remained of past dynastic rule was being rapidly and violently eroded by fragmenting regional interests. In this time of political and cultural tumult, Confucius traveled from province to province, attracting disciples and offering council to dukes and would-be kings. He advocated for a moral and spiritual renaissance that envisioned a return to what he saw as the harmonizing values, hierarchies, and traditions of early times.

Although Confucianism later became increasingly metaphysical and otherworldly, in its earliest texts it focuses on the more pragmatic concerns of how to interact politically, how to flourish within the social roles in which one finds oneself (ruler, parent, child, etc.), and how to coexist with the natural order of things. Of particular emphasis in Confucian writings is the ideal of the *junzi* 君子 (translated in our selection as "gentleman"), a sort of moral and political exemplar who embodies the core virtues of filial piety, wisdom, ritual propriety, social grace, and overall humaneness. Rather than reduce the *junzi*'s moral code to an algorithmic set of abstract formulae, however, Confucianism instead relies on anecdotal examples in the form of dialogues between Confucian teachers, pupils, and various political officials. For this reason, Confucian moral philosophy is sometimes conceived as a system of "virtue" or "role" ethics, according to which obligations are grounded in concrete individuals and situations, rather than a "rule-based" system of ethics in which moral prescriptions are given impersonal, universal expression.

The majority of the selections are taken from the *Analects*, a collection of sayings traditionally ascribed to Confucius and his followers. Each individual passage is indicated by a book number and then the number of the passage within that book, e.g., 1.13. The final selection is from a text attributed to another early Confucian thinker named Mencius (the Latinized form of Mengzi, or "Master Meng") who lived in the fourth century BCE and is known for defending an interpretation of Confucius' teachings that views human nature in a very optimistic light.

As you read these Confucian passages pertaining to lying and truthfulness, think about these questions:

1. Sometimes it appears that Confucius himself, or the sort of "gentleman" he characterizes, deploys differing degrees of truthfulness depending on his audience, e.g., immediate family members versus visiting strangers, or disciples possessed of different dispositions. Do you think that the ethics of lying vary depending on the nature of the person who is being addressed? Are there things that are okay to lie about (or at least to be more subtle about) when speaking with one's family or friends compared to speaking to strangers, subordinates, professional colleagues, etc.? If so, what could account for this distinction, given that the gentleman is not supposed to be "partial"?
2. Can other people or certain situations "trap" us into a position wherein we have to lie or deceive? Consider the scenario in which a close family member has committed a crime (*Analects* 13.18 or Shun's dilemma in *Mengzi* 5A2), or think about Confucius' own actions in *Analects* 7.31. Do such circumstances change the meaning or the ethics of truthfulness?
3. Consider Confucius' actions in *Analects* 17.20. Is there any difference between directly lying to someone's face versus intending that someone overhear something deceptive? Can an action lie (or reveal the truth) in the same way that spoken or written communication can?

Analects

1.3 The Master said, "A clever tongue and fine appearance are rarely signs of Goodness."[1]

1.13 Master You said, "Trustworthiness comes close to rightness, in that your word can be counted upon.[2] Reverence comes close to ritual propriety, in that it allows you to keep shame and public disgrace at a distance. Simply following these virtues, never letting them out of your sight—one cannot deny that this is worthy of respect."

2.22 The Master said, "I cannot see how a person devoid of trustworthiness could possibly get along in the world. Imagine a large ox-drawn cart without a linchpin for its yoke, or a small horse drawn cart without a linchpin for its collar: how could they possibly be driven?"

5.5 Someone said, "Zhonggong is Good but not eloquent (*ning* 佞)."

The Master said, "Of what use is 'eloquence'? If you go about responding to everyone with a clever tongue you will often incur resentment. I do not know whether or not Zhonggong is Good, but of what use is eloquence?"

5.25 The Master said, "Clever words, an ingratiating countenance, and perfunctory gestures of respect are all things that Zuoqiu Ming considered shameful, and I, too, consider them shameful. Concealing one's resentment and feigning friendship toward another is something Zuoqiu considered shameful, and I, too, consider shameful.[3]

6.15 The Master said, "Meng Zhifan is not given to boasting. When his forces were retreating he stayed behind to defend the rear, but as they were about to enter the city gates he spurred his horses ahead, saying, 'It was not my courage that kept me back, but merely that my horses would not advance.'"[4]

6.26 Zai Wo asked, "If someone lied to a Good person, saying 'a man has just fallen into the well!', would he go ahead and jump in after him [to save the supposed man]?"

1. ["Goodness" here is translating the term *ren* 仁, which is also frequently rendered as "benevolence" or "humaneness" (the etymology of the character has to do with interpersonal relationships). "Clever tongue" is *ning* 佞. This entire passage is duplicated later in *Analects* 17.17.]

2. ["Trustworthiness" is *xin* 信, also occasionally rendered as "integrity" or the quality of accurately matching one's credentials.]

3. ["Concealing" translates *ni* 匿, etymologically suggesting putting something inside a box.]

4. [Meng Zhifan was a minister of Lu.]

The Master replied, "Why would he do that? The gentleman can be enticed, but not trapped; he can be tricked, but not duped."[5]

7.31 The Minister of Crime in the state of Chen asked, "Can we say that Duke Zhao [of Lu] understood ritual?"

Confucius answered, "Yes, he understood ritual."

Confucius then retired. With a bow, the Minister invited Wuma Qi to approach and said to him, "I have heard it said that the gentleman is not partial. Is the gentleman in fact partial after all? His lordship took as his wife a woman from the state of Wu who was of the same clan, and then called her 'Elder Daughter of Wu.' If his lordship understood ritual, who does not understand it?"

Later, Wuma Qi reported this conversation to Confucius. Confucius said, "How fortunate I am! If I happen to make a mistake, others are sure to inform me."[6]

5. ["Tricked" here translates *qi* 欺, which also has the meanings of being cheated, deceived, or bullied. "Duped" is *wang* 罔, which connotes being slandered or made crooked. "Gentleman" is translating the term *junzi* 君子, which originally had aristocratic connotations, but which Confucianism refigures to have a primarily moral and political meaning. The point seems to be that while a *junzi* can be externally fooled or abused by deceptions, such an exemplary person can never be made to deviate internally from the proper path, and any successful deception will reflect only on the deceiver rather than the *junzi*.]

6. [Slingerland includes the following note to this passage: "It was a serious violation of ritual to take as a wife or concubine someone with the same clan-name. Therefore, when Duke Zhao took an aristocrat from Wu as his wife, he had people refer to her by the vague locution, 'Elder Daughter of Wu,' instead of using her proper name, hoping in this way to avoid attracting attention to his incestuous transgression. In this exchange, the Minister of Chen is probably trying to embarrass Confucius by citing some Confucian wisdom to criticize Confucius' actual conduct . . . the Minister is implying that Confucius is choosing loyalty to the former ruler of his home state over rightness in defending the ritually improper Duke Zhao. Confucius' final response is ironic: although the Minister mocks Duke Zhao for ignoring ritual propriety, he fails to see that asking Confucius to criticize a former lord of his home state—especially in the presence of an official of a rival state—is itself a grave violation of ritual, and that Confucius' praise of Duke Zhao was the only ritually proper response." Robert Eno, in his translation of this passage, notes that "Duke Zhao was a former duke in Lu [Confucius' home province]. The Minister has put Confucius in the difficult position of choosing between telling the truth and being loyal to his state's ruling house . . . Confucius' final remark is sarcastic. The Minister could have criticized him either way." See Eno (2015), *The Analects of Confucius: An Online Teaching Translation*, p. 34.]

11.22 Zilu asked, "Upon learning of something that needs to be done, should one immediately take care of it?"

The Master replied, "As long as one's father and elder brothers are still alive, how could one possibly take care of it immediately?"

[On a later occasion] Ran Qiu asked, "Upon learning of something that needs to be done, should one immediately take care of it?"

The Master replied, "Upon learning of it, you should immediately take care of it."

Zihua [having observed both exchanges] inquired, "When Zilu asked you whether or not one should immediately take care of something upon learning of it, you told him one should not, as long as one's father and elder brothers were still alive. When Ran Qiu asked the same question, however, you told him that one should immediately take care of it. I am confused, and humbly ask to have this explained to me."

The Master said, "Ran Qiu is overly cautious, and so I wished to urge him on. Zilu, on the other hand, is too impetuous, and so I sought to hold him back."

13.18 The Duke of She said to Confucius, "Among my people there is one we call 'Upright Gong.' When his father stole a sheep, he reported him to the authorities."

Confucius replied, "Among my people, those who we consider 'upright' are different from this: fathers cover up for their sons, and sons cover up for their fathers. 'Uprightness' is to be found in this."[7]

13.20 Zigong asked, "What does a person have to be like before he could be called a true scholar-official?"

The Master said, "Conducing himself with a sense of shame, and not dishonoring his ruler's mandate when sent abroad as a diplomat—such a person could be called a scholar-official."

"May I ask what the next best type of person is like?"

"His lineage and clan consider him filial, and his fellow villagers consider him respectful to his elders."

"And the next best?"

"In his speech, he insists on being trustworthy, and with regard to his actions, he insists that they bear fruit. What a narrow, rigid little man he is! And yet he might still be considered the next best."

7. [Here, "covering up" is translating *yin* 隱, meaning to keep private as if on the other side of a wall. "Upright" is *Zhi gong* 直躬, meaning "rigid and unbending person." Thus, one possible way of understanding Confucius' response is to see him as attempting to redefine moral uprightness in a way that is less uncompromising and more amenable to individual judgments of discretion.]

"How about those who today are involved in government?"

The Master exclaimed, "Oh! Those petty functionaries are not even worth considering."

14.31 The Master said, "Not anticipating betrayal, nor expecting untrustworthiness, yet still being the first to perceive it—this is a worthy person indeed."

17.20 Ru Bei [sent a messenger expressing his] wish to have an audience with Confucius, but Confucius declined, saying that he was ill. As soon as the messenger went out the door, however, Confucius picked up his zither and sang, making sure that the messenger could hear him.

Mengzi

3A4 There was a certain Xu Xing who, supporting the teachings of Shen Nong[1] went from the state of Chu to Teng . . . Chen Xiang met Xu Xing and was greatly pleased. He completely abandoned his former learning and learned from him instead . . .

[Chen told Mengzi], "If we follow the Way of Xu Xing, market prices will never vary, and there will be no artifice in the state. Even if one sends a child to go to the market, no one will cheat him. Cotton cloth or silk cloth of the same length would be of equal price. Bundles of hemp or silk of the same weight would be of equal price. The same amount of any of the five grains would be the same price. Shoes of the same size would be of equal price."

Mengzi said, "Things are inherently unequal. One thing is twice or five times more than another, another ten or a hundred times more, another a thousand or ten thousand times more. If you line them up and treat them as identical, this will bring chaos to the world. If a fine shoe and a shoddy shoe are the same price, will anyone make the former? If we follow the Way of Xu Xing, we will lead each other into artifice. How can this bring order to the state?"

---

1. [Shen Nong was a legendary sage and ruler who advocated a return to an agrarian, communal lifestyle. While Chen Xiang is attracted to this ideal for its seeming honest simplicity, Mengzi argues that such utopianism ignores real moral complexity and thus actually generates a need for *greater* dishonesty in the long run. "Artifice" in the first occurrence translates *qi* 欺, referring to being tricked or cheated, and *wei* 偽, referring to anything counterfeit, in the second occurrence.]

4B11 Mengzi said, "The words of great people are not necessarily faithful,[2] and their actions are not necessarily resolute. They rest only in righteousness."[3]

5A2 Wan Zhang asked, "The *Odes* say[4]

> How should one handle taking a bride?
> One must inform one's father and mother.

It seems that no one should be more faithful to such a teaching than Shun.[5] So why did Shun take a bride without informing his father and mother?"

Mengzi responded, "He could not have taken a bride if he had informed them. For a man and a woman to live together is the greatest of human roles. If he had informed his parents, then he would have had to abandon the greatest of human roles, which would have led to enmity with his father and mother. For this reason he did not inform them."

Wan Zhang said, "I now understand your explanation of Shun taking a wife without informing his parents. But why did Emperor Yao betroth his daughters without informing Shun's parents?"

Mengzi said, "The Emperor also knew that if he informed them Shun could not wed them."

Wang Zhang said, "Shun's parents ordered him to go up into the granary to finish building it. Then they took away the ladder, and his father set fire to the granary. They ordered him to dig a well. He had left the well, but (not knowing this) they covered the well over. Shun's brother, Xiang, said, 'The plan to bury this *ruler of the capital* was all my achievement! His oxen and sheep—those can go to our parents. His

2. ["Faithful" is *xin* 信—cf. note 2 to the *Analects* selection.]

3. [Van Norden provides an annotation to this passage, pointing to the way it was interpreted by the famous commentator Zhao Qi (108–201). On Zhao Qi's reading, what Mengzi means is that someone can still be a "great person" even if they sometimes tell a lie or fail to fulfill a particular commitment; what preserves their greatness is that they are so righteous that they possess the discretion to determine when such exceptions are warranted.]

4. [The *Odes*, or *Shijing*, refers to an ancient collection of poems and songs that early Confucians often used for philosophical inspiration or illustration.]

5. [Shun is one of the legendary sages and rulers of Chinese mythology. As the excerpt makes clear, he struggled to fulfill his filial duties to a monstrous family who prevented him from marrying and even tried on several occasions to murder him. As the legend has it, Shun's virtuous conduct eventually won over his parents and brother.]

grain storehouses—those can go to our parents. But his shields and spears—mine. His zither—mine. His bow—mine. And his two wives shall service me in my bed!' Xiang then went into Shun's home. Shun was on his couch, playing his zither. His face flushed with embarrassment, Xiang said, 'I was wracked with concern, worrying about you, my lord!'

"Shun said, 'My numerous ministers, rule them with me.'

"I wonder whether Shun did not realize that Xiang planned on killing him?"

Mengzi replied, "How could he have not realized it? But when Xiang was concerned, he was concerned too. When Xiang was delighted, he was delighted too."

Wan Zhang said, "In that case, did Shun feign his happiness?"[6]

Mengzi said, "He did not. Formerly, someone gave a gift of a live fish to Zichan of Zheng. Zichan ordered a groundskeeper to take care of it in the pond. The groundskeeper cooked it instead. But he reported back, 'When I first released it, it seemed uncertain. But in a short time it was at ease. I was satisfied and swam off.' Zichan exclaimed, 'He has found his place! He has found his place!' The groundskeeper left and said to himself, 'Who said that Zichan was wise? When I had already cooked and eaten it, he says, *He has found his place! He has found his place!*' Hence, a gentleman *can* be deceived by what is in line with his path, but it is difficult to trap him with what is not the Way.[7] Xiang came in accordance with the Way of a loving younger brother. Hence, Shun genuinely had faith in and was happy about him. How could he be feigning it?"

6. ["Feign" here is *wei* 偽, referring to anything counterfeit. The questions the passage raises, then, are whether Shun's actions constituted deception of his parents (about his marriage) and his brother (about his happiness), and whether it is the responsibility of a good person to remain faithful to family obligations, including honesty, when the family in question is despicable.]

7. ["Way" refers to *dao* 道, a complex philosophical concept which here refers to the path that the morally good person should walk.]

6
KANT

Immanuel Kant (1724–1804) is one of the most influential philosophers of the modern era, publishing major treatises in metaphysics, ethics, aesthetics, and the philosophy of religion. Kant's most well known contribution to the field of ethics is undoubtedly the articulation of what he calls the Categorical Imperative, which he derives in his *Grounding for the Metaphysics of Morals*. In order to understand Kant's account of lying, it is imperative that one understands the Categorical Imperative. Kant makes the point that everything in nature functions according to laws, and humans are no exception. Rational beings (and thus humans) are unique, however, in that they are able to act according to their conception of laws—according to principles. The principles of action that accord with duty are part of the moral law, and they must have the same universality that laws of nature have. Any maxim that cannot be coherently universalized cannot be understood as a law of nature, and thus must not be in accord with duty. Thus, reason itself dictates the form of the moral law: "I should never act except in such a way that I can also will that my maxim should become a universal law" (4.402). This insight gives rise to the first formulation of the Categorical Imperative: "Act only according to that maxim whereby you can at the same time will that it should become a universal law" (4.421).

The selections from the *Grounding* that are reprinted below include the portions in which Kant uses the false promise as a case study for how one can test a proposed course of action against the Categorical Imperative in order to learn whether that action is morally permissible. Kant asks the reader to imagine someone who finds himself in dire straits, and is tempted to borrow money on the basis of an insincere promise to repay the loan. It quickly becomes clear, Kant argues, that the principle of making a false promise to get oneself out of a jam cannot coherently be universalized: a false promise is predicated precisely on such a course of action *not* being a universal practice.

Because the moral law is universal, it does not admit of exceptions. Thus if lying is wrong, it is always wrong, regardless of consequences. The French thinker Benjamin Constant published an article challenging Kant's ethics on this ground. It cannot be immoral, Constant argues, to lie to the would-be murderer at your door who asks you about the whereabouts of your friend, the intended victim. Our second selection, "On a Supposed Right to Lie because of Philanthropic Concerns," is Kant's reply to this challenge.

Discussions of Kant's categorical prohibition on lying often focus exclusively on what he says in the *Grounding* and "On a Supposed Right to Lie." In our view this is unfortunate, because what he says in the *Metaphysics of Morals* and what is reported of him in the *Lectures on Ethics* reveal a much more nuanced and sophisticated view of lying than he is generally credited with. For instance, in "On a Supposed Right to Lie" Kant defines a lie as "an intentionally untruthful declaration." His discussion in the *Metaphysics of Morals* makes it clear, however, that both "untruthful" and "declaration" are technical terms for Kant: not every utterance that conflicts with one's beliefs is untruthful and not every assertion is a declaration. As you read the selections, consider the following questions:

1. Is Kant correct that a lying promise is necessarily based on a non-universalizable maxim? If yes, is that analysis generalizable to all lies?
2. In responding to Constant's claim that the duty to tell the truth holds only toward one who has a right to the truth, Kant claims that it makes no sense to speak of having a right to the truth. What does Kant mean when he says this, and does his response to Constant succeed?
3. What differences among these four excerpts can you identify with regard to how Kant treats lying? How significant are these differences and which account do you find most plausible?

Grounding for the Metaphysics of Morals

Section 1

But what sort of law can that be the thought of which must determine the will without reference to any expected effect, so that the will can be called absolutely good without qualification? Since I have deprived the will of every impulse that might arise for it from obeying any particular law, there is nothing left to serve the will as principle except the universal conformity of its actions to law as such, i.e., I should never act except in such a way that I can also will that my maxim should become a universal law. Here mere conformity to law as such (without having as its basis any law determining particular actions) serves the will as principle and must so serve it if duty is not to be a vain delusion and a chimerical concept. The ordinary reason of mankind in its practical judgments agrees completely with this, and always has in view the aforementioned principle.

For example, take this question. When I am in distress, may I make a promise with the intention of not keeping it? I readily distinguish here the two meanings which the question may have; whether making a false promise conforms with prudence or with duty. Doubtless the former can often be the case. Indeed I clearly see that escape from some present difficulty by means of such a promise is not enough. In addition I must carefully consider whether from this lie there may later arise far greater inconvenience for me than from what I now try to escape. Furthermore, the consequences of my false promise are not easy to foresee, even with all my supposed cunning; loss of confidence in me might prove to be far more disadvantageous than the misfortune which I now try to avoid. The more prudent way might be to act according to a universal maxim and to make it a habit not to promise anything without intending to keep it. But that such a maxim is, nevertheless, always based on nothing but a fear of consequences becomes clear to me at once. To be truthful from duty is, however, quite different from being truthful from fear of disadvantageous consequences; in the first case the concept of the action itself contains a law for me, while in the second I must first look around elsewhere to see what are the results for me that might be connected with the action. For to deviate from the principle of duty is quite certainly bad; but to abandon my maxim of prudence can often be very advantageous for me, though to abide by it is certainly safer. The most direct and infallible way, however, to answer the question as to whether a lying promise accords with duty is to ask myself whether I would really be content if my maxim (of extracting myself from difficulty by means of a false promise) were to hold as a universal law for myself as well as for others, and could I really say to myself that everyone may promise falsely when he finds himself in a difficulty from which he can find no other way to extricate himself. Then I immediately become aware that I can indeed will the lie but can not at all will a universal law to lie. For by such a law there would really be no promises at all, since in vain would my willing future actions be professed to other people who would not believe what I professed, or if they over-hastily did believe, then they would pay me back in like coin. Therefore, my maxim would necessarily destroy itself just as soon as it were made a universal law.

Section 2

Another man in need finds himself forced to borrow money. He knows well that he won't be able to repay it, but he sees also that he will not get any loan unless he firmly promises to repay it within a fixed time. He wants to make such a promise, but he still has conscience enough to ask himself whether it is not permissible and is contrary to duty to get out of difficulty in this way. Suppose, however, that he decides to do so. The maxim of his action would then be expressed as follows: when I believe myself to be in need of money, I will borrow money and promise to pay it back, although I know that I can never do so. Now this principle of self-love or personal advantage may perhaps be quite compatible with one's entire future welfare, but the question is now whether it is right. I then transform the requirement of self-love into a universal law and put the question thus: how would things stand if my maxim were to become a universal law? He then sees at once that such a maxim could never hold as a universal law of nature and be consistent with itself, but must necessarily be self-contradictory. For the universality of a law which says that anyone believing himself to be in difficulty could promise whatever he pleases with the intention of not keeping it would make promising itself and the end to be attained thereby quite impossible, inasmuch as no one would believe what was promised him but would merely laugh at all such utterances as being vain pretenses.

"On a Supposed Right to Lie because of Philanthropic Concerns"

In the periodical *France* for 1797, Part VI, No. 1, page 123, in an article bearing the title "On Political Reactions" by Benjamin Constant there is contained on p. 123 the following passage:

> "The moral principle stating that it is a duty to tell the truth would make any society impossible if that principle were taken singly and unconditionally. We have proof of this in the very direct consequences which a German philosopher has drawn from this principle. This philosopher goes as far as to assert that it would be a crime to tell a lie to a murderer who asked whether our friend who is being pursued by the murderer had taken refuge in our house."[1]

The French philosopher [Constant] on p. 124 [of the periodical *France*] refutes this [moral] principle in the following way:

> "It is a duty to tell the truth. The concept of duty is inseparable from the concept of right. A duty is what in one man corresponds to the right of another. Where there are no rights, there are no duties. To tell the truth is a duty, but is a duty only with regard to one who has a right to the truth. But no one has a right to a truth that harms others."

The πρωτον ψευδος [first fallacy] here lies in the statement, "To tell the truth is a duty, but is a duty only with regard to one who has a right to the truth."

Firstly it must be noted that the expression "to have a right to truth" is meaningless. One must say, rather, that man has a right to his own truthfulness (*veracitas*), i.e., to subjective truth in his own person. For to have objectively a right to truth would be the same as to say that it is a matter of one's will (as in cases of *mine* and *thine* generally) whether a given statement is to be true or false; this would produce an unusual logic.

Now, the first question is whether a man (in cases where he cannot avoid answering Yea or Nay) has the warrant (right) to be untruthful. The second question is whether he is not actually bound to be untruthful in a certain statement which he is unjustly compelled to make in order to prevent a threatening misdeed against himself or someone else.

1. "J. D. Michaelis in Göttingen had propounded this unusual opinion even before Kant. But the author of this article [viz., Constant] has informed me that Kant is the philosopher referred to in this passage." –K. F. Cramer [editor of the journal in which Constant published his article]. [Compare the scenario to the similar one described by Augustine in the selection from *De Mendacio*, sections 22–24, in chapter 1 of this volume.]
*I hereby admit that this was actually said by me somewhere, though I cannot now recollect the place. –I. Kant.

Truthfulness in statements that cannot be avoided is the formal duty of man to everyone,[2] however great the disadvantage that may arise therefrom for him or for any other. And even though by telling an untruth I do no wrong to him who unjustly compels me to make a statement, yet by this falsification, which as such can be called a lie (though not in a juridical sense), I do wrong to duty in general in a most essential point. That is, as far as in me lies I bring it about that statements (declarations) in general find no credence, and hence also that all rights based on contracts become void and lose their force, and this is a wrong done to mankind in general.

Hence a lie defined merely as an intentionally untruthful declaration to another man does not require the additional condition that it must do harm to another, as jurists require in their definition (*mendacium est falsiloquium in praeiudicium alterius*) [a lie is a falsehood that harms another]. For a lie always harms another; if not some other human being, then it nevertheless does harm to humanity in general, inasmuch as it vitiates the very source of right.

However, this well-intentioned lie can become punishable in accordance with civil law because of an accident (*casus*); and that which avoids liability to punishment only by accident can also be condemned as wrong even by external laws. For example, if by telling a lie you have in fact hindered someone who was even now planning a murder, then you are legally responsible for all the consequences that might result therefrom. But if you have adhered strictly to the truth, then public justice cannot lay a hand on you, whatever the unforeseen consequence might be. It is indeed possible that after you have honestly answered Yes to the murderer's question as to whether the intended victim is in the house, the latter went out unobserved and thus eluded the murderer, so that the deed would not have come about. However, if you told a lie and said that the intended victim was not in the house, and he has actually (though unbeknownst to you) gone out, with the result that by so doing he has been met by the murderer and thus the deed has been perpetrated, then in this case you may be justly accused as having caused his death. For if you had told the truth as best you knew it, then the murderer might perhaps have been caught by neighbors who came running while he was searching the house for

2. I do not want to sharpen this principle to the point of saying "Untruthfulness is a violation of one's duty to himself." For this principle belongs to ethics, but here the concern is with a duty of right. The *Doctrine of Virtue* sees in this transgression only worthlessness, the reproach of which the liar draws upon himself.

his intended victim, and thus the deed might have been prevented. Therefore, whoever tells a lie, regardless of how good his intentions may be, must answer for the consequences resulting therefrom even before a civil tribunal and must pay the penalty for them, regardless of how unforeseen those consequences may be. This is because truthfulness is a duty that must be regarded as the basis of all duties founded on contract, and the laws of such duties would be rendered uncertain and useless if even the slightest exception to them were admitted.

To be truthful (honest) in all declarations is, therefore, a sacred and unconditionally commanding law of reason that admits of no expediency whatsoever.

Monsieur Constant remarks thoughtfully and correctly with regard to the decrying of such principles that are so strict as to be alleged to lose themselves in impracticable ideas and that are therefore to be rejected. He says on page 123, "In every case where a principle that has been proved to be true appears to be inapplicable, the reason for this inapplicability lies in the fact that we do not know the middle principle that contains the means of its application." He adduces (p. 121) the doctrine of equality as being the first link of the social chain when he says (p. 122): "No man can be bound by any laws other than these to whose formation he has contributed. In a very limited society this principle can be applied directly and requires no middle principle in order to become a common principle. But in a very numerous society there must be added a new principle to the one that has been stated. The middle principle is this: individuals can contribute to the formation of laws either in their own person or through their representatives. Whoever wanted to apply the former principle to a numerous society without also using the middle principle would unfailingly bring about the destruction of such a society. But this circumstance, which would show only the ignorance or the incompetence of the legislator, would prove nothing against the principle." He concludes (p. 125) thus: "A principle acknowledged as true must hence never be abandoned, however obviously there seems to be danger involved in it." (And yet the good man himself abandoned the unconditional principle of truthfulness on account of the danger which that principle posed for society, inasmuch as he could not find any middle principle that could serve to prevent this danger; and indeed there is no such principle to do the mediating here.)

If the names of the persons as they have here been introduced be retained, then the "French philosopher" confuses the action whereby someone does harm (*nocet*) to another by telling the truth when its avowal cannot be avoided with the action whereby someone does wrong to (*laedit*) another. It was merely an accident (*casus*) that the truth of the statement did harm to the occupant of the house, but it was not a free act (in the juridical sense). For from a right to demand that another should lie for the sake of one's own advantage there would follow a claim that conflicts with all lawfulness. For every man has not only a right but even the strictest duty to be truthful in statements that are unavoidable, whether this truthfulness does harm to himself or others. Therefore he does not himself by this [truthfulness] actually harm the one who suffers because of it; rather, this harm is caused by accident. For he is not at all free to choose in such a case, inasmuch as truthfulness (if he must speak) is an unconditional duty. The "German philosopher" will, therefore, not take as his principle the proposition (p. 124), "To tell the truth is a duty, but is a duty only with regard to the man who has a right to the truth." He will not do so, first, because of the confused formulation of the proposition, inasmuch as truth is not a possession the right to which can be granted to one person but refused to another. But, secondly, he will not do so mainly because the duty of truthfulness (which is the only thing under consideration here) makes no distinction between persons to whom one has this duty and to whom one can be excused from this duty; it is, rather an unconditional duty which holds in all circumstances.

Now, in order to go from a metaphysics of right (which abstracts from all empirical determinations) to a principle of politics (which applies these concepts to instances provided by experience) and by means of this principle to gain the solution of a problem of politics in accordance with the universal principle of right, the philosopher will provide the following. First, he will present an axiom, i.e., an apodeictically certain proposition that arises directly from the definition of external right (the harmony of the freedom of each with the freedom of all others according to a universal law). Second, he will provide a postulate of external public law (the will of all united according to the principle of equality, without which no freedom would exist for anyone). Third, there is the problem of how to make arrangements so that in a society, however large, harmony can be maintained in accordance with principles of freedom and equality (namely, by means of a representative system). And this will then be a principle of politics; and establishing and arranging such a political system will involve decrees that are drawn from experiential knowledge regarding men; and such decrees will have in view only the mechanism for the administration of justice and how such mechanism is to be suitably arranged. Right must never be adapted to politics; rather, politics must always be adapted to right.

The author says, "A principle acknowledged as true (I add, acknowledged as an a priori principle, and therefore apodeictic) must never be forsaken, however apparently danger is involved in it." But here one must understand the danger not as that of (accidentally) doing harm but in general as the danger of doing wrong. And such wrongdoing would occur if I made the duty of truthfulness, which is wholly unconditional and which constitutes the supreme juridical condition in assertions, into a conditional duty subordinate to other considerations. And although by telling a certain lie I in fact do not wrong anyone, I nevertheless violate the principle of right in regard to all unavoidably necessary statements generally (i.e., the principle of right is thereby wronged formally, though not materially). This is much worse than committing an injustice against some individual person, inasmuch as such a deed does not always presuppose that there is in the subject a principle for such an act.

The man who is asked whether or not he intends to speak truthfully in the statement that he is now to make and who does not receive the very question with indignation as regards the suspicion thereby expressed that he might be a liar, but who instead asks permission to think first about possible exceptions—that man is already a liar (*in potential*) [in accordance with possibility]. This is because he shows that he does not acknowledge truthfulness as in itself a duty but reserves for himself exceptions from a rule which by its very nature does not admit of any exceptions, inasmuch as to admit of such would be self-contradictory.

All practical principles of right must contain rigorous truth; and the principles that are here called middle principles can contain only the closer determination of the application of these latter principles (according to rules of politics) to cases that happen to occur, but such middle principles can never contain exceptions to the aforementioned principles of right. This is because such exceptions would destroy the universality on account of which alone they bear the name of principles.

The Metaphysics of Morals

Doctrine of Virtue, II.I (§9): On Lying

The greatest violation of a human being's duty to himself regarded merely as a moral being (the humanity in his own person) is the contrary of truthfulness, *lying*, (*aliud lingua promptum, aliud pectore inclusion gerere*). In the doctrine of right an intentional untruth is called a lie only if it violates another's right; but in ethics, where no authorization is derived from harmlessness, it is clear of itself that no intentional untruth in the expression of one's thoughts can refuse this harsh name. For, the dishonor (being an object of moral contempt) that accompanies a lie also accompanies a liar like his shadow. A lie can be an external lie (*mendacium externum*) or also an internal lie.—By an external lie a human being makes himself an object of contempt in the eyes of others; by an internal lie he does what is still worse: he makes himself contemptible in his own eyes and violates the dignity of humanity in his own person. And so, since the harm that can come to others from lying is not what distinguishes this vice (for if it were, the vice would consist only in violating one's duty to others), this harm is not taken into account here. Neither is the harm that a liar brings upon himself; for then a lie, as a mere error in prudence, would conflict with the pragmatic maxim, not the moral maxim, and it could not be considered a violation of duty at all.—By a lie a human being throws away and, as it were, annihilates his dignity as a human being. A human being who does not himself believe what he tells another (even if the other is a merely ideal person) has even less worth than if he were a mere thing; for a thing, because it is something real and given, has the property of being serviceable so that another can put it to some use. But communication of one's thoughts to someone through words that yet (intentionally) contain the contrary of what the speaker thinks on the subject is an end that is directly opposed to the natural purposiveness of the speaker's capacity to communicate his thoughts, and is thus a renunciation by the speaker of his personality, and such a speaker is a mere deceptive appearance of a human being, not a human being himself.—*Truthfulness* in one's declarations is also called *honesty* and, if the declarations are promises, *sincerity*; but, more generally, truthfulness is called *rectitude*.

Lying (in the ethical sense of the word), intentional untruth as such, need not be *harmful* to others in order to be repudiated; for it would then be a violation of the rights of others. It may be done merely out of frivolity or even good nature; the speaker may even intend to achieve a really good end by it. But his way of pursuing this end is, by its mere form, a crime of a human being against his own person and a worthlessness that must make him contemptible in his own eyes.

It is easy to show that man is actually guilty of many **inner** lies, but it seems more difficult to explain how they are possible; for a lie requires a second person whom one intends to deceive, whereas to deceive oneself on purpose seems to contain a contradiction.

Man as a moral being (*homo noumenon*) cannot use himself as a natural being (*homo phaenomenon*) as a mere means (a speaking machine), as if his natural being were not bound to the inner end (of communicating thoughts), but is bound to the condition of using himself as a natural being in agreement with the declaration (*declaratio*) of his moral being and is under obligation to himself to *truthfulness*.—Someone tells an inner lie, for example, if he professes belief in a future judge of the world, although he really finds no such belief within himself but persuades himself that it could do no harm and might even be useful to profess in his thoughts to one who scrutinizes hearts a belief in such a judge, in order to win his favor in case he should exist. Someone also lies if, having no doubt about the existence of this future judge, he still flatters himself that he inwardly reveres his law, though the only incentive he feels is fear of punishment.

Insincerity is mere lack of *conscientiousness*, that is, of purity in one's professions before one's *inner* judge, who is thought of as another person when conscientiousness is taken quite strictly; then if someone, from self-love, takes a wish for the deed because he has a really good end in mind, his inner lie, although it is indeed contrary to his duty to himself, gets the name of a frailty, as when a lover's wish to find only good qualities in his beloved blinds him to her obvious faults.—But such insincerity in his declarations, which a human being perpetuates upon himself, still deserves the strongest censure, since it is from such a rotten spot (falsity, which seems to be rooted in human nature itself) that the ill of untruthfulness spreads into his relations with other human beings as well, once the highest principle of truthfulness has been violated.

Remark

It is noteworthy that the Bible dates the first crime, through which evil entered the world, not from *fratricide* (Cain's) but from the first *lie* (for even nature rises up against fratricide), and calls the author of all evil a liar from the beginning and the father of lies. However, reason can assign no further ground for the human propensity to *hypocrisy* (*esprit fourbe*), although this propensity must have been present before the lie; for, an act of freedom cannot (like a natural effect) be deduced and explained in accordance with the natural law of the connection of effects with their causes, all of which are appearances.

Casuistical Questions

Can an untruth from mere politeness (e.g., the "your obedient servant" at the end of a letter) be considered a lie? No one is deceived by it.—An author asks one of his readers, "How do you like my work?" One could merely seem to give an answer, by joking about the impropriety of such a question. But who has his wit always ready? The author will take the slightest hesitation in answering as an insult. May one, then, say what is expected of one?

If I say something untrue in more serious matters, having to do with what is mine or yours, must I answer for all the consequences it might have? For example, a household has ordered his servant to say "not at home" if a certain human being asks for him. The servant does this and, as a result, the master slips away and commits a serious crime, which would otherwise have been prevented by the guard sent to arrest him. Who (in accordance with ethical principles) is guilty in this case? Surely the servant, too, who violated a duty to himself by his lie, the results of which his own conscience imputes to him.

Lectures on Ethics[1]

Herder's Notes[2]

Lying is simply too restricted, as an injury to the other; as untruth, it already has an immediately abhorrent quality, for (a) this most *trenchantly* separates human society, of which truth is the bond; *truth* is simply lost, and with it, all the happiness of mankind; everything puts

1. [The *Lectures on Ethics* is a collection of notes that were taken by, and probably distributed among, students attending Kant's classes. The notes we have span some thirty years of Kant's teaching career and thus provide valuable insight into the development of his thinking over time. The fact that these notes were taken by Kant's students invites some question as to how reliable they are as a reflection of Kant's thought. While they are surely less reliable than his published writings, there is a consistency among the ideas as they are presented in the lecture notes, as well as between the lecture notes and his published writings, that supports the notion that the notes are largely accurate reflections of Kant's thinking at the times the notes were taken. For more information, see J. B. Schneewind's Introduction to the *Lectures on Ethics*, in Heath and Schneewind, eds. (1997), *Lectures on Ethics*, Cambridge: Cambridge University Press.]

2. [J. G. Herder's notes are from 1762–1764, relatively early in Kant's teaching career and before any of his well-known publications on ethics. Of all the notes we have, these are perhaps the least reliable: Herder apparently revised the notes on his own and may have inserted ideas that were not Kant's. That said, his notes are still the most accurate depiction we have of Kant's ethical views during this early period.]

on a mask, and every indication of civility becomes a deceit; we make use of other men to *our own* best advantage. The lie is thus a higher degree of untruth. (b) So soon as the lust for honour becomes a prevailing principle, it already sets no bounds to the lie. Self-interest cannot be so strong a reason, for lying is not an *enduring* means of advantage, since others shun the liar. The greediest shopkeepers of all are the *most honourable* in their dealings, simply from self-interest, and this is thus often a reason for truthfulness, etc. The lust for honour makes *lying* easier, since here the inner content is not so apparent; religion and well-being, for example, can easily be simulated, and not so readily exposed. (c) The longing for imaginary perfections, that perhaps were not thought suitable before; for example, a disinterested zeal to serve is a *fantasy* too high for us. But since we can indeed be of service to a person in certain matters, there is the wish, in fantasy, to sacrifice ourselves; and since this cannot actually *be*, there is the *wish*, at least, for it to *seem* so. Second example: The fantasied desire for infinite knowledge, that is impossible to us, creates the *semblance* of this knowledge. In the indulgence in knowledge and enjoyment, do we therefore find the *lie* that is most abhorrent of all to the *natural man*?

Value of the love of truth: It is the basis of all virtue; the first law of nature, Be truthful!, is a ground (1) of virtue towards others, for if all are truthful, a man's untruth would be exposed as a *disgrace*. (2) of virtue to oneself, for a man cannot hide from himself, nor is he able to contain his abhorrence.

The *feeling of shame* (which is *later* made subject to delusion, and envelops even the best actions), seems to be a natural means (*pudor*, not merely *pudicitium* in the pursuit of pleasure) of promoting truthfulness and betraying falsehood. If we wanted to use such shame, simply to betray the lie, it is very *practicable*. Providence would certainly not have furnished it to delude us, for it is the greatest of tortures; it is given, rather for betrayal—*involuntary* betrayal. It has never been there to cause us anxiety, but rather to betray *something* which nature did not want to hide. To thus make use of this shameful feeling as an antidote against lying, we must not employ it for any other purpose, e.g. to show up a child. Here I use merely the means for imitation; if he has behaved or spoken stupidly, I simply persuade, and *as a child* there is much that becomes him, which is not becoming to the *man*. But supposing that, regardless of his love of truth, he has *but once* told a lie, from self-interest, because the love of truth is not so lively as physical feeling; in that case I do not talk to him of *obedience* (of which no child has the *concept*, nor is of an age to do so), but simply of *untruth*. In the end he acquires as much abhorrence for it as he has for a spider.

Incest with a sister is abhorrent, not because God has forbidden it, but because the wrongness of it has been imprinted since childhood. Such is the power of ideas of dreadfulness; and if a son were to see his father's abhorrence of lying, he would by moral sympathy perceive the same himself. Suppose him now grown up, then everything would go better. I would openly declare my intention, for example, that I am working, not for the benefit of science, but from self-interest; I would yearn only for an official position that I am capable of filling. Nowadays, however, there is *untruth,* not merely in the world, but also before God, in solitude, since we cannot stand even before Him without pretence. To be truthful, we would now have to forfeit a great deal, and so each of us shies away from the truth, and most of all in a nightshirt. Untruth may end by deceiving itself, and so self-examination becomes equally slippery; the good side of kind-heartedness, for example, is put before its reprehensible aspect, and men eventually become deceivers even towards God: for example, Job's comforters. Certain untruths are not called lies, because the latter are *strictly untruths* that are contrary to *duty;* not, however, as our author thinks, merely to the duty *to myself,* but also to that *towards others.* The importance of the love of truth is so great that one can almost never make an exception to it.

Untruth, to the great *advantage of another,* still has something *sublime* in it, that is near allied to virtue. Yet to speak *truth,* to the *disadvantage of oneself,* is sublime still, and to speak untruth to *one's own advantage* is doubtless always immoral. But since the *highest morality* is not on a par with the *moral level* of man, this is not, indeed, quite settled. Yet because the bounds of a man's strength and obligation are hard to determine, this *human ethic* of untruth will be as confused as the *logica probabilis. Every coward* is a liar; Jews, for example, not only in business, but also in common life. It is hardest of all to judge Jews; they are cowards. Children, for example, that are brought up cowards, tell lies, since they are weak in conquering themselves, etc. But not every liar is a coward, for there are inveterate scoundrels as well.

With us, in many cases, a small untruth does not seem untoward, for weak persons; the case is often complicated; if another asks him something, a man cannot remain silent, for that would be to assent, etc., etc. In short, we should investigate the degree of morality that is suited to men. As with all fine inclinations, we can also enlarge the desire for holiness; but not all can be moral men, when they are weak or needy, since in few cases are we able to attain to holiness. If our untruth is in keeping with our main intent, then it is bad; but if I can avert a truly great evil only by this means, then . . . etc. Here goodness of heart takes the place of sincerity. To obtain a great good by untruthfulness is far less excusable than to ward off a great evil by that means; for (1) our inclination to our happiness is often fanciful, and morality should not be sacrificed on that account; (2) the taking away of what I have is a greater denial than a withdrawal of what I might have. A white lie is often a *contradictio in adjecto*; like pretended tipsiness, it is *untruth* that breaches no *obligation*, and is thus properly no lie. *Joking* lies, if they are not taken to be *true*, are not immoral. But if it be that the other is *ever* meant to *believe* it, then, even though no harm is done, it is a lie, since at least there is always deception. If untruth presupposes cleverness and skill, we get *artful* lying and repute; courtiers and politicians, for example, have to achieve their aims by lying, and everyone should flee any position in which *untruth* is indispensable to him.

Collins' Notes[3]

Of Ethical Duties Towards Others, and Especially Truthfulness

In human social life, the principal object is to communicate our attitudes, and hence it is of the first importance that everyone be truthful in respect of his thoughts, since without that, social intercourse ceases to be of any value. Only when a person voices his opinions can another tell what he thinks, and if he declares that he wishes to express his thoughts, he must also do it, for otherwise there can be no sociality among men. Fellowship among men is only the second condition of sociality; but the liar destroys this fellowship, and hence we despise a liar, since the lie makes it impossible for people to derive any benefit from what he has to say. Man has an impulse towards holding himself back, and disguising himself. The former is dissimulatio, the latter simulatio. Man holds back in regard to his weaknesses and transgressions, and can also pretend and adopt an appearance. The proclivity for reserve and concealment rests on this, that providence has willed that man should not be wholly open, since he is full of iniquity; because we have so many characteristics and tendencies that are

3. [G. W. Collins attended Kant's course on ethics during the winter term 1784–1785, right before the *Grounding for the Metaphysics of Morals* was published. The lecture notes are very thorough, and often provide more subtle distinctions than we find in Kant's published writings. These notes are also strikingly consistent with other students' notes from the same time frame, possibly indicating that a professional note-taker was involved in transcribing—and maybe even in distributing—them.]

objectionable to others, we would be liable to appear before them in a foolish and hateful light. But the result, in that case, might be this, that people would tend to grow accustomed to such bad points, since they would see the same in everyone. Hence we order our behavior in such a way that in part we conceal our faults, and in part also put a different face on them, and have the knack for appearing other than we are; so other people see nothing of our sins and weaknesses beyond the appearances of well-being, and hence we habituate ourselves to dispositions that produce good conduct. Hence nobody, in the true sense, is open-hearted. Had it been as Momus wanted, that Jupiter should have installed a window in the heart, so that every man's disposition might be known, then men would have had to be better constituted, and have good principles, for if all men were good, nobody could hold anything back; but since this is not so, we must keep our shutters closed. When domestic nastiness is confined to the privy, and a person is not invited into the bedroom, where the chamber-pots are, though he knows we have them, just as he does himself, we refrain from these things lest we get into the habit of it and corrupt our taste. In just the same way, we conceal our faults, and try to give a different impression, and make a show of politeness, despite our mistrust; yet by this we grow used to politeness, and at length it becomes natural to us, and we thereby set a good example, at least to the eye; if this were not so, everybody would neglect these things, finding nobody the better for them. So by this endeavor to look well we actually end up doing so, later on. If men were all good, they could afford to be open-hearted; but not at present.

Reserve consists in not expressing one's mind. This can be done, in the first place, by complete silence. That is a short way of being reserved. But it represents a want of sociability. It robs a man of the pleasure of company, and such silent men are not only unwanted in social circles, but also incur suspicion, and everyone thinks he is watching them. For if he is asked his opinion of a thing, and says: I have nothing to say, that is as much as if he were to speak against it, for if he thought well of it, he could surely say so. Since silence always gives us away, it is not even a prudent form of reserve; but we can also be prudent in our reserve without it. For such prudence in reserve we need deliberation. We must speak and pass judgement on everything, save that on which we wish to keep our counsel.

Secretiveness is quite a different thing from reserve. I can hold a thing back, when I have no desire to speak of it, and am reserved about my misdeeds, for example, since nature by no means impels me to betray them; thus every man has his secrets, and these he can easily keep quiet about; but there are matters where it needs strength to preserve discretion. Secrets have a way of getting out, and it takes strength not to betray them, and this is secretiveness. Secrets are always deposits lodged by others, and I must not release them for the use of third parties. But since human garrulity is very interesting, the telling of secrets is what chiefly sustains it, for the other views it as a gift. How are secrets to be kept? Men who are not themselves very garrulous, generally keep secrets well, but better still are those who talk freely, but with prudence; from the former, something might yet be elicited, but not so from the latter, for they always know how to interpose with something else.

Just as practical taciturnity is an excess on the one side, so loquacity is on the other. The first is a male shortcoming, the second a female one. Some writer has said that women are talkative, because the upbringing of infants is entrusted to their care, and that by reason of their chattiness they soon teach children to talk, since they are able to keep babbling to them all day long; among men, however, it would take the children much longer to speak. Taciturnity is an odious habit. We are irritated by people who say nothing. They betray a sort of pride. Loquacity in men breeds contempt, and is unbecoming to their strength. All these were merely matters of pragmatic interest. We now turn to something more important.

If a man announces that he means to disclose his opinions, should he knowingly disclose them in full, or keep something to himself? If he says that he intends to speak his mind, but does not, and makes a false statement instead, that is a *falsiloquium*, or untruth. *Falsiloquium* may occur, even though the other cannot presume that I shall state my views. One may impose on a person, without actually saying anything to him. I can make a pretence, and give expression to something, from which the other may deduce what I want him to; but he has no right to infer from my utterance a declaration of intent, and in that case I have told him no lie, for I never declared that I was opening my mind to him; if I pack my bags, for example, people will think I am off on a journey, and that is what I want them to believe; but they have no right to demand any declaration of will from me. That is what the famous John Law did; he kept on building, and when everyone was thinking: He'll never leave, off he went.

I can also, however, commit a *falsiloquium*, when my intent is to hide my intentions from the other, and he can also presume that I shall do so, since his own purpose is to make a wrongful use of the truth. If an enemy, for example, takes me by the throat and demands to know where my money is kept, I can hide the information here, since he means to misuse the truth. That is still no *mendacium*, for the other knows that I shall withhold the information, and that he also has no right whatever to demand the truth from me. Suppose, however, that I actually state that I mean to speak my mind, and that the other is perfectly well aware that he has no right to require this of me, since he is a swindler; the question arises: Am I then a liar? If the other has cheated me, and I cheat him in return, I have certainly done this fellow no wrong; since he has cheated me, he cannot complain about it, yet I am a liar nonetheless, since I have acted contrary to the right of humanity. It is therefore possible for a *falsiloquium* to be a *mendacium*—a lie—though it contravenes no right of any man in particular. Whoever may have told me a lie, I do him no wrong if I lie to him in return, but I violate the right of mankind; for I have acted contrary to the condition, and the means, under which a society of men can come about, and thus contrary to the right of humanity.

When one country has broken the peace, the other cannot do so in retaliation, for if that were allowable, no peace would be secure. And thus though something may not infringe on the particular right of a man, it is still already a lie, since it is contrary to the right of humanity. If a man publishes a false report, he thereby does no wrong to anyone in particular, but offends against mankind, for if that were to become general, the human craving for knowledge would be thwarted; apart from speculation, I have only two ways of enlarging my store of information: by experience, and by testimony. But now since I cannot experience everything myself, if the reports of others were to be false tidings, the desire for knowledge could not be satisfied. A *mendacium* is thus a *falsiloquium in praejudicium humanitatis*, even when it is not also in violation of any particular *jus quaesitum* of another. In law a *mendacium* is a *falsiloquium in praejudicium alterius*, and cannot be anything else there, but from the moral viewpoint it is a *falsiloquium in preajudicium humanitatis*. Not every untruth is a lie; it is so only if there is an express declaration of my willingness to inform the other of my thought. Every lie is objectionable and deserving of contempt, for once we declare that we are telling the other our thoughts, and fail to do it, we have broken the *pactum*, and acted contrary to the right of humanity. But if, in all cases, we were to remain faithful to every detail of the truth, we might often expose ourselves to the wickedness of others, who wanted to abuse our truthfulness. If everyone were well disposed, it would not only be a duty not to lie, but nobody would need to do it, since he would have nothing to worry about. Now, however, since men are malicious, it is true that we often court danger by punctilious observance of the truth, and hence has arisen the concept of the necessary lie, which is a very critical point for the moral philosopher. For seeing that one may steal, kill or cheat from necessity, the case of emergency subverts the whole of morality, since if that is the plea, it rests upon everyone to judge whether he deems it an emergency or not; and since the ground here is not determined, as to where emergency arises, the moral rules are not certain. For example, somebody, who knows that I have money, asks me: Do you have money at home? If I keep silent, the other concludes that I do. If I say yes, he takes it away from me; if I say no, I tell a lie, so what am I to do? So far as I am constrained, by force used against me, to make an admission, and a wrongful use is made of my statement, and I am unable to save myself by silence, the lie is a weapon of defence; the declaration extorted, that is then misused, permits me to defend myself, for whether my admission or my money is extracted, is all the same. Hence there is no case in which a necessary lie should occur, save where the declaration is wrung from me, and I am also convinced that the other means to make a wrongful use of it.

The question arises, whether a lie that affects nobody's interests, and does nobody any harm, is likewise a lie? It is, for I promise to speak my mind, and if I fail to speak it truly, I do not, indeed, act *in praejudicium* of the particular individual concerned, but I do so act in regard to humanity. There are also lies whereby the other is cheated. To cheat is to make a lying promise. Breach of faith is when we promise something truthfully, but do not have so high a regard for the promise as to keep it. The lying promise is offensive to the other, and though it does not invariably cause offence, there is still always something mean about it. If I promise, for example, to send a person wine, but subsequently make light of it, that is already a cheat, for though he certainly has no right to demand such a gift from me, it is still cheating, in that it was already, as he saw it, a part of his property.

Reservatio mentalis is a form of dissimulation, and *aequivocatio* of simulation. *Aequivocatio* is permitted, in order to reduce the other to silence and get rid of him, so that he shall no longer try to extract the truth from us, once he sees that we cannot give it to him, and do not wish to tell him a lie. If the other is wise, he will also let it go at that. It is quite difficult, though, to employ equivocation when we state and declare that we are expressing our views, for in that case the other may infer something else from the equivocation, and then I have deceived him. Such lies, professing to achieve some good result, were called by the Jesuits *peccatum philosophicum*, or *peccatillum*, from which comes the word 'bagatelle'. But the lie is intrinsically a worthless thing, whether its intentions be good or bad, because it is evil as to form; it is still more worthless, however, when it is also evil as to matter. For by lies something evil may always result. A liar is a cowardly fellow, for since he has no other way of obtaining something, or getting out of trouble, he starts to tell lies. But a bold man will love the truth, and never let a *casus necessitatis* arise. All such methods, whereby the other man cannot be on his guard, are utterly vile. Lying, assassination and poisoning are amongst them. A highwayman's attack is not so low, for there one may take precautions, but not so against the poisoner, since one does, after all, have to eat. Flattery is not always mendacity, but rather a want of self-esteem, where we do not scruple to demean our own worth beneath another's, and elevate his, in order to gain something thereby. But one may also flatter from kindheartedness, and this is done by some kindly souls, who have a high opinion of others. So we have both well-meaning and false flattery. The former is weak, but the other low. When men do not flatter, they lapse into censoriousness.

Now if a man is often the subject of comment in society, he is criticized. But of a friend we should not always have good to tell, for others will then grow jealous and grudging, since, seeing that he, too, is only human, they will not believe it possible for him to have only good qualities; hence we must concede something to their grudging attitude, and mention some flaws in him; he will not think ill of me for that; in emphasizing his merits, I can grant him such faults as are common and inessential. Parasites are those who cry up others in company to gain something. Men are designed for the purpose of passing judgement on others, but nature has also made them judges, for otherwise, in matters outside the scope of external legal authority, we might not stand at the bar of public opinion as we do before a court of law. If somebody, for example, has brought shame upon a person, authority does not punish it, but others judge, and also punish him, although only insofar as it lies in their power to do so, and hence no violence is done to him. People ostracize him, for example, and that is punishment enough. But for this, the actions that authority does not penalize might go altogether unpunished. What does it mean, then, to say that we ought not to judge others? We cannot pass any complete moral judgment on another, as to whether he is punishable or not before the divine judgement-seat, since we do not know his disposition. The moral dispositions of others are therefore a matter for God, but in regard to my own, I am fully competent to judge. So as to the core of morality we cannot judge, since no man can know it. But in external matters we do have competence. In the moral sphere, therefore, we are not judges of men; but nature has given us the right to judge them, and determined us to judge ourselves in accordance with their verdict upon us. He who pays no heed to the judgement of others is low and reprehensible. There is nothing that happens in the world, on which we are not allowed to pass judgement, and we are also very subtle in the assessment of actions. The best friends are those who are exact in judging each other's actions, and only between two friends can such open-heartedness occur.

In judging a man, the next question to arise is: What are we to say of him? We should frame all our judgements so that we find mankind loveable, and never pass sentence of condemnation or acquittal, especially in regard to wickedness. We pronounce such a verdict when, in virtue of his actions, we hold a man worthy of being damned or exonerated. Though we are entitled to form opinions of others, we have no right to spy on them. Everybody has a right to prevent the other from investigating and spying out his actions; such a man is arrogating to himself a right over the acts and omissions of other people. Nobody should do that; for example, by eavesdropping when someone says something to the other in private; better to move away so as not to hear a word of it. Again, if we pay a call on a person, and are left alone, and there is a letter lying open on the table, it is a very disreputable thing to try to read it. A right-thinking man will even try to avoid any suspicion or mistrust; he will not care to remain alone in a room where there is money on the table, nor will he want to hear secrets from others, lest he fall under the suspicion of having let them out; and because such secrets always bother him, for even in the closest friendship, suspicion may always arise. The man who from inclination or appetite deprives his friend of anything, his intended bride, for example, is acting very basely in doing so; for just as he has taken a fancy to my intended, so he can also take a fancy to my purse. It is very mean to lie in wait for, or spy upon, a friend or anyone else; for example, if one tries to find out what he is doing from servants; in that case we have to lower ourselves to their level, and the servants, thereafter, will always consider themselves our equals. By everything that tells against candour, a man loses his dignity; for example, by doing something ill-natured behind the back, for this is a use of means in which a man cannot be open and honest, and all social life is destroyed thereby. All such furtive measures are far more vile than violent wickedness, since we can, after all, take precautions against that; but he who does not even have the courage to demonstrate his wickedness in public has no trace of nobility in him. A person who is violent, but otherwise abhors all pettiness, can still become good, however, if he is tamed. Thus even in England, the attempt of a wife to poison her husband is punished by burning, because if that were to spread, no husband would be safe from his wife.

Just as I am not entitled to spy upon another, so I also have no right to tell him his faults; for even if he should ask for this, the other never hears it without offence; he knows better than I that he has such faults. He thinks, however, that others are not aware of them, and if they tell him, he learns that other people know of them. It is not good, therefore, for people to say: Friends must tell each other their faults, because the other can know them better; nobody, after all, can know my faults better than I do; the other, admittedly, can know better than I, whether or not I stand and walk upright; but who is to know better than I do myself, if only I choose to examine myself? It is forwardness in the other, if he tells someone his faults, and if it comes to that in a friendship, then the latter, too, will no longer last long. We must be blind to the other's faults, for otherwise he sees that we have lost respect for him, and then he also loses all respect for us. Faults must be pointed out if we are placed in authority over someone; in that case we are entitled to give lessons and indicate shortcomings, as a husband, for example, does to his wife; but here kindness, benevolence and respect must prevail; if displeasure alone is present, the outcome is censure and bitterness. But censure can be mitigated by love, good-will and respect. Nothing else makes any contribution to improvement.

7

MAHĀBHĀRATA, KARṆA PARVAN

Our second selection from the *Mahābhārata* begins right after Yudhiṣṭhira has insulted his brother Arjuna (see the introduction to chapter 4 of this volume for more context). Yudhiṣṭhira, frustrated at the slow pace of the war and at what he perceives to be Arjuna's reluctance to fight to his fullest ability, says that Arjuna's bow, Gāṇḍīva, is useless in his arms and that it would be better if he were to give it to Krishna to fight with. This presents Arjuna with a dilemma, as he has taken a vow to kill anyone who would dare to insult his bow or suggest that he give it to someone else. Arjuna thus sees himself as committed, in order not to break his vow, to killing his brother.

In order to help Arjuna resolve this dilemma, Krishna tells him two stories: the story of Balāka the hunter and the story of the famed truth-teller Kauśika. In interpreting the story of Balāka, it is important to remember that hunting and killing animals was considered to be a sinful act. Thus Balāka's ascent to heaven as a result of killing an animal would have struck both the characters in the story and those reading or listening to recitals of the *Mahābhārata* as decidedly counterintuitive.

The story of Kauśika calls to mind the example from Kant's "On a Supposed Right to Lie" (see chapter 6 of this volume). The lesson here, though, is supposed to be that there is something morally obtuse about insisting on telling the truth. Further, given that Kauśika's situation is presented as casting light on Arjuna's, this renders implausible the middle ground that people sometimes advocate with regard to Kant's example: refusing to answer the question at all. No such middle ground is available to Arjuna: either he keeps his vow and kills his brother, or he fails to stay true to his word. It would seem to follow, then, that Krishna would not think that Kauśika can stay true to his vow to tell only the truth by refusing to answer the bandits. For starters, the bandits may be particularly determined to find their targets and thus willing to resort to violence and torture to extract the information from Kauśika. It would then become a question of how much Kauśika is—or should be expected to be—willing to endure to avoid breaking his vow.[1] But the problem is avoided if he were simply

1. [Compare Kauśika's situation with that of Bishop Firmus, described by Augustine in section 23 of De Mendacio (chapter 1 of this volume).]

willing to utter a falsehood at the beginning. More importantly, a refusal to speak would leave the bandits with the knowledge that they are ignorant of the travelers' whereabouts and may lead to a redoubled effort to find them. A successful deception would thus be more likely to succeed at saving the innocent lives than would principled silence.

As you read this selection, consider the following questions:

1. How does the story of Balāka help to illuminate the story of Kauśika and Arjuna's situation? Since it's not about lying or truthfulness, why would Krishna start with it rather than just telling the story of Kauśika?
2. Arjuna's dilemma arises as the result of a vow—a vow, as Krishna points out, that he took carelessly. The same is true of Kauśika. Several of the other selections in this volume consider dilemmas in which there is no explicit vow (e.g., Kant's would-be murderer, Augustine's robber-beset road, etc.). Does this difference matter in one's assessment of the situations, or of the morality of various possible responses?
3. Given that Krishna criticizes Arjuna for foolishly taking the vow that has led to this dilemma, why should he then propose the solution that appears in the last paragraph of the reading? Why might it be important to keep an unethical vow—even if only nominally—rather than simply to ignore it?

Mahābhārata

Karṇa Chapter, Section 69

Thus addressed by Yudhiṣṭhira, Arjuna, filled with rage, drew his sword in order to slay that bull of Bharata's race. Beholding his wrath, Krishna, conversant with the workings of the human heart, said, "Why, O Partha, do you draw your sword? I do not see anyone here with whom you need to fight! The Dhartarāṣṭras[1] have now been assailed by the intelligent Bhīmasena. You come from battle, O son of Kunti, to see the king. The king has been seen by you. Indeed, Yudhiṣṭhira is well. Having seen that tiger among kings who is endued with prowess equal to that of a tiger, why this folly at a time when you should rejoice? I do not see here, O son of Kunti, the person whom you may slay. Why then do you desire to strike? What is this delusion of your mind? Why do you, with such speed, take up that formidable sword? I ask you this, O son of Kunti!"

Thus addressed by Krishna, Arjuna, casting his eyes on Yudhiṣṭhira, and breathing like an angry snake, said to Govinda,[2] "I would cut off the head of that man who would tell me to give my bow Gāṇḍīva to another person. This is my sacred vow. Those words have been spoken by this king, in your presence, O Govinda! I dare not forgive them. For that I will slay this king who himself fears the slightest falling from virtue. Slaying this best of men, I will keep my vow. It is for this that I have drawn my sword. In slaying Yudhiṣṭhira, I will fulfill my debt to truth, and I will dispel my grief and fever, O Janārdana. I ask you, what do you think suitable to the circumstances that have arisen? You know the entire past and future of this universe. I will do what you tell me to."

Krishna then replied to Arjuna, "I now know, Arjuna, that you have not waited upon the old, since you have yielded to wrath at a time when you should not have done so. No one who is acquainted with the distinctions of morality would act in the way in which you, who are not acquainted with them, are acting today. He, O Partha, is the worst of men who commits acts that should not be done and that are apparently proper but condemned by the scriptures. You don't know the decisions of those learned men who, waited upon by students, declare their opinions, following the dictates of morality. The man

1. ["Dhartarāṣṭras," literally, "sons of Dhṛtarāṣṭra," is another name for the Kauravas.]

2. ["Govinda" is another name for Krishna.]

who is not acquainted with those rulings becomes confounded and stupefied, O Partha, just as you have been stupefied, in discriminating between what should be done and what should not. What should be done and what should not cannot be ascertained easily. Everything can be ascertained by the aid of the scriptures. You, however, are not acquainted with the scriptures. Since, believing yourself conversant with morality, you strive to observe morality, you are motivated by ignorance. You believe yourself to be conversant with virtue, but you do not know that the slaughter of living creatures is a sin. Abstention from injury to animals is, I think, the highest virtue. One may even speak an untruth, but one should never kill. How, then, O foremost of men, could you wish to slay your eldest brother, the king, who is conversant with morality? The righteous never applaud the slaughter of a person not engaged in battle, or of a foe who has turned his face from battle or who flies away or seeks protection or joins his hands or yields himself up or who is not in his chariot. Yudhiṣṭhira possesses all of these attributes. You adopted your vow earlier out of foolishness. As a consequence of that vow you are now, from folly, striving to perpetrate a sinful act. Why, O Partha, do you rush toward your eldest brother in order to slay him, without having resolved the exceedingly subtle course of morality that is, again, difficult to understand?

"I will now tell you, O son of Pāṇḍu, this mystery connected with morality, this mystery that was declared by Bhīṣma, by the righteous Yudhiṣṭhira, by Vidura otherwise called Kṣatri, and by Kunti, of great celebrity. I will tell you that mystery in all its details. Listen to it, O Dhananjaya! One who speaks truth is righteous. There is nothing higher than truth. Behold, however: it is exceedingly difficult to understand the essential attributes of the practice of truth. Truth may be unutterable, and even falsehood may be utterable where falsehood would become truth and truth would become falsehood. In a situation of peril to life and in marriage, falsehood becomes utterable. In a situation involving the loss of one's entire property, falsehood becomes utterable. On an occasion of marriage, or of enjoying a woman, or when life is in danger, or when one's entire property is about to be taken away, or for the sake of a Brahmin, falsehood may be uttered. These five kinds of falsehood have been declared to be sinless. On these occasions falsehood would become truth and truth would become falsehood. He is a fool who practices truth without knowing the difference between truth and falsehood. One is said to be conversant with morality when one is able to distinguish between truth and falsehood. What wonder then in this that a man of wisdom, by perpetrating even a cruel act, may obtain great merit like Balāka by the slaughter of the blind beast? What wonder, again, in this that a foolish and ignorant person, from the desire to gain merit, incurs great sin like Kauśika the river dweller?"

Arjuna said, "Tell me, O holy one, this story that I may understand it, viz., this illustration about Balāka and about Kauśika the river dweller."

Vasudeva said,[3] "There was a certain hunter of animals, O Bharata, of the name of Balāka. For the sake of the well-being of his son and wives, and not from a desire to kill, he used to slay animals. Devoted to the duties of his own order and always speaking the truth and never harboring malice, he used also to support his parents and others who depended upon him. One day, searching for animals with perseverance and care, he found none. At last he saw, drinking water, a beast of prey whose sense of smell supplied the defect of his eyes. Although he had never seen such an animal before, still he slew it immediately. After the slaughter of that blind beast, a floral shower fell from the skies. A celestial chariot also, exceedingly delightful and resounding with the songs of Apsarases[4] and the music of their instruments, came from heaven to take away that hunter of animals. That beast of prey, having undergone ascetic austerities, had obtained a boon and had become the cause of the destruction of all creatures. For this reason he was made blind by the Self-Born.[5] Having slain that animal which had resolved to slay all creatures, Balāka went to heaven. Morality is even so difficult to understand as this.

"There was an ascetic named Kauśika without much knowledge of the scriptures. He lived in a spot much removed from a village, at a point where many rivers met. He made a vow, saying, 'I shall always speak the truth.' He then became celebrated, O Dhananjaya, as a speaker of truth. One time some people, fleeing from bandits, entered that wood. The bandits, following behind and filled with rage, searched for them carefully. Approaching Kauśika then, that speaker of truth, they asked him, 'O holy one, by which path have a multitude of men gone a little while before? Asked in the name of Truth, answer us. If thou hast seen them, tell us this.' Thus addressed, Kauśika told them the truth, saying, 'Those men have entered this wood crowded with many trees and creepers and plants.' Even thus, O Partha, did Kauśika give them the information. Then those cruel men, it is heard,

3. ["Vasudeva" is another name for Krishna.]

4. [Apsaras (or Apsarases) are divine dancers, sometimes compared to nymphs or muses from Western mythology.]

5. ["The Self-Born" is a reference to Brahmā, the Hindu god of creation.]

finding the persons they sought, slew them all. In consequence of that great sin consisting in the words spoken, Kauśika, ignorant of the subtleties of morality, fell into a grievous hell, even as a foolish man, of little knowledge, and unacquainted with the distinctions of morality, falls into painful hell by not having asked persons of age for the solution to his doubts.

"There must be some indications for distinguishing virtue from sin. Sometimes that high and unattainable knowledge may be had by the exercise of reason. Many persons say, on the one hand, that the scriptures indicate morality. I do not contradict this. The scriptures, however, do not provide for every case. It is for the growth of creatures that precepts of morality have been declared. That which is connected with inoffensiveness is religion. Dharma protects and preserves the people. So it is the conclusion of the paṇdits that what maintains is dharma. O Partha, I have narrated to you the signs and indications of dharma. Hearing this, you decide whether you ought to slaughter Yudhiṣṭhira or not."

Arjuna said, "Krishna, your words are fraught with great intelligence and imbued with wisdom. You are to us like our parents and our refuge. Nothing in the three worlds is unknown to you, so you are conversant with the canons of morality. O Keśava of the Vṛṣṇi clan, you know my vow that whoever among men would tell me to give my bow Gāṇḍīva to someone else, I shall at once put an end to his life. Bhīma has also made a promise that whoever would call him 'tularak' would be slaughtered by him there and then. Now Yudiṣṭhira has repeatedly used those very words to me in your presence. If I slay him, O Keśava, I will not be able to live in this world for even a moment. Having intended again the slaughter of the king through folly and the loss of my mental faculties, I have been polluted by sin. It behooves you, O foremost of all who are righteous, to give me such counsel that my vow, known throughout the world, may become true while at the same time both I and the eldest son of Pāṇḍu may live."

Vasudeva said, "The king was fatigued, and under the influence of grief. He had been mangled in battle by Karṇa with numerous arrows. After that, O hero, he was repeatedly struck by the Suta's son,[6] while he was retreating from battle. It was for this that, laboring under a load of sorrow, he spoke those improper words to you in wrath. He provoked you by those words so that you might slay Karṇa in battle. The son of Pāṇḍu knows that the wretched Karṇa is incapable of being defeated by anyone else in the world. It was for this, O Partha, that

6. ["The Suta's son" is Karṇa.]

the king in great wrath said those harsh words to you. The stake in the game of today's battle has been made to lie in the ever alert and always unbeatable Karṇa. That Karṇa being slain, the Kauravas would necessarily be vanquished. This is what the royal son of Dharma had thought. For this the son of Dharma does not deserve death.

"Your vow also, O Arjuna, should be kept. Listen now to my advice that will be agreeable to you, to advice in which Yudhiṣṭhira, without being actually deprived of life may yet be dead. As long as one who is deserving of respect continues to receive respect, one is said to live in the world of men. When, however, such a person meets with disrespect, he is spoken of as one who is dead though alive. This king has always been respected by you and by Bhīma and the twins,[7] as also by all heroes and all persons in the world who are venerable for years. In some trifle then show him disrespect. Therefore, O Partha, address this Yudhiṣṭhira as 'you' when his usual form of address is 'your honor.' A superior, O Bharata, by being addressed in the familiar is killed though not deprived of life. Bear thyself thus, O son of Kunti, towards king Yudhiṣṭhira the just. Adopt this censurable behavior, O perpetrator of Kuru's race! This best advice of all advice, has been declared by both Atharvan and Aṅgiras.[8] Men desiring good should always act in this way without scruples of any kind. Without being deprived of life a superior is yet said to be killed if that venerable one is addressed in the familiar. Conversant with duty as you are, address king Yudhiṣṭhira the just in the manner I have indicated. This death, O son of Pāṇḍu, at your hands, king Yudhiṣṭhira will never regard as an offense committed by you. Having addressed him in this way, you may then worship his feet and speak words of respect to him and soothe his wounded honor. Your brother is wise. The royal son of Pāṇḍu, therefore, will never be angry with you. Freed from falsehood as also from fratricide, you will then, O Partha, cheerfully slay the Suta's son Karṇa!"

7. [The twins are Nakula and Sahadeva, the youngest of the five Pāṇḍava brothers.]

8. [Atharvan and Aṅgiras are the legendary authors of the *Atharva Veda*.]

8

PLATO'S *GORGIAS*

The *Gorgias* is considered to be one of the earlier dialogues composed by the Greek philosopher Plato (427–347 BCE). In this excerpt, the character of Socrates has encountered the visiting Sophist (alleged "wise-person") Gorgias, a well-known orator and teacher from Sicily. After exchanging some pleasantries, Socrates proceeds to interrogate Gorgias, asking him to define and defend the practice of oratory.[1] The topic is an especially poignant (or ironic) one, given that Socrates himself was to be convicted and sentenced to death partly due to his alleged affiliation with the Sophists and their practice of using rhetoric to turn words around, thereby "making the weaker argument appear stronger" (one of the actual accusations against Socrates, as recounted by Plato in the *Apology*, Plato's account of Socrates' trial).

Gorgias initially characterizes his profession of oratory as a "craft" which aims at producing emotions in an audience (*peithesthai*—"to persuade") and thereby "leading the mind" (*psychogogia*) of an audience member to whatever purpose the orator desires. Oratory may even, suggests Gorgias, help teach people to be morally virtuous. In the latter half of the selection, Gorgias' young pupil Polus enters the discussion and attempts to reinforce his teacher's position, the logic of which Socrates has been gradually chipping away at by identifying inconsistencies, disanalogies (oratory seems quite different from other recognized crafts such as sculpture and medicine), and unintended consequences (such as orators being potentially tyrannical).

The view that seems to emerge—we may call it Platonic or Socratic—is that rhetoric cannot truly be a craft (*techne*) at all. For something to qualify as a proper craft according to Socrates, it must permit of universal and abstract principles capable of being clearly and rationally articulated. Moreover, genuine crafts must aim at the truth (*aletheia*), understood as accurately imitating (*mimesis*) the way things actually are. Oratory, by contrast, is shown to be grounded merely in inchoate hunches, individual psychologies and emotional reactions, and past

1. "Oratory" is translating the Greek word *rhetorikes*, whence the English word "rhetoric," which we are treating as synonymous. Compare to Aristotle's treatment of the same word in the selection in chapter 3 (there translated instead as "rhetoric").

experiences. For Socrates, this renders it merely a "knack" (*empeiria*) rather than a true *techne*. Furthermore, instead of trying to correspond to reality, oratory is more akin to lying and flattery, i.e., oratory distorts reality to make it conform to our desires, rather than trying to conform our desires to reality. In this light, oratory is a poor shadow of what Socrates claims philosophy actually does—just as cosmetics imitate the real physical beauty which gymnastics brings to the body, or as junk food provides pleasure but not actual medical health. The following differences also emerge in Socrates' treatment of oratory:

Oratory	Philosophy
• attempts to implant new ideas by manipulating emotions;	• attempts to extract new ideas by using reason;
• produces emotional conviction;	• produces knowledge;
• leads to pleasure;	• leads to happiness;
• ultimately disempowers;	• ultimately empowers;
• can be used for good or evil, truth or deceit.	• always seeks the good and true.

For the topic of lying and truthfulness, what is most noteworthy about this exchange is the high standards to which Socrates holds truthfulness: oratory is deceitful because it fails to explicitly aim at verisimilitude between word and reality. Moreover, Plato connects deception with emotionality, moral wickedness, and sensory pleasures (which partially undergirds his suspicion of much poetry and art as inherently deceitful, which we see in our excerpt from his *Republic*).

Here are some questions for further consideration:

1. Because he associates it with a form of deception, Socrates suggests that rhetorical persuasion is (or should be) always bad and undesirable, or at least that it needs the mitigating influence of true philosophy to properly direct it. Are there instances, however, where flattery might be morally appropriate? Can certain things, which might themselves distort reality (e.g., works of art), nevertheless reveal deeper truths?
2. Part of Socrates' argument hinges on the claim that we only ever desire truth (at least insofar as we are being rational).

How would such a claim be proved or disproved? Can you think of possible counterexamples?

3. Is it even possible to fully avoid oratory in everyday life? Oratory, as a form of flattery and thus arguably a lie, produces pleasure. Give examples of specific instances of persuasion or deception that are pleasurable. Are they pleasurable to both the deceived and the deceiver? What, ultimately, is wrong with pursuing pleasant falsehoods?

Gorgias

Socrates: Come then. You claim to be an expert in the craft of oratory and to be able to make someone else an orator, too. With which of the things there are is oratory concerned? Weaving, for example, is concerned with the production of clothes, isn't it?

Gorgias: Yes.

Soc: And so, too, music is concerned with the composition of tunes?

Gor: Yes.

Soc: By Hera, Gorgias, I do like your answers. They couldn't be shorter!

Gor: Yes, Socrates, I daresay I'm doing it quite nicely.

Soc: And so you are. Come and answer me then that way about oratory, too. About which, of the things there are, is *it* expertise?

Gor: About speeches.

Soc: What sort of speeches, Gorgias? Those that explain how sick people should be treated to get well?

Gor: No.

Soc: So oratory isn't concerned with *all* speeches.

Gor: Oh, no.

Soc: But it does make people capable of speaking.

Gor: Yes.

Soc: And also to be wise in what they're speaking about?

Gor: Of course.

Soc: Now does the medical craft, the one we were talking about just now, make people able both to have wisdom about and to speak about the sick?

Gor: Necessarily.

Soc: This craft, then, is evidently concerned with speeches too.

Gor: Yes.

Soc: Speeches about diseases, that is?

Gor: Exactly.

Soc: Isn't physical training also concerned with speeches, speeches about good and bad physical condition?

Gor: Yes, it is.

Soc: In fact, Gorgias, the same is true of the other crafts, too. Each of them is concerned with those speeches that are about the object of the particular craft.

Gor: Apparently.

Soc: Then why don't you call the other crafts oratory, since you call any craft whatever that's concerned with speeches oratory? They're concerned with speeches, too!

Gor: The reason, Socrates, is that in the case of the other crafts the expertise consists almost completely in working with your hands and activities of that sort. In the case of oratory, on the other hand, there isn't any such manual work. Its activity and influence depend entirely on speeches. That's the reason I consider the craft of oratory to be concerned with speeches. And I say I'm right about this.

Soc: I'm not sure I understand what sort of craft you want to call it. I'll soon know more clearly. Tell me this. There are crafts at our disposal, aren't there?

Gor: Yes.

Soc: Of all the crafts there are, I take it that there are those that consist for the most part of making things and that call for little speech, and some that call for none at all, ones whose tasks could be done even silently. Take painting, for instance, or sculpture, or many others. When you say that oratory has nothing to do with other crafts, it's crafts of this sort I think you're referring to. Or aren't you?

Gor: Yes, Socrates. You take my meaning very well.

Soc: And then there are other crafts, the ones that perform their whole task by means of speeches and that call for practically no physical work besides, or very little of it. Take arithmetic or computation or geometry, even checkers and many other crafts. Some of these involve speeches to just about the same degree as they do activity, while others involve speeches more. All their activity and influence depend entirely on speeches. I think you mean that oratory is a craft of this sort.

Gor: True.

Soc: But you certainly don't want to call any of *these* crafts oratory, do you, even though, as you phrase it, oratory is the craft that exercises its influence through speech. Somebody might take you up, if he wanted to make a fuss in argument, and say, "So you're saying that arithmetic is oratory, are you, Gorgias?" I'm sure, however, that you're not saying either arithmetic or geometry is oratory.

Gor: Yes, you're quite correct, Socrates. You take my meaning rightly.

Soc: Come on, then. Please complete your answer in the terms of my question. Since oratory is one of those crafts which mostly uses speech, and since there are also others of that sort, try to say *what* it is that oratory, which exercises its influence through speeches, is about. Imagine someone asking me about any of the crafts I mentioned just now, "Socrates, what is the craft of arithmetic?" I'd tell him, just as you told me, that it's one of those that exercise their influence by means of speech. And if he continued, "What are they crafts about?" I'd say that they're about even and odd, however many of each there might be. If he then asked, "What is the craft you call computation?" I'd say that this one, too, is one of those that exercise their influence entirely by speech. And if he then continued, "What is it about?" I'd answer in the style of those who draw up motions in the Assembly that in other respects computation is like arithmetic—for it's about the same thing, even and odd—yet it differs from computation insofar as the latter examines the quantity of odd and even, both in relation to themselves and in relation to each other. And if someone asked about astronomy and I replied that it, too, exercises its influence by means of speech, then if he asked, "What are the speeches of astronomy about, Socrates?" I'd say that they're about the motions of the stars, the sun and the moon, and their relative velocities.

Gor: And you'd be quite right to say so, Socrates.

Soc: Come, Gorgias, you take your turn. For oratory is in fact one of those crafts that carry out and exercise their influence entirely by speech, isn't it?

Gor: That's right.

Soc: Tell us then: what are they crafts about? Of the things there are, which is the one that these speeches used by oratory are concerned with?

Gor: The greatest of human concerns, Socrates, and the best.

Soc: But that statement, too, is debatable, Gorgias. It isn't at all clear yet, either. I'm sure that you've heard people at drinking parties singing that song in which they count out as they sing that "to enjoy good health is the best thing; second is to have turned out good looking; and third"—so the writer of the song puts it—"is to be honestly rich."

Gor: Yes, I've heard it. Why do you mention it?

Soc: Suppose that the producers of the things the songwriter praised were here with you right now: a doctor, a physical trainer, and a financial expert. Suppose that first the doctor said, "Socrates, Gorgias is telling you a lie. It isn't his craft that is concerned with the greatest good for mankind, but mine." If I then asked him, "what are you, to say that?" I suppose he'd say that he's a doctor. "What's this you're saying? Is the product of your craft really the greatest good?" "Of course, Socrates," I suppose he'd say, "seeing that its product is health. What greater good for mankind is there than health?" And suppose that next in his turn the trainer said, "I too would be amazed, Socrates, if Gorgias could present you with a greater good derived from his craft than the one I could provide from mine." I'd ask this man, too, "What are you sir, and what's your product?" "I'm a physical trainer," he'd say, "and my product is making people physically good-looking and strong." And following the trainer the financial expert would say, I'm sure with an air of considerable scorn for all, "Do consider, Socrates, whether you know of any good, Gorgias' or anyone else's, that's a greater good than wealth." We'd say to him, "Really? Is that what you produce?" He'd say yes. "As what?" "As a financial expert." "Well," we'll say, "is wealth in your judgment the greatest good for people?" "Of course," he'll say. "Ah, but Gorgias here disputes that. He claims that his craft is the source of a good that's greater than yours," we'd say. And it's obvious what question he'd ask next. "And what is this good, please? Let Gorgias answer me that!" So come on, Gorgias. Consider yourself questioned by both these men and myself, and give us your answer. What is this thing that you claim is the greatest good for mankind, a thing you claim to be a producer of?

Gor: The thing that is in actual fact the greatest good, Socrates. It is the source of freedom for mankind itself and at the same time it is for each person the source of rule over others in one's own city.

Soc: And what is this thing you're referring to?

Gor: I'm referring to the ability to persuade by speeches judges in a law court, councilors in a council meeting, and assemblymen in an assembly or in any other political gathering that might take place. In point of fact, with this ability you'll have the doctor for your slave, and the physical trainer, too. As for this financial expert of yours, he'll turn out to be making more money for somebody else instead of himself; for you, in fact, if you've got the ability to speak and to persuade the crowds.[1]

Soc: *Now* I think you've come closest to making clear what craft you take oratory to be, Gorgias. If I follow you at all, you're saying that oratory is a producer of persuasion. Its whole business comes to that, and that's the long and short of it. Or can you mention anything else

1. [The term used for "persuasion" here and throughout the rest of the selection is *peitho*. Aristotle uses cognate terms to refer to persuasion in the selection from *Rhetoric* (chapter 3 of this volume), but with rather different connotations.]

oratory can do besides instilling persuasion in the souls of an audience?

Gor: None at all, Socrates. I think you're defining it quite adequately. That is indeed the long and short of it.

Soc: Listen then, Gorgias. You should know that I'm convinced I'm one of those people who in a discussion with someone else really want to have knowledge of the subject the discussion's about. And I consider you one of them, too.

Gor: Well, what's the point, Socrates?

Soc: Let me tell you now. You can know for sure that I don't know what this persuasion derived from oratory that you're talking about is, or what subjects it's persuasion about. Even though I do have my suspicions about which persuasion you mean, I suppose, and what it's about, I'll still ask you just the same what you say this persuasion produced by oratory is, and what it's about. And why, when I have my suspicions do I ask you and refrain from expressing them myself? It's not you I'm after, it's our discussion, to have it proceed in such a way as to make the thing we're talking about most clear to us. Consider, then, whether you think I'm being fair in resuming my questions to you. Suppose I were to ask you which of the painters Zeuxis is.[2] If you told me that he's the one who paints pictures, wouldn't it be fair for me to ask, "Of what sort of pictures is he the painter, and where?"

Gor: Yes, it would.

Soc: And isn't the reason for this the fact that there are other painters, too, who paint many other pictures?

Gor: Yes.

Soc: But if no one besides Zeuxis were a painter, your answer would have been a good one?

Gor: Of course.

Soc: Come then, and tell me about oratory. Do you think that oratory alone instills persuasion, or do other crafts do so

2. Zeuxis was the most famous painter of the late fifth century B.C.

too? This is the sort of thing I mean: Does a person who teaches some subject or other persuade people about what he's teaching, or not?

Gor: He certainly does, Socrates. He persuades most of all.

Soc: Let's talk once more about the same crafts we were talking about just now. Doesn't arithmetic or the arithmetician teach us everything that pertains to number?

Gor: Yes, he does.

Soc: And he also persuades?

Gor: Yes.

Soc: So arithmetic is also a producer of persuasion.

Gor: Apparently.

Soc: Now if someone asks us what sort of persuasion it produces and what it's persuasion about, I suppose we'd answer him that it's the persuasion of teaching about the extent of even and odd. And we'll be able to show that all the other crafts we were just now talking about are producers of persuasion, as well as what the persuasion is and what it's about. Isn't that right?

Gor: Yes.

Soc: So oratory isn't the only producer of persuasion.

Gor: That's true.

Soc: In that case, since it's not the only one to produce this product but other crafts do it too, we'd do right to repeat to our speaker the question we put next in the case of the painter: "Of what sort of persuasion is oratory a craft, and what is its persuasion about?" Or don't you think it's right to repeat that question?

Gor: Yes, I do.

Soc: Well then, Gorgias, since you think so too, please answer.

Gor: The persuasion I mean, Socrates, is the kind that takes place in law courts and in those other large gatherings, as I was saying a moment ago. And it's concerned with those matters that are just and unjust.

Soc: Yes, Gorgias, I suspected that this was the persuasion you meant, and that these are the matters it's persuasion about. But so you won't be surprised if in a moment I ask you again another question like this, about what seems to be clear, and yet I go on with my questioning—as I say, I'm asking questions so that we can conduct an orderly discussion. It's not you I'm after; it's to prevent our getting in the habit of second-guessing and snatching each other's statements away ahead of time. It's to allow you to work out your assumption in any way you want to.

Gor: Yes, I think that you're quite right to do this, Socrates.

Soc: Come then, and let's examine this point. Is there something you call "to have learned"?

Gor: There is.

Soc: Very well. And also something you call "to be convinced"?

Gor: Yes, there is.

Soc: Now, do you think that to have learned, and learning, are the same as to be convinced and conviction, or different?

Gor: I certainly suppose that they're different, Socrates.

Soc: You suppose rightly. This is how you can tell: If someone asked you, "Is there such a thing as true and false conviction, Gorgias?" you'd say yes, I'm sure.

Gor: Yes.

Soc: Well now, is there such a thing as true and false knowledge?

Gor: Not at all.

Soc: So it's clear they're not the same.

Gor: That's true.

Soc: But surely both those who have learned and those who are convinced have come to be persuaded?

Gor: That's right.

Soc: Would you like us then to posit two types of persuasion, one providing conviction without knowledge, the other providing knowledge?

Gor: Yes, I would.

Soc: Now which type of persuasion does oratory produce in law courts and other gatherings concerning things that are just and unjust? The one that results in being convinced without knowing or the one that results in knowing?

Gor: It's obvious, surely, that it's the one that results in conviction.

Soc: So evidently oratory is a producer of conviction-persuasion and not of teaching-persuasion concerning what's just and unjust.

Gor: Yes.

Soc: And so an orator is not a teacher of law courts and other gatherings about things that are just and unjust, either, but merely a persuader, for I don't suppose that he could teach such a large gathering about matters so important in a short time.

Gor: No, he certainly couldn't.

Soc: Well now, let's see what we're really saying about oratory. For, mind you, even I myself can't get clear yet about what I'm saying. When the city holds a meeting to appoint doctors or shipbuilders or some other variety of craftsmen, that's surely not the time when the orator will give advice, is it? For obviously it's the most accomplished craftsman who should be appointed in each case. Nor will the orator be the one to give advice at a meeting that concerns the building of walls or the equipping of harbors or dockyards, but the master builders will be the ones. And when there is a deliberation about the appointment of generals or an arrangement of troops against the enemy or an occupation of territory, it's not the orators but the generals who'll give advice then. What do you say about such cases, Gorgias? Since you yourself claim both to be an orator and to make others orators, we'll do well to find out from you the characteristics of your craft. You must think of me now as eager to serve your interests, too. Perhaps there's actually someone inside who wants to become your pupil. I notice some, in fact a good many, and they may well be embarrassed to question you. So, while you're being questioned by me, consider yourself being questioned by them as well: "What will we get if we associate with you, Gorgias? What will we be able to advise the city on? Only about what's just and unjust or also about the things Socrates was mentioning just now?" Try to answer them.

Gor: Well, Socrates, I'll try to reveal to you clearly everything oratory can accomplish. You yourself led the way nicely, for you do know, don't you, that these dockyards and walls of the Athenians and the equipping of the harbor came about through the advice of Themistocles and in some cases through that of Pericles, but not through that of the craftsmen?[3]

Soc: That's what they say about Themistocles, Gorgias. I myself heard Pericles when he advised us on the middle wall.

Gor: And whenever those craftsmen you were just now speaking of are appointed, Socrates, you see that the orators are the ones who give advice and whose views on these matters prevail.

Soc: Yes, Gorgias, my amazement at that led me long ago to ask what it is that oratory can accomplish. For as I look at it, it seems to me to be something supernatural in scope.

3. Themistocles (c. 528–c. 462 B.C.) was the leading statesman of Athens after the death of Miltiades in 489. He was largely responsible for the fortification of the Piraeus and the development of Athens' naval power during the first two decades of the fifth century. Pericles (c. 495–429 B.C.) rose to prominence in the late 460s, and in 443 and every year of his life thereafter was elected as general. He was the architect of Athenian strategy against Sparta at the outbreak of the Peloponnesian war in 431. He died in 429 from the effects of the plague that had struck Athens a year earlier.

Gor: Oh yes, Socrates, if only you knew all of it, that it encompasses and subordinates to itself just about everything that can be accomplished. And I'll give you ample proof. Many a time I've gone with my brother or with other doctors to call on some sick person who refuses to take his medicine or allow the doctor to perform surgery or cauterization on him. And when the doctor failed to persuade him, I succeeded, by means of no other craft than oratory. And I maintain too that if an orator and a doctor came to any city anywhere you like and had to compete in speaking in the assembly or some other gathering over which of them should be appointed doctor, the doctor wouldn't make any showing at all, but the one who had the ability to speak would be appointed, if he so wished. And if he were to compete with any other craftsman whatever, the orator more than anyone else would persuade them that they should appoint him, for there isn't anything that the orator couldn't speak more persuasively about to a gathering than could any other craftsman whatever. That's how great the accomplishment of this craft is, and the sort of accomplishment it is! One should, however, use oratory like any other competitive skill, Socrates. In other cases, too, one ought not to use a competitive skill against any and everybody, just because he has learned boxing, or boxing and wrestling combined, or fighting in armor, so as to make himself be superior to his friends as well as to his enemies. That's no reason to strike, stab, or kill one's own friends! Imagine someone who after attending wrestling school, getting his body into good shape and becoming a boxer, went on to strike his father and mother or any other family member or friend. By Zeus, that's no reason to hate physical trainers and people who teach fighting in armor, and to exile them from their cities! For while these people imparted their skills to be used justly against enemies and wrongdoers, and in defense, not aggression, their pupils pervert their strength and skill and misuse them. So it's not their teachers who are wicked, nor is this a reason why the craft should be a cause of wickedness; the ones who misuse it are supposedly the wicked ones. And the same is true for oratory as well. The orator has the ability to speak against everyone on every subject, so as in gatherings to be more persuasive, in short, about anything he likes, but the fact that he has the ability to rob doctors or other craftsmen of their reputations doesn't give him any more of a reason to do it. He should use oratory justly, as he would any competitive skill. And I suppose that if a person who has become an orator goes on with this ability and this craft to commit wrongdoing, we shouldn't hate his teacher and exile him from our cities. For while the teacher imparted it to be used justly, the pupil is making the opposite use of it. So it's the misuser whom it's just to hate and exile or put to death, not the teacher.

Soc: Gorgias, I take it that you, like me, have experienced many discussions and that you've observed this sort of thing about them: it's not easy for the participants to define jointly what they're undertaking to discuss, and so, having learned from and taught each other, to conclude their session. Instead, if they're disputing some point and one maintains that the other isn't right or isn't clear, they get irritated, each thinking the other is speaking out of spite. They become eager to win instead of investigating the subject under discussion. In fact, in the end some have a most shameful parting of the ways, abuse heaped upon them, having given and gotten to hear such things that make even the bystanders upset with themselves for having thought it worthwhile to come to listen to such people. What's my point in saying this? It's that I think you're now saying things that aren't very consistent or compatible with what you were first saying about oratory. So, I'm afraid to pursue my examination of you, for fear that you should take me to be speaking with eagerness to win against you, rather than to have our subject become clear. For my part, I'd be pleased to continue questioning you if you're the same kind of man I am, otherwise I would drop it. And what kind of man am I? One of those who would be pleased to be refuted if I say anything untrue, and who would be pleased to refute anyone who says anything untrue; one who, however, wouldn't be any less pleased to be refuted than to refute. For I count being refuted a greater good, insofar as it is a greater good to be rid of the greatest evil from oneself than to rid someone else of it. I don't suppose that any evil for a man is as great as false belief about the things we're discussing right now. So if you say you're this kind of man, too, let's continue the discussion; but if you think we should drop it, let's be done with it and break it off.

Gor: Oh yes, Socrates, I say that I myself, too, am the sort of person you describe. Still, perhaps we should keep in mind the people who are present here, too. For quite a while ago now, even before you came, I gave them a long presentation, and perhaps we'll stretch things out too long if we continue the discussion. We should think about them, too, so as not to keep any of them who want to do something else.

Chaerephon: You yourselves hear the commotion these men are making, Gorgias and Socrates. They want to hear anything you have to say. And as for myself, I hope I'll never be so busy that I'd forego discussions such as this, conducted in the way this one is, because I find it more practical to do something else.

Callicles: By the gods, Chaerephon, as a matter of fact I, too, though I've been present at many a discussion before now, don't know if I've ever been so pleased as I am at the moment. So if you're willing to discuss, even if it's all day long, you'll be gratifying me.

Soc: For my part there's nothing stopping me, Callicles, as long as Gorgias is willing.

Gor: It'll be to my shame ever after, Socrates, if I weren't willing, when I myself have made the claim that anyone may ask me anything he wants. All right, if it suits these people, carry on with the discussion, and ask what you want.

Soc: Well then, Gorgias, let me tell you what surprises me in the things you've said. It may be that what you said was correct and that I'm not taking your meaning correctly. Do you say that you're able to make an orator out of anyone who wants to study with you?

Gor: Yes.

Soc: So that he'll be persuasive in a gathering about all subjects, not by teaching but by persuading?

Gor: Yes, that's right.

Soc: You were saying just now, mind you, that the orator will be more persuasive even about health than a doctor is.

Gor: Yes I was, more persuasive in a gathering, anyhow.

Soc: And doesn't "in a gathering" just mean "among those who don't have knowledge"? For, among those who do have it, I don't suppose that he'll be more persuasive than the doctor.

Gor: That's true.

Soc: Now if he'll be more persuasive than a doctor, doesn't he prove to be more persuasive than the one who has knowledge?

Gor: Yes, that's right.

Soc: Even though he's not a doctor, right?

Gor: Yes.

Soc: And a non-doctor, I take it, lacks expertise in the things a doctor's an expert in?

Gor: That's obvious.

Soc: So when an orator is more persuasive than a doctor, a non-knower will be more persuasive than a knower among non-knowers. Isn't this exactly what follows?

Gor: Yes it is, at least in this case.

Soc: The same is true about the orator and oratory relative to the other crafts, too, then. Oratory doesn't need to have any knowledge of the state of their subject matters; it only needs to have discovered a persuasion device in order to make itself appear to those who don't have knowledge that it knows more than those who actually do have it.

Gor: Well, Socrates, aren't things made very easy when you come off no worse than the craftsmen even though you haven't learned any other craft but this one?

Soc: Whether the orator does or does not come off worse than the others because of this being so, we'll examine in a moment if it has any bearing on our argument. For now, let's consider this point first. Is it the case that the orator is in the same position with respect to what's just and unjust, what's shameful and admirable, what's good and bad, as he is about what's healthy and about the subjects of the other crafts? Does he lack knowledge, that is, of what these are, of what is good or what is bad, of what is admirable or what is shameful, or just or unjust? Does he devise persuasion about them, so that—even though he doesn't know—he seems, among those who don't know either, to know more than someone who actually does know? Or is it necessary for him to know, and must the prospective student of oratory already possess this expertise before coming to you? And if he doesn't will you, the oratory teacher, not teach him any of these things when he comes to you—for that's not your job—and will you make him seem among most people to have knowledge of such things when in fact he doesn't have it, and to seem good when in fact he isn't? Or won't you be able to teach him oratory at all, unless he knows the truth about these things to begin with? How do matters such as these stand, Gorgias? Yes, by Zeus, do give us your revelation and tell us what oratory can accomplish, just as you just now said you would.

Gor: Well, Socrates, I suppose that if he really doesn't have this knowledge, he'll learn these things from me as well.

Soc: Hold it there. You're right to say so. If you make someone an orator, it's necessary for him to know what's just and what's unjust, either beforehand, or by learning it from you afterwards.

Gor: Yes, it is.

Soc: Well? A man who has learned carpentry is a carpenter, isn't he?

Gor: Yes.

Soc: And isn't a man who has learned music a musician?

Gor: Yes.

Soc: And a man who has learned medicine a doctor? And isn't this so too, by the same reasoning, with the other crafts? Isn't a man who has learned a particular subject the sort of man his expertise makes him?

Gor: Yes, he is.

Soc: And, by this line of reasoning, isn't a man who has learned what's just a just man too?

Gor: Yes, absolutely.

Soc: And a just man does just things, I take it?

Gor: Yes.

Soc: Now isn't an orator necessarily just, and doesn't a just man necessarily want to do just things?

Gor: Apparently so.

Soc: Therefore an orator will never want to do what's unjust.

Gor: No, apparently not.

Soc: Do you remember saying a little earlier that we shouldn't complain against physical trainers or exile them from our cities if the boxer uses his boxing skill to do what's unjust, and that, similarly, if an orator uses his oratorical skill unjustly we shouldn't complain against his teacher or banish him from the city, but do so to the one who does what's unjust, the one who doesn't use his oratorical skill properly? Was that said or not?

Gor: Yes, it was.

Soc: But now it appears that this very man, the orator, would never have done what's unjust, doesn't it?

Gor: Yes, it does.

Soc: And at the beginning of our discussion, Gorgias, it was said that oratory would be concerned with speeches, not those about even and odd, but those about what's just and unjust. Right?

Gor: Yes.

Soc: Well, at the time you said that, I took it that oratory would never be an unjust thing, since it always makes its speeches about justice. But when a little later you were saying that the orator could also use oratory unjustly, I was surprised and thought that your statements weren't consistent, and so I made that speech in which I said that if you, like me, think that being refuted is a profitable thing, it would be worthwhile to continue the discussion, but if you don't to let it drop. But now, as we subsequently examine the question, you see for yourself too that it's agreed that, quite to the contrary, the orator is incapable of using oratory unjustly and of being willing to do what's unjust. By the Dog, Gorgias, it'll take more than a short session to go through an adequate examination of how these matters stand!

Polus: Really, Socrates? Is what you're now saying about oratory what you actually think of it? Or do you really think, just because Gorgias was too ashamed not to concede your further claim that the orator also knows what's just, what's admirable, and what's good, and that if he came to him without already having this knowledge to begin with, he said that he would teach him himself, and then from this admission maybe some inconsistency crept into his statements—just the thing that gives you delight, you're the one who leads him on to face such questions—who do you think would deny that he himself knows what's just and would teach others? To lead your arguments to such an outcome is a sign of great rudeness.[4]

Soc: Most admirable Polus, it's not for nothing that we get ourselves companions and sons. It's so that, when we ourselves have grown older and stumble, you younger men might be on hand to straighten our lives up again, both in what we do and what we say. And if Gorgias and I are stumbling now in what we say—well, you're on hand, straighten us up again. That's only right. And if you think we were wrong to agree on it, I'm certainly

4. Polus' indignation at the outcome of Socrates' discussion with Gorgias is evident from the lack of grammatical structure in this speech.

willing to retract any of our agreements you like, provided that you're careful about just one thing.

Pol: What do you mean?

Soc: That you curb your long style of speech, Polus, the style you tried using at first.

Pol: Really? Won't I be free to say as much as I like?

Soc: You'd certainly be in a terrible way, my good friend, if upon coming to Athens, where there's more freedom of speech than anywhere else in Greece, you alone should miss out on it here. But look at it the other way. If you spoke at length and were unwilling to answer what you're asked, wouldn't *I* be in a terrible way if I'm not to have the freedom to stop listening to you and leave? But if you care at all about the discussion we've had and want to straighten it up, please retract whatever you think best, as I was saying just now. Take your turn in asking and being asked questions the way Gorgias and I did, and subject me and yourself to refutation. You say, I take it, that you're an expert in the same craft as Gorgias is? Or don't you?

Pol: Yes, I do.

Soc: And don't you also invite people to ask you each time whatever they like, because you believe you give expert answers?

Pol: Certainly.

Soc: So now please do whichever of these you like: either ask questions or answer them.

Pol: Very well, I shall. Tell me, Socrates, since you think Gorgias is confused about oratory, what do *you* say it is?

Soc: Are you asking me what *craft* I say it is?

Pol: Yes, I am.

Soc: To tell you the truth, Polus, I don't think it's a craft at all.

Pol: Well then, what do you think oratory is?

Soc: In the treatise that I read recently, it's the thing that you say has produced craft.

Pol: What do you mean?

Soc: I mean a knack.[5]

Pol: So you think oratory's a knack?

Soc: Yes, I do, unless you say it's something else.

Pol: A knack for what?

Soc: For producing a certain gratification and pleasure.

Pol: Don't you think that oratory's an admirable thing, then, to be able to give gratification to people?

Soc: Really, Polus! Have you already discovered from me what I say it is, so that you go on to ask me next whether I don't think it's admirable?

Pol: Haven't I discovered that you say it's a knack?

Soc: Since you value gratification, would you like to gratify me on a small matter?

Pol: Certainly.

Soc: Ask me now what craft I think pastry baking is.[6]

Pol: All right, I will. What craft is pastry baking?

Soc: It isn't one at all, Polus. Now say, "What is it then?"

Pol: All right.

Soc: It's a knack. Say, "A knack for what?"

Pol: All right.

Soc: For producing gratification and pleasure, Polus.

Pol: So oratory is the same thing as pastry baking?

Soc: Oh no, not at all, although it *is* a part of the same practice.

Pol: What practice do you mean?

5. Gr. *Empeiria*, tr. "experience" . . . Socrates uses this word here to deny that oratory meets his conditions of being a *technē*.

6. Gr. *Opsopoiia*. The term has a wider use than the translation suggests and can refer to cooking or baking delicacies of various kinds.

Soc: I'm afraid it may be rather crude to speak the truth. I hesitate to do so for Gorgias' sake, for fear that he may think I'm satirizing what he practices. I don't know whether this is the kind of oratory that Gorgias practices—in fact in our discussion a while ago we didn't get at all clear on just what he thinks it is. But what *I* call oratory is a part of some business that isn't admirable at all.

Gor: Which one's that, Socrates? Say it, and don't spare my feelings.

Soc: Well then, Gorgias, I think there's a practice that's not craftlike, but one that a mind given to making hunches takes to, a mind that's bold and naturally clever at dealing with people. I call it flattery, basically. I think that this practice has many other parts as well, and pastry baking, too, is one of them. This part *seems* to be a craft, but in my account of it it isn't a craft but a knack and a routine. I call oratory a part of this, too, along with cosmetics and sophistry. These are four parts, and they're directed to four objects. So if Polus wants to discover them, let him do so. He hasn't discovered yet what sort of part of flattery I say oratory is. Instead, it's escaped him that I haven't answered that question yet, and so he goes on to ask whether I don't consider it to be admirable. And I won't answer him whether I think it's admirable or shameful until I first tell what it is. That wouldn't be right, Polus. If, however, you do want to discover this, ask me what sort of part of flattery I say oratory is.

Pol: I shall. Tell me what sort of part it is.

Soc: Would you understand my answer? By my reasoning, oratory is an image of a part of politics.

Pol: Well? Are you saying that it's something admirable or shameful?

Soc: I'm saying that it's a shameful thing—I call bad things shameful—since I must answer you as though you already know what I mean.

Gor: By Zeus, Socrates, I myself don't understand what you mean, either!

Soc: Reasonably enough, Gorgias. I'm not saying anything clear yet. This colt[7] here is youthful and impulsive.

Gor: Never mind him. Please tell me what you mean by saying that oratory is an image of a part of politics.

Soc: All right, I'll try to describe my view of oratory. If this isn't what it actually is, Polus here will refute me. There is, I take it, something you call *body* and something you call *soul*?

Gor: Yes, of course.

Soc: And do you also think that there's a state of fitness for each of these?

Gor: yes, I do.

Soc: All right. Is there also an apparent state of fitness, one that isn't real? The sort of thing I mean is this. There are many people who *appear* to be physically fit, and unless one is a doctor or one of the fitness experts, one wouldn't readily notice that they're not fit.

Gor: That's true.

Soc: I'm saying that this sort of thing exists in the case of both the body and the soul, a thing that makes the body and the soul *seem* fit when in fact they aren't any the more so.

Gor: That's so.

Soc: Come then, and I'll show you more clearly what I'm saying, if I can. I'm saying that of this pair of subjects there are two crafts. The one for the soul I call politics; the one for the body, though it is one, I can't give you a name for offhand, but while the care of the body is a single craft, I'm saying it has two parts: gymnastics and medicine. And in politics, the counterpart of gymnastics is legislation, and the part that corresponds to medicine is justice. Each member of these pairs has features in common with the other, medicine with gymnastics and justice with legislation, because they're concerned with the same thing. They do, however, differ in some

7. A pun on Polus' name; *pōlos* means "colt."

way from each other. These, then, are the four parts, and they always provide care, in the one case for the body, in the other for the soul, with a view to what's best. Now flattery takes notice of them, and—I won't say by *knowing*, but only by *guessing*—divides itself into four, masks itself with each of the parts, and then pretends to be the characters of the masks. It takes no thought at all of whatever is best; with the lure of what's most pleasant at the moment, it sniffs out folly and hoodwinks it, so that it gives the impression of being most deserving. Pastry baking has put on the mask of medicine, and pretends to know the foods that are best for the body, so that if a pastry baker and a doctor had to compete in front of children, or in front of men just as foolish as children, to determine which of the two, the doctor or the pastry baker, had expert knowledge of good food and bad, the doctor would die of starvation. I call this flattery,[8] and I say that such a thing is shameful, Polus—it's you I'm saying this to—because it guesses at what's pleasant with no consideration for what's best. And I say that it isn't a craft, but a knack, because it has no account of the nature of whatever things it applies by which it applies them, so that it's unable to state the cause of each thing. And I refuse to call anything that lacks such an account a craft. If you have any quarrel with these claims, I'm willing to submit them for discussion.

So pastry baking, as I say, is the flattery that wears the mask of medicine. Cosmetics is the one that wears that of gymnastics in the same way; a mischievous, deceptive, disgraceful and liberal thing; one that perpetrates deception by means of shaping and coloring, smoothing out and dressing up, so as to make people assume an alien beauty and neglect their own, which comes through gymnastics. So that I won't make a long-style speech, I'm willing to put it to you the way the geometers do—for perhaps you follow me now—that what cosmetics is to gymnastics, pastry baking is to medicine; or rather, like this: what cosmetics is to gymnastics, sophistry is to legislation, and what pastry baking

8. [Greek *kolakeia*.]

is to medicine, oratory is to justice. However, as I was saying, although these activities are naturally distinct in this way, yet because they are so close, sophists and orators tend to be mixed together as people who work in the same area and concern themselves with the same things. They don't know what to do with themselves, and other people don't know what to do with them. In fact, if the soul didn't govern the body but the body governed itself, and if pastry baking and medicine weren't kept under observation and distinguished by the soul, but the body itself made judgments about them, making its estimates by reference to the gratification it receives, then the world according to Anaxagoras would prevail,[9] Polus my friend—you're familiar with these views—all things would be mixed together in the same place and then there would be no distinction between matters of medicine and health, and matters of pastry baking.

You've now heard what I say oratory is. It's the counterpart in the soul to pastry baking, its counterpart in the body. Perhaps I've done an absurd thing: I wouldn't let you make long speeches, and here I've just composed a lengthy one myself. I deserve to be forgiven, though, for when I made my statements short you didn't understand and didn't know how to deal with the answers I gave you, but you needed a narration. So if I don't know how to deal with your answers either, you must spin out a speech, too. But if I do, just let me deal with them. That's only fair. And if you now know how to deal with my answer, please deal with it.

9. [Anaxagoras (c. 510–428 BCE) taught that the world is composed of primordial and eternal material, which is chaotically intermixed, and attains organization only through the activity of reason (*nous*).]

9
PLATO'S *REPUBLIC*

Republic spans ten full books and deals with the topic of justice, broadly construed. In the first book, Socrates initiates a discussion about both the nature and justification of morality. An analogy is developed between the sort of political/institutional justice that can exist in cities and the kind of psychic "justice" that can exist within an individual's own personality and moral character. Common to both species of justice is the idea of a proper balancing of parts, attained through the cultivation of rationality in the case of psychic justice and the delicate training of a caste of benevolent rulers in the case of political justice.

Plato believes that in both instances of justice, much hinges on the sorts of influences to which impressionable youths are exposed. One of the main ways the privileged children of Plato's time were educated was through the poetry and mythology of writers such as Homer and Hesiod. As readers familiar with Greek mythology may recall, much of the poetry of these authors is devoted to graphic depictions of often morally suspicious characters and actions. In the selection from *Republic* Book 2, Socrates expresses his worries to a man named Adeimantus about the developmental effects that such art will have on audiences, in virtue of the powerful emotional seductions of the poetry as well as the predisposition of untutored minds to imitate (*mimesis*) that to which they are exposed.

With so much at stake, Socrates hesitantly condones a form of censorship (*epistataiteos*—literally "one must stand over") in which enlightened rulers and teachers may justifiably deceive (*prosaikei pseudesthai*) "on account of enemies or citizens for the benefit of the state." Earlier in *Republic*, Socrates had convinced his interlocutors that it would not constitute the breaking of a promise to refuse to return a weapon that had been borrowed from a friend who turned out to be crazy or suicidal. Such a person is no longer in their right mind and so their current crazed self is not the same person to whom the original promise was made. In a similar vein, rulers and teachers may deceive their young charges whose minds are not yet capable of understanding the complexities of reality or of separating truth from imitation. Moreover, Socrates claims that censoring Homeric art is not technically deception at all. By representing the gods as sometimes imperfect, Socrates thinks it is *Homer* who has distorted reality; and a deception intended to redress a previous lie is not itself a lie.

This sort of deception can take the form of the redaction of existing art and stories, but Socrates also advocates the creation of *new* art and stories which, though still deceptive, deceive for a greater pedagogical purpose. This latter form of deception is called a "noble falsehood" (*gennaios pseudos*), and when pressed by another interlocutor, Glaucon, in Book 3 for a concrete example of such a thing, Socrates offers a fable about the origins of humans—the so-called "Myth of the Metals"—according to which different classes of people were conceived underground and hewn from different substances.

As you evaluate Socrates' arguments, consider these additional questions:

1. Compared to the selection from *Gorgias*, these excerpts from *Republic* would seem to endorse a much more permissive, even manipulative, conception of lying. How can the imitative deceptiveness of oratory be condemned in *Gorgias*, while paternalistic censorship is condoned in *Republic*? Or has Plato changed his mind on the ethics of lying?
2. Given that Socrates is primarily addressing political censorship, to what extent do political contexts differ from other contexts with respect to deception? Does it ever make sense to hold rulers, politicians, or other authorities to different standards of truthfulness compared to other people? Are there any "noble falsehoods" that authority figures tell us?
3. To what extent might Socrates' advocacy of censorship be limited to the particular examples he discusses (Homer, etc.)? Are there forms of art, entertainment, or other activities in society today that might similarly worry Socrates?

Republic (Book 2)

Socrates: You know, don't you, that the beginning of any process is most important, especially for anything young and tender? It's at that time that it is most malleable and takes on any pattern one wishes to impress on it.

Adeimantus: Exactly.

Soc: Then shall we carelessly allow the children to hear any old stories, told by just anyone, and to take beliefs into their souls that are for the most part opposite to the ones we think they should hold when they are grown up?

Ade: We certainly won't.

Soc: Then we must first of all, it seems, supervise the storytellers. We'll select their stories whenever they are fine or beautiful and reject them when they aren't. And we'll persuade nurses and mothers to tell their children the ones we have selected, since they will shape their children's souls with stories much more than they shape their bodies by handling them. Many of the stories they tell now, however, must be thrown out.

Ade: Which ones do you mean?

Soc: We'll first look at the major stories, and by seeing how to deal with them, we'll see how to deal with the minor ones as well, for they exhibit the same pattern and have the same effects whether they're famous or not. Don't you think so?

Ade: I do, but I don't know which ones you're calling major.

Soc: Those that Homer, Hesiod, and other poets tell us, for surely they composed false stories, told them to people, and are still telling them.

Ade: Which stories do you mean, and what fault do you find in them?

Soc: The fault one ought to find first and foremost, especially if the falsehood isn't well told.

Ade: For example?

Soc: When a story gives a bad image of what the gods and heroes are like, the way a painter does whose picture is not at all like the things he's trying to paint.

Ade: You're right to object to that. But what sort of thing in particular do you have in mind?

Soc: First, telling the greatest falsehood about the most important things doesn't make a fine story—I mean Hesiod telling us about how Ouranos behaved, how Cronos punished him for it, and how he was in turn punished by his own son.[1] But even if it were true, it should be passed over in silence, not told to foolish young people. And if, for some reason, it has to be told, only a very few people—pledged to secrecy and after sacrificing not just a pig but something great and scarce—should hear it, so that their number is kept as small as possible.

Ade: Yes, such stories are hard to deal with.

Soc: And they shouldn't be told in our city, Adeimantus. Nor should a young person hear it said that in committing the worst crimes he's doing nothing out of the ordinary, or that if he inflicts every kind of punishment on an unjust father, he's only doing the same as the first and greatest of the gods.

Ade: No, by god, I don't think myself that these stories are fit to be told.

Soc: Indeed, if we want the guardians of our city to think that it's shameful to be easily provoked into hating one another, we mustn't allow *any* stories about gods warring, fighting, or plotting against one another, for they aren't true. The battles of gods and giants, and all the various stories of the gods hating their families or friends, should neither be told nor even woven in embroideries. If we're to persuade our people that no citizen has ever hated another and that it's impious to do so, then *that's* what should be told to children from the beginning by old men and women; and as these children grow older,

1. [Ouranos is an elder deity associated with the heavens. Cronos is his son and he castrates his father to protect his mother Gaia (Earth). This pattern later repeats when Cronos' own son, Zeus, rebels against him.]

poets should be compelled to tell them the same sort of thing. We won't admit stories into our city—whether allegorical or not—about Hera being chained by her son, nor about Hephaestus being hurled from heaven by his father when he tried to help his mother, who was being beaten, nor about the battle of the gods in Homer. The young can't distinguish what is allegorical from what isn't, and the opinions they absorb at that age are hard to erase and apt to become unalterable. For these reasons, then, we should probably take the utmost care to insure that the first stories they hear about virtue are the best ones for them to hear.

Ade: That's reasonable. But if someone asked us what stories these are, what should we say?

Soc: You and I, Adeimantus, aren't poets, but we *are* founding a city. And it's appropriate for the founders to know the patterns on which poets must base their stories and from which they mustn't deviate. But we aren't actually going to compose their poems for them.

Ade: All right. But what precisely are the patterns for theology or stories about the gods?

Soc: Something like this: Whether in epic, lyric, or tragedy, a god must always be represented as he is.

Ade: Indeed, he must.

Soc: Now, a god is really good, isn't he, and must be described as such?

Ade: What else?

Soc: And surely nothing good is harmful, is it?

Ade: I suppose not.

Soc: And can what isn't harmful do harm?

Ade: Never.

Soc: Or can what does no harm do anything bad?

Ade: No.

Soc: And can what does nothing bad be the cause of anything bad?

Ade: How could it?

Soc: Moreover, the good is beneficial?

Ade: Yes.

Soc: It is the cause of doing well?

Ade: Yes.

Soc: The good isn't the cause of all things, then, but only of good ones; it isn't the cause of bad ones.

Ade: I agree entirely.

Soc: Therefore, since a god is good, he is not—as most people claim—the cause of everything that happens to human beings but of only a few things, for good things are fewer than bad ones in our lives. He alone is responsible for the good things, but we must find some other cause for the bad ones, not a god.

Ade: That's very true, and I believe it.

Soc: Then we won't accept from anyone the foolish mistake Homer makes about the gods when he says:

There are two urns at the threshold of Zeus,
One filled with good fates, the other with bad ones . . .
and the person to whom he gives a mixture of these
Sometimes meets with a bad fate, sometimes with good,
but the one who receives his fate entirely from the second urn,
Evil famine drives him over the divine earth.
We won't grant either that Zeus is for us
The distributor of both good and bad.[2]

And as to the breaking of the promised truce by Pandarus, if anyone tells us that it was brought about by Athena and Zeus or that Themis and Zeus were responsible for strife and contention among the gods, we will not praise him.[3] Nor will we allow the young to hear the words of Aeschylus:

2. [Homer, *Iliad* 24.527–532.]

3. [In Homer's telling of the Trojan War in *Iliad*, a tentative truce between the warring Trojans and Achaeans is destroyed when an archer named

A god makes mortals guilty
When he wants utterly to destroy a house.[4]

And if anyone composes a poem about the sufferings of Niobe, such as the one in which these lines occur, or about the house of Pelops, or the tale of Troy, or anything else of that kind, we must require him to say that these things are not the work of a god.[5] Or, if they are, then poets must look for the kind of account of them that we are now seeking, and say that the actions of the gods are good and just, and that those they punish are benefited thereby. We won't allow poets to say that the punished are made wretched and that it was a god who made them so. But we will allow them to say that bad people are wretched because they are in need of punishment and that, in paying the penalty, they are benefited by the gods. And, as for saying that a god, who is himself good, is the cause of bad things, we'll fight that in every way, and we won't allow anyone to say it in his own city, if it's to be well governed, or anyone else to hear it either—whether young or old, whether in verse or prose. These stories are not pious, not advantageous to us, and not consistent with one another.

Ade: I like your law, and I'll vote for it.

Soc: This, then, is one of the laws or patterns concerning the gods to which speakers and poets must conform, namely, that a god isn't the cause of all things but only of good ones.

Ade: And it's a fully satisfactory law.

Pandarus accidentally lets fly an arrow. As Homer relates the episode, though, Pandarus' action was the result of divine intervention by gods who wished to see the fighting continue. See *Iliad* 4.73–126.]

4. [The source of this Aeschylus quote is unknown.]

5. [Niobe was punished by the gods for boasting of her flourishing family, in retaliation for which the deities Artemis and Apollo killed all of her children. Pelops was her brother, and he was killed by their father Tantalus who attempted to serve him as food to the gods. Pelops was eventually resurrected, only to suffer a curse on himself and his descendants as punishment for his betrayal of a friend.]

Soc: What about this second law? Do you think that a god is a sorcerer, able to appear in different forms at different times, sometimes changing himself from his own form into many shapes, sometimes deceiving us by making us think that he has done it? Or do you think he's simple and least of all likely to step out of his own form?

Ade: I can't say offhand.

Soc: Well, what about this? If he steps out of his own form, mustn't he either change himself or be changed by something else?

Ade: He must.

Soc: But the best things are least liable to alteration or change, aren't they? For example, isn't the healthiest and strongest body least changed by food, drink, and labor, or the healthiest and strongest plant by sun, wind, and the like?

Ade: Of course.

Soc: And the most courageous and most rational soul is least disturbed or altered by any outside affection?

Ade: Yes.

Soc: And the same account is true of all artifacts, furniture, houses, and clothes. The ones that are good and well made are least altered by time or anything else that happens to them.

Ade: That's right.

Soc: Whatever is in good condition, then, whether by nature or craft or both, admits least of being changed by anything else.

Ade: So it seems.

Soc: Now, surely a god and what belongs to him are in every way in the best condition.

Ade: How could they fail to be?

Soc: Then a god would be least likely to have many shapes.

Ade: Indeed.

Soc: Then does he change or alter himself?

Ade: Clearly he does, if indeed he is altered at all.

Soc: Would he change himself into something better and more beautiful than himself or something worse and uglier?

Ade: It would have to be into something worse, if he's changed at all, for surely we won't say that a god is deficient in either beauty or virtue.

Soc: Absolutely right. And do you think, Adeimantus, that anyone, whether god or human, would deliberately make himself worse in any way?

Ade: No, that's impossible.

Soc: Is it impossible then, for gods to want to alter themselves? Since they are the most beautiful and best possible, it seems that each always and unconditionally retains his own shape.

Ade: That seems entirely necessary to me.

Soc: Then let no poet tell us about Proteus or Thetis,[6] or say that

The gods, in the likeness of strangers from foreign lands,
Adopt every sort of shape and visit our cities.[7]

Nor must they present Hera, in their tragedies or other poems, as a priestess collecting alms for

the life-giving sons of the Argive river Inachus,[8]

or tell us other stories of that sort. Nor must mothers, believing bad stories about the gods wandering at night in the shapes of strangers from foreign lands,

6. [Proteus is a shape-shifting god. Thetis is the mother of Achilles and she transformed herself as a way of escaping courtship.]

7. [Socrates is quoting from Homer's *Odyssey* 17.485–486.]

8. [The river Inachus was thought to be the first king of Argos and so the progenitor of the Argive people, one of the major ethnicities of ancient Greece and a group who participated heavily in the Trojan War. The quote is from Aeschylus' play *Xantriae,* no longer extant.]

terrify their children with them. Such stories blaspheme the gods and, at the same time, make children more cowardly.

Ade: They mustn't be told.

Soc: But though the gods are unable to change, do they nonetheless make us believe that they appear in all sorts of ways, deceiving us through sorcery?

Ade: Perhaps.

Soc: What? Would a god be willing to be false, either in word or deed, by presenting an illusion?

Ade: I don't know.

Soc: Don't you know that a *true* falsehood, if one may call it that, is hated by all gods and humans?

Ade: What do you mean?

Soc: I mean that no one is willing to tell falsehoods to the most important part of himself about the most important things, but of all places he is most afraid to have falsehood there.

Ade: I still don't understand.

Soc: That's because you think I'm saying something deep. I simply mean that to be false to one's soul about things that are, to be ignorant and to have and hold falsehood there, is what everyone would least of all accept, for everyone hates a falsehood in that place most of all.

Ade: That's right.

Soc: Surely, as I said just now, this would be most correctly called true falsehood—ignorance in the soul of someone who has been told a falsehood. Falsehood in words is a kind of imitation of this affection in the soul, an image of it that comes into being after it and is not a pure falsehood. Isn't that so?

Ade: Certainly.

Soc: And the thing that is really a falsehood is hated not only by the gods but by human beings as well.

Ade: It seems so to me.

Soc: What about falsehood in words? When and to whom is it useful and so not deserving of hatred? Isn't it useful against one's enemies? And when any of our so-called friends are attempting, through madness or ignorance to do something bad, isn't it a useful drug for preventing them? It is also useful in the case of those stories we were just talking about, the ones we tell because we don't know the truth about those ancient events involving the gods. By making a falsehood as much like the truth as we can, don't we also make it useful?

Ade: We certainly do.

Soc: Then in which of these ways could a falsehood be useful to a god? Would he make false likenesses of ancient events because of his ignorance of them?

Ade: It would be ridiculous to think that.

Soc: Then there is nothing of the false poet in a god?

Ade: Not in my view.

Soc: Would he be false, then, through fear of his enemies?

Ade: Far from it.

Soc: Because of the ignorance or madness of his family or friends, then?

Ade: No one who is ignorant or mad is a friend of the gods.

Soc: Then there's no reason for a god to speak falsely?

Ade: None.

Soc: Therefore the daimonic and the divine are in every way free from falsehood.[9]

Ade: Completely.

Soc: A god, then, is simple and true in word and deed. He doesn't change himself or deceive others by images, words, or signs, whether in visions or in dreams.

Ade: That's what I thought as soon as I heard you say it.

9. ["Daimonic" refers to the concept of a *daimon* (whence the English word *demon*), a secret or private divine power. In other works by Plato, Socrates theorizes the *daimon* to be an inner voice of reason and conscience.]

Soc: You agree, then, that this is our second pattern for speaking or composing poems about the gods: They are not sorcerers who change themselves, nor do they mislead us by falsehoods in words or deeds.

Ade: I agree.

Soc: So, even though we praise many things in Homer, we won't approve of the dream Zeus sent to Agamemnon, nor of Aeschylus when he makes Thetis say that Apollo sang in prophecy at her wedding:

About the good fortune my children would have,
Free of disease throughout their long lives,
And of all the blessings that the friendship of the gods would bring me.
I hoped that Phoebus' divine mouth would be free of falsehood,
Endowed as it is with the craft of prophecy.
But the very god who sang, the one at the feast,
The one who said all this, he himself it is
Who killed my son.[10]

Whenever anyone says such things about a god, we'll be angry with him, refuse him a chorus, and not allow his poetry to be used in the education of the young, so that our guardians will be as god-fearing and godlike as human beings can be.

Ade: I completely endorse these patterns . . . and I would enact them as laws.

Republic (Book 3)

Soc: Moreover, we have to be concerned about truth as well, for if what we said just now is correct, and falsehood, though of no use to the gods, is useful to people as a

10. [In Homer's *Iliad* 2.1–42, Zeus uses a dream to inspire the general Agamemnon to foolishly overcommit his troops on one day of battle during the Trojan War. The Aeschylus quote is from a surviving fragment: Apollo (also referred to as Phoebus) helps bring about the death of Thetis' son Achilles during the Trojan War.]

form of drug, clearly we must allow only doctors to use it, not private citizens.

Ade: Clearly.

Soc: Then if it is appropriate for anyone to use falsehoods for the good of the city, because of the actions of either enemies or citizens, it is the rulers. But everyone else must keep away from them, because for a private citizen to lie to a ruler is just as bad a mistake as for a sick person or athlete not to tell the truth to his doctor or trainer about his physical condition or for a sailor not to tell the captain the facts about his own condition or that of the ship and the rest of its crew—indeed it is a worse mistake than either of these.

Ade: That's completely true.

Soc: And if the ruler catches someone else telling falsehoods in the city—any one of the craftsmen, whether a prophet, a doctor who heals the sick, or a maker of spears—he'll punish him for introducing something as subversive and destructive to a city as it would be to a ship.

Ade: He will, if practice is to follow theory.

. . .

Socrates: How, then, could we devise one of those useful falsehoods we were talking about a while ago, one noble falsehood that would, in the best case, persuade even the rulers, but if that's not possible, then the others in the city?

Glaucon: What sort of falsehood?

Soc: Nothing new, but a Phoenician story which describes something that has happened in many places.[1] At least, that's what the poets say, and they've persuaded many people to believe it too. It hasn't happened among us, and I don't even know if it could. It would certainly take a lot of persuasion to get people to believe it.

1. [The Phoenicians were ancient sea-faring peoples prominent in the eastern Mediterranean. The specific story being referred to remains a matter of debate.]

Gla: You seem hesitant to tell the story.

Soc: When you hear it, you'll realize that I have every reason to hesitate.

Gla: Speak, and don't be afraid.

Soc: I'll tell it, then, though I don't know where I'll get the audacity or even what words I'll use. I'll first try to persuade the rulers and the soldiers and then the rest of the city that the upbringing and the education we gave them, and the experiences that went with them, were a sort of dream, that in fact they themselves, their weapons, and the other craftsmen's tools were at that time really being fashioned and nurtured inside the earth, and that when the work was completed, the earth, who is their mother, delivered all of them up into the world. Therefore, if anyone attacks the land in which they live, they must plan on its behalf and defend it as their mother and nurse and think of the other citizens as their earthborn brothers.

Gla: It isn't for nothing that you were so shy about telling your falsehood.

Soc: Appropriately so. Nevertheless, listen to the rest of the story. "All of you in the city are brothers," we'll say to them in telling our story, "but the god who made you mixed some gold into those who are adequately equipped to rule, because they are most valuable. He put silver in those who are auxiliaries and iron and bronze in the farmers and other craftsmen. For the most part you will produce children like yourselves, but, because you are all related, a silver child will occasionally be born from a golden parent, and vice versa, and all the others from each other. So the first and most important command from the god to the rulers is that there is nothing that they must guard better or watch more carefully than the mixture of metals in the souls of the next generation. If an offspring of theirs should be found to have a mixture of iron or bronze, they must not pity him in any way, but give him the rank appropriate to his nature and drive him out to join the craftsmen and farmers. But if an offspring of these people is found to have a mixture of gold or silver, they will honor him and take him up to join the guardians or the auxiliaries, for there is an oracle which says that the city will be ruined if it ever has an iron or a bronze guardian." So, do you have any device that will make our citizens believe this story?

Gla: I can't see any way to make them believe it themselves, but perhaps there is one in the case of their sons and later generations and all the other people who come after them.

Soc: I understand pretty much what you mean, but even that would help to make them care more for the city and each other. However, let's leave this matter wherever tradition takes it.

10
SUNZI & HAN FEIZI

This chapter pairs two ancient Chinese thinkers who each articulate powerful and unapologetic defenses of an alleged need for deception in certain spheres of life, such as war and political intrigue. The first selection is from the *Art of War* (*Bingfa* 兵法), traditionally attributed to an elusive figure named Sunzi, but now thought to be composed by a man named Sun Bin in the fourth century BCE. Sunzi stresses that war is an unavoidable aspect of statecraft, which may have struck his contemporaries as a truism given the brutality and chaos of the Warring States Period (475–221 BCE). Within this context, Sunzi argues that it is part of the nature of war to utilize a variety of deceptions, ranging from organized stratagems to the employment of spies.[1] The implications of Sunzi's philosophy, however, extend far beyond military concerns, insofar as his word for "deception" (*gui* 詭) is composed of the radical for "speech" and so connotes *verbal* deceptions more generally. Indeed, the *Art of War* today enjoys a degree of popularity and notoriety for the ways in which modern thinkers have mined it for insight into political and business philosophies.

The second selection in this chapter is from the eponymous text *Han Feizi*. Han Feizi (280–233 BCE) was brought up in the Confucianism of his day (see the Kongzi and Mengzi selections in chapter 5 of this volume) but traces of Daoist influence are also evident in the way he writes about shadows, the power of passivity, and the "Way" (*dao* 道)—a normative and largely inexpressible state of ultimate reality. Han Feizi, however, also developed a new philosophical and political movement of his own—Legalism (*fajia* 法家)—that proved instrumental in bringing King Zheng of Qin into power as China's first unifying emperor (Qin Shi Huang) after centuries of war and strife. In subsequent dynasties, Legalism fell into increasing disrepute and even the twentieth-century consensus has tended to read Han Feizi as a sort of Chinese Machiavelli. Complicating the interpretation of Han Feizi is the fact that he seems to be addressing different readerships in different parts of his writing—sometimes rulers, other times ministers and advisors—with seemingly differing advice for each. (As you

1. "Spies" translates *jian* 間, which refers to something that divides a space, and depicts the moon peeking through a crack in a gate.

read these selections, see if you can identify whom Han Feizi may be addressing and whether this context makes his points more or less palatable.)

As with Sunzi, Han Feizi seems to praise certain deceptive tactics. But the literal warzone that Sunzi had in mind has become, in the *Han Feizi*, the more figurative (but no less lethal) battleground of politics. Against this backdrop, Han Feizi is sometimes read as an amoral opportunist, providing pragmatic advice about how to stay alive and get ahead in the dangerous world of court politics, where blunt honesty and high-minded integrity rarely pay. There is also the more totalitarian Han Feizi who seems to approve of harsh punishments and uncompromising standards for the sake of maintaining law, order, and balance. Perhaps we can also reconstruct a Han Feizi who is genuinely committed to moral reform and simply wants to eschew naiveté and work realistically within the parameters of human nature. Or it could be that Han Feizi is himself a political idealist who thinks that the power to deceive should be exercised only under certain extreme conditions and only by the rare "enlightened" or "worthy" political individual.

Here are some additional questions to ponder:

1. In what ways are Sunzi and Han Feizi similar and different? Can you identify an example of an act of deception which one of them, but not the other, might condone or condemn?
2. Do the peculiar natures of war, espionage, or politics warrant making moral exceptions to the ethics of lying and truthfulness? Why or why not, and are there other spheres of human life which might permit of similar exceptions?
3. Sunzi stresses that "if one is not benevolent and righteous, one cannot deploy spies," and Han Feizi sometimes constrains his advice only to those rulers who are "enlightened" or "worthy." Do you agree that moral character legitimizes the sorts of deceptions they have in mind? What do benevolence and righteousness entail and how (if at all) can they be preserved while engaging in war, espionage, or politics?
4. Several of the examples Han Feizi provides in §12 depict individuals whose hyper-honesty undoes them. Are there contemporary examples of individuals who are "too honest" for their own good or who use high-handed accusations of dishonesty against others in inappropriate ways?

Sunzi

Ch. 1 The way of war is deception. And so, when you have the ability to strike, appear as if you have none. When busy deploying your troops and equipment, appear unengaged. When you are near, appear far away. When far away, appear near. Use the prospect of advantage to lure the enemy in. If they are chaotic and confused, seize them. If they are solid and secure, prepare for them. If they are strong, avoid them. If they are angry, irritate them. If they are mean and cowardly, encourage them to be arrogant and haughty. If they are resting, harry them. If they are united, divide them. Attack whenever they are ill prepared. Appear where they least expect it. This is how the enlightened warrior wins victory; it is not something that can be taught prior to knowing how to prepare for war.

Prior to battle, carry out a proper assessment in one's ancestral temple.[1] Those with the most factors in their favor shall win. Those with the fewest factors in their favor shall lose. How much poorer the prospects of those who have *no* factors in their favor!

When I look at things in this way, it is easy to see who will win.

Ch. 13 When you raise an army of a hundred thousand men and send them off on a distant campaign a thousand leagues away, the cost to private households and public coffers will come to a thousand pieces of gold a day. There will be great turmoil throughout the state, people will wear themselves out transporting supplies on the highways and roads, and some seven hundred thousand households will be unable to attend to their normal affairs.[2] Opposing forces can battle each other for years in order to win victory decided upon a single day. And yet some, who covet high office and salary or begrudge but a hundred pieces of gold, will fail to use spies to ascertain the enemy's situation and condition.[3] This is the height of inhumanity! Such people are not fit to serve as generals; they are not true counselors, nor are they masters of victory.

1. The ancestral temple is where ancestral tablets were kept and where important sacrifices to the ancestors took place. It is also where the most important affairs of state were decided. Here, Sunzi is concerned with the final strategic calculations before going to war. He is not endorsing or advocating any type of divination, a practice which he thinks has no place in war.

2. Among the vital work that will be disrupted are things such as agriculture and weaving.

3. The thought is that such people would rather not risk their own position or salary or spend even a relatively small amount of money to secure the services of spies.

What enables the enlightened ruler or worthy general to conquer others whenever they deploy their forces and realize achievements that far surpass the common run of men is that they know things beforehand. Such knowledge cannot be obtained from ghosts or spirits, it is not prefigured in situations or events nor can one determine it through calculation[4]—it must be gained from people who know the enemy's situation and condition.

And so there are five types of spies that one can use: local, inside, double, dead, and alive. If all five types of spies are working at the same time and no one knows of their activities, this is called a "divine net" and is a ruler's treasure.[5]

Local spies are agents you recruit from among the local population. Inside spies are officials you recruit from within the enemy's own ranks. Double agents are enemy spies you successfully recruit to your side. Dead spies are your own agents who are provided with false information to be given to the enemy.[6] Live spies are agents who can return and report to you about the enemy's situation and condition.

And so, within the army, no one is closer to the ruler than his spies, no one is rewarded more lavishly, and no one is more secretive. If one is not sagely and wise, one cannot use spies. If one is not benevolent and righteous, one cannot deploy spies. If one is not subtle and sensitive, one cannot get the truth out of spies. How subtle! How subtle! Spies can be used everywhere! If confidential information about a spy's mission is prematurely disclosed, the spy and all those told about the mission must be put to death.

Whenever there is an army you want to attack, a city you want to lay siege to, or a person you want to assassinate, you first must know the family and personal names of your enemy's commanding general, his closest associates, messengers, gatekeepers, and attendants.

4. [Sunzi seems to be critiquing, among other things, the traditional practice of consulting oracle readings, as outlined in the ancient text *Yijing* 易經 or *Book of Changes*, according to which every discrete moment or event contains within it a synecdoche of the wider state of affairs.]

5. "Divine net" translates *shen ji* 神紀. Using all five types of spies is a "net" in that it allows the ruler to *draw in* information as a fisherman draws in fish with his net. It is "divine" in accomplishing its work in ways that do not rely on any discernable action.

6. I take "dead" *si* to indicate that one no longer has contact with these spies: one sends them off with misinformation but does not expect them to report back. In this way, they differ from "live" spies, the last type described. Commentators tend to take *si* as meaning these spies are most at risk and will almost certainly be killed.

Dispatch your spies to search out and discover as much as you can about them. You also must discover those the enemy has sent to spy on you. You must attract them with bribes and persuade them to defect to your side. In this way, you can gain double agents and put them to use. By employing such double agents to further understand the enemy, you can gain local and inside spies and make use of them. By employing local and inside spies to further understand the enemy, you can find ways for your dead spies to convey false information to them. By employing your dead spies to further understand the enemy, your live spies can tell you of your enemy's plans when they return at the appointed time.

A ruler must be well-informed about the work of the five types of spies, and the key to his being well-informed is the double agent. And so double agents must be rewarded the most lavishly of all.

In the past, the Yin flourished because it made use of Yi Zhi, who was serving the Xia; the Zhou flourished because it made use of Lü Ya, who was serving the Yin.[7] And so, only the enlightened ruler and worthy general, who are capable of getting the most wise to serve as their spies, always succeed in producing great achievements. This is essential in war and what an army relies upon in order to take action.

Han Feizi

§5 The Way is the beginning of all beings and the measure of right and wrong. Therefore the enlightened ruler holds fast to the beginning in order to understand the wellspring of all beings, and minds the measure in order to know the source of good and bad. He waits, empty and still, letting names define themselves and affairs reach their own settlement. Being empty, he can comprehend the true aspect

7. The Yin refers to the Yin 殷 or Shang 商 Dynasties (1766–1122 BCE). The Xia refers to the Xia 夏 Dynasty (2205–1766 BCE) and the Zhou refers to the Zhou 周 Dynasty (1122–256 BCE). Yi Zhi 伊摯 (better known as Yi Yin 伊尹) was a minister of the Xia who defected to the Yin. Lü Ya 呂牙 or Lü Shang 呂尚 (better known as Jiang Ziya 姜子牙, Tai Gongwang 太公望, or Shi Shangfu 師尚父) was a minister of the Yin who crossed over to the Zhou. Normally, loyalty would require a minister to die with his lord, much less spy for the enemy, but these two men are generally regarded as exceptions because they recognized that the rulers they served were fundamentally corrupt. For Yi Zhi, see *Mengzi* 5A6, etc. Lü Ya's biography appears in chapter 32 of Sima Qian's *The Grand Scribe's Records* (*Shiji* 史記). For an English translation, see William H. Nienhauser, Jr., ed., *The Grand Scribe's Records*, Volume V. I (Bloomington: Indiana University Press, 2006): 31–130.

of fullness; being still, he can correct the mover. Those whose duty it is to speak will come forward to name themselves; those whose duty it is to act will produce results. When names and results match, the ruler need do nothing more and the true aspect of all things will be revealed. Hence it is said: the ruler must not reveal his desires; for if he reveals his desires his ministers will put on the mask that pleases him. He must not reveal his will; for if he does so his ministers will show a different face. So it is said: Discard likes and dislikes and the ministers will show their true form; discard wisdom and wile and the ministers will watch their step. Hence, though the ruler is wise, he hatches no schemes from his wisdom, but causes all men to know their place. Though he has worth, he does not display it in his deeds, but observes the motives of his ministers. Though he is brave, he does not flaunt his bravery in shows of indignation, but allows his subordinates to display their valor to the full. Thus, though he discards wisdom, his rule is enlightened; though he discards worth, he achieves merit; and though he discards bravery, his state grows powerful. When the ministers stick to their posts, the hundred officials have their regular duties, and the ruler employs each according to his particular ability, this is known as the state of manifold constancy. Hence it is said: "So still he seems to dwell nowhere at all; so empty no one can seek him out." The enlightened ruler reposes in non-action above, and below his ministers tremble with fear.[1]

§12 On the whole, the difficult thing about persuasion is to know the mind of the person one is trying to persuade and to be able to fit one's words to it. . . .[2]

The important thing in persuasion is to learn how to play up the aspects that the person you are talking to is proud of, and play down the aspects he is ashamed of. Thus, if the person has some urgent personal desire, you should show him that it is his public duty to carry it out and urge him not to delay. If he has some mean objective in mind

1. ["Non action" translates *wuwei* 無爲, a key concept in Daoist philosophy that refers to the sort of spontaneous and instinctual movements that flow from someone who has been properly habituated or is living in accord with the *Dao*. See note 7 to the *Mengzi* selection in chapter 5 in this volume.]

2. ["Persuasion" translates *shui* 說 and may refer specifically to the art of diplomatically opposing or advocating laws that affect communal welfare. In this respect, *shui* may be distinguished from *ning* 佞, which is also sometimes translated as "persuasion," but which connotes more individualistic ambitions. For a discussion of this distinction in classical Chinese rhetoric, see Xing Lu (1998) *Rhetoric in Ancient China* (Columbia, SC: University of South Carolina Press).]

and yet cannot restrain himself, you should do your best to point out to him whatever admirable aspects it may have and to minimize the reprehensible ones. If he has some lofty objective in mind and yet does not have the ability needed to realize it, you should do your best to point out to him the faults and bad aspects of such an objective and make it seem a virtue not to pursue it. If he is anxious to make a show of wisdom and ability, mention several proposals which are different from the one you have in mind but of the same general nature in order to supply him with ideas; then let him build on your words, but pretend that you are unaware that he is doing so, and in this way abet his wisdom. . . .

Yi Yin became a cook and Boli Xi a captive slave, so they could gain the ear of the ruler. These men were sages, and yet they could not avoid shouldering hard tasks for the sake of advancement and demeaning themselves in this way. Therefore you too should become a cook or a slave when necessary; if this enables you to gain the confidence of the ruler and save the state, then it is no disgrace for a man of nobility to take such a course.

In ancient times Duke Wu of Zheng wanted to attack the state of Hu, and so he first married his daughter to the ruler of Hu in order to fill his mind with thoughts of pleasure. Then he told his ministers, "I want to launch a military campaign. What would be a likely state to attack?" The high official Guan Qisi replied, "Hu could be attacked," whereupon Duke Wu flew into a rage and had him executed, saying, "Hu is a brother state! What do you mean by advising me to attack it!" The ruler of Hu, hearing of this, assumed that Zheng was friendly towards him and therefore took no precautions to defend himself from Zheng. The men of Zheng then made a surprise attack on Hu and seized it.

Once there was a rich man of Song. When the dirt wall around his house collapsed in a heavy rain, his son said, "If you don't rebuild it, thieves will surely break in," and the old man who lived next door told him the same thing. When night fell, thieves actually broke in and made off with a large share of the rich man's wealth. The rich man's family praised the son for his wisdom, but eyed the old man next door with suspicion.

Both these men—the high official Guan Qisi and the old man next door—spoke the truth, and yet one was actually executed for his words, while the other cast suspicion on himself. It is not difficult to know a thing; what is difficult is to know how to use what you know. Rao Zhao spoke the truth but, though he was regarded as a sage by the men of Jin, he was executed by those of Qin. This is something you cannot afford not to examine.

§49 In the state of Chu there was a man named Honest Gong.[3] When his father stole a sheep, he reported the theft to the authorities. But the local magistrate, considering that the man was honest in the service of his sovereign but a villain to his own father, replied, "Put him to death!", and the man was accordingly sentenced and executed. Thus we see that a man who is an honest subject of his sovereign may be an infamous son to his father.

If people regard those who act with integrity and good faith as worthy, it must be because they value men who have no deceit, and they value men of no deceit because they themselves have no means to protect themselves from deceit.[4] The common people in selecting their friends, for example, have no wealth by which to win others over, and no authority by which to intimidate others. For that reason they seek for men who are without deceit to be their friends. But the ruler occupies a position whereby he may impose his will upon others, and he has the whole wealth of the nation at his disposal; he may dispense lavish rewards and severe penalties and, by wielding these two handles, may illuminate all things through his wise policies. In that case, even traitorous ministers like Tian Chang and Zihan would not dare to deceive him. Why should he have to wait for men who are by nature not deceitful?

3. [*Zhi gong* 直躬, literally "rigid or overly literal man." This is the same person referred to in *Analects* 13.18 (see the selection in chapter 5 of this volume).]

4. [Here "deceit" is translating *miao* 妙, more literally "feminine wiles."]

11
AQUINAS

Saint Thomas Aquinas (1225–1274) is considered one of the most influential philosophers of the European Middle Ages, famous for his magisterial attempts to integrate Christian religious content with Greek philosophical method. While classical Greek philosophy had been largely lost to northern Europe, it had been preserved in the Muslim world, and through the increased cultural contact brought about by the Crusades, theologians such as Aquinas became reacquainted with the powerful secular metaphysical and ethical arguments of the ancient Greeks. The Dominican Order in general and the University of Paris in particular were chartered partly to deal with this controversy—that is, to show that secular or "natural" reason is compatible with Christian doctrine and revelation.

Aquinas represents the pinnacle of the Scholastic Method that developed in response to the rediscovery of Greek thought. Central to this method was the *disputation*—a formal debate in which a theologian

1. poses a question;
2. recognizes potential answers to the question that are contrary to doctrine ("objections");
3. states the official doctrine with reference to either scripture or earlier Church teachings ("On the contrary . . . "); and then
4. rebuts the objections ("I answer that . . . ") by bringing to bear rational counterarguments in the style of Greek philosophical dialectic.

In this way, the resulting argument was designed to be persuasive to both faith and reason, and to those within the tradition as well as those outside it. Aquinas was a master of this technique and his *Summa Theologiae* (the "summary of theology") from which our selection is taken, attempts to comprehensively tackle all manner of doctrinal debates.

In these particular excerpts, Aquinas addresses the definition and ethics of oaths, vows, and perjury specifically as well as lying more generally. The particular kind of oath that interests Aquinas is where someone swears by God, thereby calling God to serve as witness for the truth of the oath. Insofar as God is conceived as perfect, such an oath establishes a standard of truthfulness and expectation in a radically different way than does swearing by alternate things. In a similar way, oaths are distinguished from vows: both are special kinds of pledges, but oaths can sometimes be taken person-to-person, whereas Aquinas thinks vows always (implicitly) are ultimately promises of fidelity to God. For this reason, the violation of vows is a more serious matter than the breaking of oaths. Perjury is regarded as more serious still, for it involves a degree of deliberateness and forethought beyond the mere breaking of an oath or vow. Indeed, Aquinas argues that perjuring oneself by swearing falsely by God is not merely a venial sin (capable of being forgiven or atoned for in purgatory), but is always a mortal sin (damning one to Hell unless confessed) even if uttered in casual conversation or in jest.

Of lying more generally, Aquinas claims that the following are conceptually necessary: (i) the intent to deceive, (ii) falsehood (i.e., one cannot technically "lie" about the truth), and (iii) the end or goal (other than deception itself) which the lie is intended to bring about. The intent to deceive in turn is subdivided according to whether the deception is aimed at benefitting another (what Aquinas calls an "officious" lie), making fun (a "jocose" lie), or deliberate injury (a so-called "mischievous" lie). Whereas perjury, oaths, and vows are deemed unethical on the basis of the standards of truthfulness and expectation they invoke (e.g., swearing in the name of something sacred), lies are wrong more generally because they violate what Aquinas sees as a necessary presumption of all communication itself—namely, that words be taken as "natural signs" of thought, a correspondence which all uttered falsehoods jeopardize, but which lies intentionally fracture.

As you read Aquinas' disputations, here are some questions to consider:

1. Do any of the other authors in this volume defend views similar to those expressed in the various objections Aquinas considers? Do those authors furnish additional arguments that Aquinas either ignores or misinterprets?
2. Aquinas claims that swearing by God establishes a special standard of truthfulness. Why does he think this and what are the theological assumptions being made? Are there other things on which people swear and can these things have the same sort of sacredness that Aquinas thinks religious vows have?
3. In what ways are words the natural signs of thought? Does this mean that we necessarily think in words? What counts as a word in the first place, and are spoken and written words "natural" in the same ways?

Summa Theologiae

OF OATHS (II-II. Q.89)[1]

Whether to swear is to call God to witness?

Objection 1: It would seem that to swear is not to call God to witness. Whoever invokes the authority of Holy Writ calls God to witness, since it is His word that Holy Writ contains. Therefore, if to swear is to call God to witness, whoever invoked the authority of Holy Writ would swear. But this is false. Therefore the antecedent is false also.

Objection 2: Further, one does not pay anything to a person by calling him to witness. But he who swears by God pays something to Him for it is written (Matthew 5:33): "Thou shall pay thy oaths to the Lord"; and Augustine says that to swear is "to pay the right of truth to God." Therefore to swear is not to call God to witness.

Objection 3: Further, the duties of a judge differ from the duties of a witness. Now sometimes a man, by swearing, implores the Divine judgment, according to Psalms 7:5, "If I have rendered to them that repaid me evils, let me deservedly fall empty before my enemies." Therefore to swear is not to call God to witness.

On the contrary, Augustine says in a sermon on perjury: "When a man says: 'By God,' what else does he mean but that God is his witness?"[2]

I answer that, as the Apostle [Paul] says (Hebrews 6:16), oaths are taken for the purpose of confirmation. Now speculative propositions receive confirmation from reason, which proceeds from principles known naturally and infallibly true. But particular contingent facts regarding man cannot be confirmed by a necessary reason, wherefore propositions regarding such things are wont to be confirmed by witnesses. Now a human witness does not suffice to confirm such matters for two reasons. First, on account of man's lack of truth, for many give

1. [This notation refers to the second part of the second part of the *Summa* and to question number 89. Aquinas also sometimes uses "A" to refer to earlier *articles*, by which he means the subsidiary questions he poses. For example, Q.89, A.1 would refer to the first sub-question he poses (namely, "Whether to swear is to call God to witness?") under the larger question about oaths.]

2. [Aquinas is quoting from Augustine's *Sermons on the New Testament*, number 180, in which Augustine addresses the directive in James 1:12 not to swear.]

way to lying, according to Psalms 16:10, "Their mouth hath spoken lies." Secondly, on account of this lack of knowledge, since he can know neither the future, nor secret thoughts, nor distant things: and yet men speak about such things, and our everyday life requires that we should have some certitude about them. Hence the need to have recourse to a Divine witness, for neither can God lie, nor is anything hidden from Him. Now to call God to witness is named "*jurare*" [to swear] because it is established as though it were a principle of law [*jure*] that what a man asserts under the invocation of God as His witness should be accepted as true. Now sometimes God is called to witness when we assert present or past events, and this is termed a "declaratory oath"; while sometimes God is called to witness in confirmation of something future, and this is termed a "promissory oath." But oaths are not employed in order to substantiate necessary matters, and such as come under the investigation of reason; for it would seem absurd in a scientific discussion to wish to prove one's point by an oath.

Reply to Objection 1: It is one thing to employ a Divine witness already given, as when one adduces the authority of Holy Scripture; and another to implore God to bear witness, as in an oath.

Reply to Objection 2: A man is said to pay his oaths to God because he performs what he swears to do, or because, from the very fact that he calls upon God to witness, he recognizes Him as possessing universal knowledge and unerring truth.

Reply to Objection 3: A person is called to give witness, in order that he may make known the truth about what is alleged. Now there are two ways in which God makes known whether the alleged facts are true or not. In one way He reveals the truth simply, either by inward inspiration, or by unveiling the facts, namely, by making public what was hitherto secret: in another way by punishing the lying witness, and then He is at once judge and witness, since by punishing the liar He makes known his lie. Hence oaths are of two kinds: one is a simple contestation of God, as when a man says "God is my witness," or, "I speak before God," or, "By God," which has the same meaning, as Augustine states; the other is by cursing, and consists in a man binding himself or something of his to punishment if what is alleged be not true.

Whether three accompanying conditions of an oath are suitably assigned, namely, justice, judgment, and truth?

Objection 1: It would seem that justice, judgment and truth are unsuitably assigned as the conditions accompanying an oath. Things should not be enumerated as diverse, if one of them includes the other. Now of these three, one includes another, since truth is a part of justice, according to Tully:[3] and judgment is an act of justice. Therefore the three accompanying conditions of an oath are unsuitably assigned.

Objection 2: Further, many other things are required for an oath, namely, devotion, and faith whereby we believe that God knows all things and cannot lie. Therefore the accompanying conditions of an oath are insufficiently enumerated.

Objection 3: Further, these three are requisite in man's every deed: since he ought to do nothing contrary to justice and truth, or without judgment, according to 1 Timothy 5:21, "Do nothing without prejudice," i.e. without previous judgment. Therefore these three should not be associated with an oath any more than with other human actions.

On the contrary, it is written (Jerome 4:2): "Thou shalt swear: As the Lord liveth, in truth, and in judgment, and in justice": which words Jerome expounds, saying: "Observe that an oath must be accompanied by these conditions, truth, judgment and justice."

I answer that, an oath is not good except for one who makes good use of it. Now two conditions are required for the good use of an oath. First, that one swear, not for frivolous, but for urgent reasons, and with discretion; and this requires judgment or discretion on the part of the person who swears. Secondly, as regards the point to be confirmed by oath, that it be neither false, nor unlawful, and this requires both truth, so that one employ an oath in order to confirm what is true, and justice, so that one confirm what is lawful. A rash oath lacks judgment, a false oath lacks truth, and a wicked or unlawful oath lacks justice.

Reply to Objection 1: Judgment does not signify here the execution of justice, but the judgment of discretion, as stated above. Nor is truth here to be taken for the part of justice, but for a condition of speech.

Reply to Objection 2: Devotion, faith and like conditions requisite for the right manner of swearing are implied by judgment: for the other two regard the things sworn to as stated above. We might also reply that justice regards the reason for swearing.

Reply to Objection 3: There is great danger in swearing, both on account of the greatness of God Who is called upon to bear witness, and on account of the frailty of the human tongue, the words of which are confirmed by oath. Hence these conditions are more requisite for an oath than for other human actions.

3. ["Tully" is the Anglicized name for the classical Roman orator Cicero.]

Whether an oath has a binding force?

Objection 1: It would seem that an oath has no binding force. An oath is employed in order to confirm the truth of an assertion. But when a person makes an assertion about the future his assertion is true, though it may not be verified. Thus Paul lied not (2 Corinthians 1:15) though he went not to Corinth, as he had said he would (1 Corinthians 16:5). Therefore it seems that an oath is not binding.

Objection 2: Further, virtue is not contrary to virtue.[4] Now an oath is an act of virtue. But it would sometimes be contrary to virtue, or an obstacle thereto, if one were to fulfill what one has sworn to do: for instance, if one were to swear to commit a sin, or to desist from some virtuous action. Therefore an oath is not always binding.

Objection 3: Further, sometimes a man is compelled against his will to promise something under oath. Now, "such a person is loosed by the Roman Pontiffs from the bond of his oath." Therefore an oath is not always binding.

Objection 4: Further, no person can be under two opposite obligations. Yet sometimes the person who swears and the person to whom he swears have opposite intentions. Therefore an oath cannot always be binding.

On the contrary, It is written (Matthew 5:33): "Thou shalt perform thy oaths to the Lord."

I answer that, an obligation implies something to be done or omitted; so that apparently it regards neither the declaratory oath (which is about something present or past), nor such oaths as are about something to be effected by some other cause (as, for example, if one were to swear that it would rain tomorrow), but only such as are about things to be done by the person who swears.

Now just as a declaratory oath, which is about the future or the present, should contain the truth, so too ought the oath which is about something to be done by us in the future. Yet there is a difference: since, in the oath that is about the past or present, this obligation affects, not the thing that already has been or is, but the action of the swearer, in the point of his swearing to what is or was already true; whereas, on the contrary, in the oath that is made about something to be done by us, the obligation falls on the thing guaranteed by oath. For a man is bound to make true what he has sworn, else his oath lacks truth.

Now if this thing be such as not to be in his power, his oath is lacking in judgment of discretion: unless perchance what was possible when

4. [See Aristotle's *Categories* 8.22.]

he swore become impossible to him through some mishap, as when a man swore to pay a sum of money, which is subsequently taken from him by force or theft. For then he would seem to be excused from fulfilling his oath, although he is bound to do what he can. If, on the other hand, it be something that he can do, but ought not to, either because it is essentially evil, or because it is a hindrance to a good, then his oath is lacking in justice: wherefore an oath must not be kept when it involves a sin or a hindrance to good. For in either case "its result is evil."

Accordingly we must conclude that whoever swears to do something is bound to do what he can for the fulfillment of truth; provided always that the other two accompanying conditions be present, namely, judgment and justice.

Reply to Objection 1: It is not the same with a simple assertion, and with an oath wherein God is called to witness: because it suffices for the truth of an assertion, that a person say what he proposes to do, since it is already true in its cause, namely, the purpose of the doer. But an oath should not be employed, save in a matter about which one is firmly certain: and, consequently, if a man employ an oath, he is bound, as far as he can, to make true what he has sworn, through reverence of the Divine witness invoked, unless it leads to an evil result, as stated.

Reply to Objection 2: An oath may lead to an evil result in two ways. First, because from the very outset it has an evil result, either through being evil of its very nature (as, if a man were to swear to commit adultery), or through being a hindrance to a greater good, as if a man were to swear not to enter religion, or not to become a cleric, or that he would not accept a prelacy, supposing it would be expedient for him to accept, or in similar cases. For oaths of this kind are unlawful from the outset: yet with a difference: because if a man swear to commit a sin, he sinned in swearing, and sins in keeping his oath: whereas if a man swear not to perform a greater good, which he is not bound to do withal, he sins indeed in swearing (through placing an obstacle to the Holy Ghost, Who is the inspirer of good purposes), yet he does not sin in keeping his oath, though he does much better if he does not keep it.

Secondly, an oath leads to an evil result through some new and unforeseen emergency. An instance is the oath of Herod, who swore to the damsel, who danced before him, that he would give her what she would ask of him. For this oath could be lawful from the outset, supposing it to have the requisite conditions, namely, that the damsel asked what it was right to grant, but the fulfillment of the oath was unlawful. Hence Ambrose says (*De Officiis* 1.50): "Sometimes it is wrong to fulfill a promise, and to keep an oath; as Herod, who granted the slaying of John, rather than refuse what he had promised."

Reply to Objection 3: There is a twofold obligation in the oath which a man takes under compulsion: one, whereby he is beholden to the person to whom he promises something; and this obligation is cancelled by the compulsion, because he that used force deserves that the promise made to him should not be kept. The other is an obligation whereby a man is beholden to God, in virtue of which he is bound to fulfill what he has promised in His name. This obligation is not removed in the tribunal of conscience, because that man ought rather to suffer temporal loss, than violate his oath. He can, however, seek in a court of justice to recover what he has paid, or denounce the matter to his superior even if he has sworn to the contrary, because such an oath would lead to evil results since it would be contrary to public justice. The Roman Pontiffs, in absolving men from oaths of this kind, did not pronounce such oaths to be unbinding, but relaxed the obligation for some just cause.

Reply to Objection 4: When the intention of the swearer is not the same as the intention of the person to whom he swears, if this be due to the swearer's guile, he must keep his oath in accordance with the sound understanding of the person to whom the oath is made. Hence Isidore says (*De Summo Bono* 2.31): "However artful a man may be in wording his oath, God Who witnesses his conscience accepts his oath as understood by the person to whom it is made." And that this refers to the deceitful oath is clear from what follows: "He is doubly guilty who both takes God's name in vain, and tricks his neighbor by guile." If, however, the swearer uses no guile, he is bound in accordance with his own intention. Wherefore [Pope] Gregory I says (*Moralia on Job* 26.7): "The human ear takes such like words in their natural outward sense, but the Divine judgment interprets them according to our inward intention."

Whether an oath is more binding than a vow?

Objection 1: It would seem that an oath is more binding than a vow. A vow is a simple promise: whereas an oath includes, besides a promise, an appeal to God as witness. Therefore an oath is more binding than a vow.

Objection 2: Further, the weaker is wont to be confirmed by the stronger. Now a vow is sometimes confirmed by an oath. Therefore an oath is stronger than a vow.

Objection 3: Further, the obligation of a vow arises from the deliberation of the mind; while the obligation of an oath results from the truth of God Whose testimony is invoked. Since therefore God's truth is something greater than human deliberation, it seems that the obligation of an oath is greater than that of a vow.

On the contrary, a vow binds one to God while an oath sometimes binds one to man. Now one is more bound to God than to man. Therefore a vow is more binding than an oath.

I answer that, the obligation both of vow and of an oath arises from something Divine; but in different ways. For the obligation of a vow arises from the fidelity we owe God, which binds us to fulfill our promises to Him. On the other hand, the obligation of an oath arises from the reverence we owe Him which binds us to make true what we promise in His name. Now every act of infidelity includes an irreverence, but not conversely, because the infidelity of a subject to his lord would seem to be the greatest irreverence. Hence a vow by its very nature is more binding than an oath.

Reply to Objection 1: A vow is not any kind of promise, but a promise made to God; and to be unfaithful to God is most grievous.

Reply to Objection 2: An oath is added to a vow not because it is more stable, but because greater stability results from "two immutable things" [see Hebrews 6:18].

Reply to Objection 3: Deliberation of the mind gives a vow its stability, on the part of the person who takes the vow: but it has a greater cause of stability on the part of God, to Whom the vow is offered.

Whether anyone can dispense from an oath?[5]

Objection 1: It would seem that no one can dispense from an oath. Just as truth is required for a declaratory oath, which is about the past or the present, so too is it required for a promissory oath, which is about the future. Now no one can dispense a man from swearing to the truth about present or past things. Therefore neither can anyone dispense a man from making truth that which he has promised by oath to do in the future.

Objection 2: Further, a promissory oath is used for the benefit of the person to whom the promise is made. But, apparently, he cannot release the other from his oath, since it would be contrary to the

5. [By "dispense," Aquinas just means whether oaths may be forgivably broken. In Catholic canon law, *dispensation* refers to the suspension of general laws in particular cases.]

reverence of God. Much less therefore can a dispensation from this oath be granted by anyone.

Objection 3: Further, any bishop can grant a dispensation from a vow, except certain vows reserved to the Pope alone. Therefore in like manner, if an oath admits of dispensation, any bishop can dispense from an oath. And yet seemingly this is to be against the law. Therefore it would seem that an oath does not admit of dispensation.

On the contrary, a vow is more binding than an oath. But a vow admits of dispensation and therefore an oath does also.

I answer that the necessity of a dispensation both from the law and from a vow arises from the fact that something which is useful and morally good in itself and considered in general, may be morally evil and hurtful in respect of some particular emergency: and such a case comes under neither law nor vow. Now anything morally evil or hurtful is incompatible with the matter of an oath: for if it be morally evil it is opposed to justice, and if it be hurtful it is contrary to judgment. Therefore an oath likewise admits of dispensation.

Reply to Objection 1: A dispensation from an oath does not imply a permission to do anything against the oath: for this is impossible, since the keeping of an oath comes under a Divine precept, which does not admit of dispensation: but it implies that what hitherto came under an oath no longer comes under it, as not being due matter for an oath. Now the matter of a declaratory oath, which is about something past or present, has already acquired a certain necessity, and has become unchangeable, wherefore the dispensation will regard not the matter but the act itself of the oath: so that such a dispensation would be directly contrary to the Divine precept. On the other hand, the matter of a promissory oath is something future, which admits of change, so that, to wit, in certain emergencies, it may be unlawful or hurtful, and consequently undue matter for an oath. Therefore a promissory oath admits of dispensation, since such dispensation regards the matter of an oath, and is not contrary to the Divine precept about the keeping of oaths.

Reply to Objection 2: One man may promise something under oath to another in two ways. First, when he promises something for his benefit: for instance, if he promise to serve him, or to give him money: and from such a promise he can be released by the person to whom he made it: for he is understood to have already kept his promise to him when he acts towards him according to his will. Secondly, one man promises another something pertaining to God's honor or to the benefit of others: for instance, if a man promise another under oath that he will enter religion, or perform some act of kindness. In this case the person to whom the promise is made cannot release him that made the promise, because it was made principally not to him but to God: unless perchance it included some condition, for instance, "provided he give his consent" or some such like condition.

Reply to Objection 3: Sometimes that which is made the matter of a promissory oath is manifestly opposed to justice, either because it is a sin, as when a man swears to commit a murder, or because it is an obstacle to a greater good, as when a man swears not to enter a religion: and such an oath requires no dispensation. But in the former case a man is bound not to keep such an oath, while in the latter it is lawful for him to keep or not to keep the oath. Sometimes what is promised on oath is doubtfully right or wrong, useful or harmful, either in itself or under the circumstance. In this case any bishop can dispense. Sometimes, however, that which is promised under oath is manifestly lawful and beneficial. An oath of this kind seemingly admits not of dispensation but of commutation, when there occurs something better to be done for the common good, in which case the matter would seem to belong chiefly to the power of the Pope, who has charge over the whole Church; and even of absolute relaxation, for this too belongs in general to the Pope in all matters regarding the administration of things ecclesiastical. Thus it is competent to any man to cancel an oath made by one of his subjects in matters that come under his authority: for instance, a father may annul his daughter's oath, and a husband his wife's (Numbers 30:6).

Whether an oath is voided by a condition of person or time?

Objection 1: It would seem that an oath is not voided by a condition of person or time. An oath, according to the Apostle (Hebrews 6:16), is employed for the purpose of confirmation. Now it is competent to anyone to confirm his assertion, and at any time. Therefore it would seem that an oath is not voided by a condition of person or time.

Objection 2: Further, to swear by God is more than to swear by the Gospels: wherefore Chrysostom says: "If there is a reason for swearing, it seems a small thing to swear by God, but a great thing to swear by the Gospels. To those who think thus, it must be said: Nonsense! the Scriptures were made for God's sake, not God for the sake of the Scriptures." Now men of all conditions and at all times are wont to swear by God. Much more, therefore, is it lawful to swear by the Gospels.

Objection 3: Further, the same effect does not proceed from contrary causes, since contrary causes produce contrary effects. Now some are debarred from swearing on account of some personal defect; children, for instance, before the age of fourteen, and persons who have already committed perjury. Therefore it would seem that a person ought not to be debarred from swearing either on account of his dignity, as clerics, or on account of the solemnity of the time.

Objection 4: Further, in this world no living man is equal in dignity to an angel: for it is written (Matthew 11:11) that "he that is the lesser in the kingdom of heaven is greater than he," namely than John the Baptist, while yet living. Now an angel is competent to swear, for it is written (Apocrypha 10:6) that the angel "swore by Him that liveth for ever and ever." Therefore no man ought to be excused from swearing, on account of his dignity.

On the contrary, it is stated, "Let a priest be examined 'by his sacred consecration,' instead of being put on his oath"; and "Let no one in ecclesiastical orders dare to swear on the Holy Gospels to a layman."

I answer that, two things are to be considered in an oath. One is on the part of God, whose testimony is invoked, and in this respect we should hold an oath in the greatest reverence. For this reason children before the age of puberty are debarred from taking oaths, and are not called upon to swear, because they have not yet attained the perfect use of reason, so as to be able to take a oath with due reverence. Perjurers also are debarred from taking an oath, because it is presumed from their antecedents that they will not treat an oath with the reverence due to it. For this same reason, in order that oaths might be treated with due reverence the law says: "It is becoming that he who ventures to swear on holy things should do so fasting, with all propriety and fear of God."

The other thing to be considered is on the part of the man, whose assertion is confirmed by oath. For a man's assertion needs no confirmation save because there is a doubt about it. Now it derogates from a person's dignity that one should doubt about the truth of what he says, wherefore "it becomes not persons of great dignity to swear." For this reason the law says that "priests should not swear for trifling reasons." Nevertheless it is lawful for them to swear if there be need for it, or if great good may result therefrom. Especially is this the case in spiritual affairs, when moreover it is becoming that they should take oath on days of solemnity, since they ought then to devote themselves to spiritual matters. Nor should they on such occasions take oaths in temporal matters, except perhaps in cases of grave necessity.

Reply to Objection 1: Some are unable to confirm their own assertions on account of their own defect: and some there are whose words should be so certain that they need no confirmation.

Reply to Objection 2: The greater the thing sworn by, the holier and the more binding is the oath, considered in itself, as Augustine states: and accordingly is a graver matter to swear by God than the Gospels. Yet the contrary may be the case on account of the manner of swearing for instance, an oath by the Gospels might be taken with deliberation and solemnity, and an oath by God frivolously and without deliberation.

Reply to Objection 3: Nothing prevents the same thing from arising out of contrary causes, by way of superabundance and defect. It is in this way that some are debarred from swearing, through being of so great authority that it is unbecoming for them to swear; while others are of such little authority that their oaths have no standing.

Reply to Objection 4: The angel's oath is adduced not on account of any defect in the angel, as though one ought not to credit his mere word, but in order to show that the statement made issues from God's infallible disposition. Thus too God is sometimes spoken of by Scripture as swearing, in order to express the immutability of His word, as the Apostle declares (Hebrews 6:17).

OF PERJURY (II-II. Q98)

Whether it is necessary for perjury that the statement confirmed on oath be false?

Objection 1: It would seem that it is not necessary for perjury that the statement confirmed on oath be false. An oath should be accompanied by judgment and justice no less than by truth. Since therefore perjury is incurred through lack of truth, it is incurred likewise through lack of judgment, as when one swears indiscreetly, and through lack of justice, as when one swears to something unjust.

Objection 2: Further, that which confirms is more weighty than the thing confirmed thereby: thus in a syllogism the premises are more weighty than the conclusion. Now in an oath a man's statement is confirmed by calling on the name of God. Therefore perjury seems to consist in swearing by false gods rather than in a lack of truth in the human statement which is confirmed on oath.

Objection 3: Further, Augustine says, "Men swear falsely both in deceiving others and when they are deceived themselves"; and he gives three examples. The first is: "Supposing a man to swear, thinking that what he swears to is true, whereas it is false"; the second is: "Take the instance of another who knows the statement to be false, and swears to it as though it were true"; and the third is: "Take another, who thinks his statement false, and swears to its being true, while perhaps it is true," of whom he says afterwards that he is a perjurer. Therefore one may be a perjurer while swearing to the truth. Therefore falsehood is not necessary for perjury.

On the contrary, perjury is defined "a falsehood confirmed by oath."

I answer that, moral acts take their species from their end. Now the end of an oath is the confirmation of a human assertion. To this confirmation falsehood is opposed: since an assertion is confirmed by being firmly shown to be true; and this cannot happen to that which is false. Hence falsehood directly annuls the end of an oath: and for this reason, that perversity in swearing, which is called perjury, takes its species chiefly from falsehood. Consequently falsehood is essential to perjury.

Reply to Objection 1: As Jerome says on Jerome 4:2, "whichever of these three be lacking, there is perjury," but in different order. For first and chiefly perjury consists in a lack of truth, for the reason stated in the Article. Secondly, there is perjury when justice is lacking, for in whatever way a man swears to that which is unlawful, for this very reason he is guilty of falsehood, since he is under an obligation to do the contrary. Thirdly, there is perjury when judgment is lacking, since by the very fact that a man swears indiscreetly, he incurs the danger of lapsing into falsehood.

Reply to Objection 2: In syllogisms the premises are of greater weight, since they are in the position of active principle, as stated in [Aristotle's] *Physics* 2.3: whereas in moral matters the end is of greater importance than the active principle. Hence though it is a perverse oath when a man swears to the truth by false gods, yet perjury takes its name from that kind of perversity in an oath, that deprives the oath of its end, by swearing what is false.

Reply to Objection 3: Moral acts proceed from the will, whose object is the apprehended good. Wherefore if the false be apprehended as true, it will be materially false, but formally true, as related to the will. If something false be apprehended as false, it will be false both materially and formally. If that which is true be apprehended as false, it will be materially true, and formally false. Hence in each of these cases the conditions required for perjury are to be found in some way, on account of some measure of falsehood. Since, however, that which is formal in anything is of greater importance than that which is material, he that swears to a falsehood thinking it true is not so much of a perjurer as he that swears to the truth thinking it false. For Augustine says: "It depends how the assertion proceeds from the mind, for the tongue is not guilty except the mind be guilty."

Whether all perjury is sinful?

Objection 1: It would seem that not all perjury is sinful. Whoever does not fulfill what he has confirmed on oath is seemingly a perjurer. Yet sometimes a man swears he will do something unlawful (adultery, for instance, or murder): and if he does it, he commits a sin. If therefore he would commit a sin even if he did it not, it would follow that he is perplexed.

Objection 2: Further, no man sins by doing what is best. Yet sometimes by committing a perjury one does what is best: as when a man swears not to enter religion, or not to do some kind of virtuous deed. Therefore not all perjury is sinful.

Objection 3: Further, he that swears to do another's will would seem to be guilty of perjury unless he do it. Yet it may happen sometimes that he sins not, if he do not the man's will: for instance, if the latter order him to do something too hard and unbearable. Therefore seemingly not all perjury is sinful.

Objection 4: Further, a promissory oath extends to future, just as a declaratory oath extends to past and present things. Now the obligation of an oath may be removed by some future occurrence: thus a state may swear to fulfill some obligation, and afterwards other citizens come on the scene who did not take the oath; or a canon may swear to keep the statutes of a certain church, and afterwards new statutes are made. Therefore seemingly he that breaks an oath does not sin.

On the contrary, Augustine says, in speaking of perjury: "See how you should detest this horrible beast and exterminate it from all human business."

I answer that, to swear is to call God as witness. Now it is an irreverence to God to call Him to witness to a falsehood, because by so doing one implies either that God ignores the truth or that He is willing to bear witness to a falsehood. Therefore perjury is manifestly a sin opposed to religion, to which it belongs to show reverence to God.

Reply to Objection 1: He that swears to do what is unlawful is thereby guilty of perjury through lack of justice: though, if he fails to keep his oath, he is not guilty of perjury in this respect, since that which he swore to do was not a fit matter of an oath.

Reply to Objection 2: A person who swears not to enter religion, or not to give an alms, or the like, is guilty of perjury through lack of judgment. Hence when he does that which is best it is not an act of perjury, but contrary thereto: for the contrary of that which he is doing could not be a matter of an oath.

Reply to Objection 3: When one man swears or promises to do another's will, there is to be understood this requisite condition—that the thing commanded be lawful and virtuous, and not unbearable or immoderate.

Reply to Objection 4: An oath is a personal act, and so when a man becomes a citizen of a state, he is not bound, as by oath, to fulfill whatever the state has sworn to do. Yet he is bound by a kind of fidelity, the nature of which obligation is that he should take his share of the state's burdens if he takes a share of its goods.

The canon who swears to keep the statutes that have force in some particular "college" is not bound by his oath to keep any that may be made in the future, unless he intends to bind himself to keep all, past and future. Nevertheless he is bound to keep them by virtue of the statutes themselves, since they are possessed of coercive force.

Whether all perjury is a mortal sin?[6]

Objection 1: It would seem that not all perjury is a mortal sin. It is laid down: "Referring to the question whether an oath is binding on those who have taken one in order to safeguard their life and possessions, we have no other mind than that which our predecessors the Roman Pontiffs are known to have had, and who absolved such persons from the obligations of their oath. Henceforth, that discretion may be observed, and in order to avoid occasions of perjury, let them not be told expressly not to keep their oath: but if they should not keep it, they are not for this reason to be punished as for a mortal sin." Therefore not all perjury is a mortal sin.

Objection 2. Further, as [St. John] Chrysostom says, "it is a greater thing to swear by God than by the Gospels." Now it is not always a mortal sin to swear by God to something false; for instance, if we were to employ such an oath in fun or by a slip of the tongue in the course of an ordinary conversation. Therefore neither is it always a mortal sin to break an oath that has been taken solemnly on the Gospels.

Objection 3: Further, according to the Law a man incurs infamy through committing perjury. Now it would seem that infamy is not incurred through any kind of perjury, as it is prescribed in the case of

6. [In Catholic doctrine, a sin is *mortal* when its seriousness jeopardizes one's eternal salvation unless it is confessed and forgiven; by contrast, *venial* sins are less egregious offenses that can be forgiven and atoned for in purgatory.]

a declaratory oath violated by perjury. Therefore, seemingly, not all perjury is a mortal sin.

On the contrary, Every sin that is contrary to a divine precept is a mortal sin. Now perjury is contrary to a divine precept, for it is written (Leviticus 19:12): "Thou shalt not swear falsely by My name." Therefore it is a mortal sin.

I answer that, According to the teaching of the Philosopher (*Posterior Analytics* 1.2), "that which causes a thing to be such is yet more so." Now we know that an action which is, by reason of its very nature, a venial sin, or even a good action, is a mortal sin if it be done out of contempt of God. Wherefore any action that of its nature, implies contempt of God is a mortal sin. Now perjury, of its very nature implies contempt of God, since, the reason why it is sinful is because it is an act of irreverence towards God. Therefore it is manifest that perjury, of its very nature, is a mortal sin.

Reply to Objection 1: Coercion does not deprive a promissory oath of its binding force, as regards that which can be done lawfully. Wherefore he who fails to fulfill an oath which he took under coercion is guilty of perjury and sins mortally. Nevertheless the Sovereign Pontiff can, by his authority, absolve a man from an obligation even of an oath, especially if the latter should have been coerced into taking the oath through such fear as may overcome a high-principled man.

When, however, it is said that these persons are not to be punished as for a mortal sin, this does not mean that they are not guilty of mortal sin, but that a lesser punishment is to be inflicted on them.

Reply to Objection 2: He that swears falsely in fun is nonetheless irreverent to God, indeed, in a way, he is more so, and consequently is not excused from mortal sin. He that swears falsely by a slip of tongue, if he adverts to the fact that he is swearing, and that he is swearing to something false, is not excused from mortal sin, as neither is he excused from contempt of God. If, however, he does not advert to this, he would seem to have no intention of swearing, and consequently is excused from the sin of perjury.

It is, however, a more grievous sin to swear solemnly by the Gospels, than to swear by God in ordinary conversation, both on account of scandal and on account of the greater deliberation. But if we consider them equally in comparison with one another, it is more grievous to commit perjury in swearing by God than in swearing by the Gospels.

Reply to Objection 3: Not every sin makes a man infamous in the eye of the law. Wherefore, if a man who has sworn falsely in a declaratory oath be not infamous in the eye of the law, but only when he has been so declared by sentence in a court of law, it does not follow that he has not sinned mortally. The reason why the law attaches infamy rather to one who breaks a promissory oath taken solemnly is that he still has it in his power after he has sworn to substantiate his oath, which is not the case in a declaratory oath.

Whether he sins who demands an oath of a perjurer?

Objection 1: It would seem that he who demands an oath of a perjurer commits a sin. Either he knows that he swears truly, or he knows that he swears falsely. If he knows him to swear truly, it is useless for him to demand an oath: and if he believes him to swear falsely, for his own part he leads him into sin. Therefore nowise seemingly should one enjoin an oath on another person.

Objection 2: Further, to receive an oath from a person is less than to impose an oath on him. Now it would seem unlawful to receive an oath from a person, especially if he swear falsely, because he would then seem to consent in his sin. Much less therefore would it seem lawful to impose an oath on one who swears falsely.

Objection 3: Further, it is written (Leviticus 5:1): "If anyone sin, and hear the voice of one swearing falsely [NB: "falsely" is not in the Vulgate], and is a witness either because he himself hath seen, or is privy to it: if he do not utter it, he shall bear his iniquity." Hence it would seem that when a man knows another to be swearing falsely, he is bound to denounce him. Therefore it is not lawful to demand an oath of such a man.

Objection 4: On the other hand, Just as it is a sin to swear falsely so is it to swear by false gods. Yet it is lawful to take advantage of an oath of one who has sworn by false gods, as Augustine says. Therefore it is lawful to demand an oath from one who swears falsely.

I answer that, As regards a person who demands an oath from another, a distinction would seem to be necessary. For either he demands the oath on his own account and of his own accord, or he demands it on account of the exigencies of a duty imposed on him. If a man demands an oath on his own account as a private individual, we must make a distinction, as does Augustine: "For if he knows not that the man will swear falsely, and says to him accordingly: 'Swear to me' in order that he may be credited, there is no sin: yet it is a human temptation" (because, to wit, it proceeds from his weakness in doubting whether the man will speak the truth). "This is the evil whereof Our Lord says (Matthew 5:37): That which is over and above these, is of evil. But if he knows the man to have done so," i.e. the contrary of what he swears to, "and yet forces him to swear, he is a murderer: for the other destroys himself by his perjury, but it is he who urged the hand of the slayer."

If, on the other hand, a man demands an oath as a public person, in accordance with the requirements of the law, on the requisition of a third person: he does not seem to be at fault, if he demands an oath of a person, whether he knows that he will swear falsely or truly, because seemingly it is not he that exacts the oath but the person at whose instance he demands it.

Reply to Objection 1: This argument avails in the case of one who demands an oath on his own account. Yet he does not always know that the other will swear truly or falsely, for at times he has doubts about the fact, and believes he will swear truly. In such a case he exacts an oath in order that he may be more certain.

Reply to Objection 2: As Augustine says, "though we are forbidden to swear, I do not remember ever to have read in the Holy Scriptures that we must not accept oaths from others." Hence he that accepts an oath does not sin, except perchance when of his own accord he forces another to swear, knowing that he will swear falsely.

Reply to Objection 3: As Augustine says, Moses in the passage quoted did not state to whom one man had to denounce another's perjury: wherefore it must be understood that the matter had to be denounced "to those who would do the perjurer good rather than harm." Again, neither did he state in what order the denunciation was to be made: wherefore seemingly the Gospel order should be followed, if the sin of perjury should be hidden, especially when it does not tend to another person's injury: because if it did, the Gospel order would not apply to the case.

Reply to Objection 4: It is lawful to make use of an evil for the sake of good, as God does, but it is not lawful to lead anyone to do evil. Consequently it is lawful to accept the oath of one who is ready to swear by false gods, but it is not lawful to induce him to swear by false gods. Yet it seems to be different in the case of one who swears falsely by the true God, because an oath of this kind lacks the good of faith, which a man makes use of in the oath of one who swears truly by false gods, as Augustine says. Hence when a man swears falsely by the true God his oath seems to lack any good that one may use lawfully.

OF LYING (II-II. Q.110)

We must now consider the vices opposed to truth, and (1) lying: (2) dissimulation or hypocrisy: (3) boasting and the opposite vice. Concerning lying there are four points of inquiry:

(1) Whether lying, as containing falsehood, is always opposed to truth?
(2) Of the species of lying;
(3) Whether lying is always a sin?
(4) Whether it is always a mortal sin?

Whether lying is always opposed to truth?

Objection 1: It seems that lying is not always opposed to truth. For opposites are incompatible with one another. But lying is compatible with truth, since that speaks the truth, thinking it to be false, lies, according to Augustine (*De Mendacio*). Therefore lying is not opposed to truth.

Objection 2: Further, the virtue of truth applies not only to words but also to deeds, since according to the Philosopher (*Nicomachean Ethics* 4.7) by this virtue one tells the truth both in one's speech and in one's life. But lying applies only to words, for Augustine says (*Against Lying* 12) that "a lie is a false signification by words." Accordingly, it seems that lying is not directly opposed to the virtue of truth.

Objection 3: Further, Augustine says (*De Mendacio*) that the "liar's sin is the desire to deceive." But this is not opposed to truth, but rather to benevolence or justice. Therefore lying is not opposed to truth.

On the contrary, Augustine says (*Against Lying* 10): "Let no one doubt that it is a lie to tell a falsehood in order to deceive. Wherefore a false statement uttered with intent to deceive is a manifest lie." But this is opposed to truth. Therefore lying is opposed to truth.

I answer that, a moral act takes its species from two things, its object, and its end: for the end is the object of the will, which is the first mover in moral acts. And the power moved by the will has its own object, which is the proximate object of the voluntary act, and stands in relation to the will's act towards the end, as material to formal.[7]

The virtue of truth—and consequently the opposite vices—regards a manifestation made by certain signs: and this manifestation or statement is an act of reason comparing sign with the thing signified; because every representation consists in comparison, which is the proper act of the reason. Wherefore though dumb animals manifest something, yet they do not intend to manifest anything: but they do something by natural instinct, and a manifestation is the result. But when this manifestation or statement is a moral act, it must needs be voluntary, and dependent on the intention of the will. Now the proper object of a manifestation or statement is the true or the false. And the intention of a bad will may bear on two things: one of which is that a

7. ["Material" and "formal" are being used here in a technical Scholastic sense, derived from Aristotle's remarks in the *Physics* and elsewhere that things admit of four different types of "cause" or explanation: the *material* cause involves accounting for the thing in terms of what it is bodily composed of; the *formal* cause involves accounting for the thing in terms of its abstract concept or shape.]

falsehood may be told; while the other is the proper effect of a false statement, namely, that someone may be deceived.

Accordingly if these three things concur, namely, falsehood of what is said, the will to tell a falsehood, and finally the intention to deceive, then there is falsehood—materially, since what is said is false, formally, on account of the will to tell an untruth, and effectively, on account of the will to impart a falsehood.[8]

However, the essential notion of a lie is taken from formal falsehood, from the fact namely, that a person intends to say what is false; wherefore also the word *"mendacium"* [lie] is derived from its being in opposition to the "mind." Consequently if one says what is false, thinking it to be true, it is false materially, but not formally, because the falseness is beside the intention of the speaker so that it is not a perfect lie, since what is beside the speaker's intention is accidental for which reason it cannot be a specific difference. If, on the other hand, one utters falsehood formally, through having the will to deceive, even if what one says be true, yet inasmuch as this is a voluntary and moral act, it contains falseness essentially and truth accidentally, and attains the specific nature of a lie.

That a person intends to cause another to have a false opinion, by deceiving him, does not belong to the species of lying, but to perfection thereof, even as in the physical order, a thing acquires its species if it has its form, even though the form's effect be lacking; for instance a heavy body which is held up aloft by force, lest it come down in accordance with the exigency of its form. Therefore it is evident that lying is directly and formally opposed to the virtue of truth.

Reply to Objection 1: We judge of a thing according to what is in it formally and essentially rather than according to what is in it materially and accidentally. Hence it is more in opposition to truth, considered as a moral virtue, to tell the truth with the intention of telling a falsehood than to tell a falsehood with the intention of telling the truth.

Reply to Objection 2: As Augustine says, words hold the chief place among other signs. And so when it is said that "a lie is a false signification by words," the term "words" denotes every kind of sign. Wherefore if a person intended to signify something false by means of signs, he would not be excused from lying.

8. [For Aquinas' meaning of "material" and "formal," see the previous note. In the same vein, an *efficient* explanation of a thing focuses on whence or by what means that thing comes.]

Reply to Objection 3: The desire to deceive belongs to the perfection of lying, but not to its species, as neither does any effect belong to the species of its cause.

Whether lies are sufficiently divided into officious, jocose, and mischievous lies?

Objection 1: It seems that lies are not sufficiently divided into "officious," "jocose" and "mischievous" lies. For a division should be made according to that which pertains to a thing by reason of its nature, as the Philosopher states (*Metaphysics* 7.43; *On the Parts of Animals* 1.3). But seemingly the intention of the effect resulting from a moral act is something beside and accidental to the species of that act, so that an indefinite number of effects can result from one act. Now this division is made according to the intention of the effect: for a "jocose" lie is told in order to make fun, an "officious" lie for some useful purpose, and a "mischievous" lie in order to injure someone. Therefore lies are unfittingly divided in this way.

Objection 2: Further, Augustine (*Against Lying* 14) gives eight kinds of lies. The first is "in religious doctrine"; the second is "a lie that profits no one and injures someone"; the third "profits one party so as to injure another"; the fourth is "told out of mere lust of lying and deceiving"; the fifth is "told out of the desire to please"; the sixth "injures no one, and profits someone in saving his money"; the seventh "injures no one and profits someone in saving him from death"; the eighth "injures no one, and profits someone in saving him from defilement of the body." Therefore it seems that the first division of lies is insufficient.

Objection 3: Further, the Philosopher (*Nicomachean Ethics* 4.7) divides lying into "boasting," which exceeds the truth in speech, and "irony," which falls short of the truth by saying something less: and these two are not contained under any one of the kinds mentioned above. Therefore it seems that the aforesaid division of lies is inadequate.

On the contrary, a gloss on Psalms 5:7, "Thou wilt destroy all that speak a lie," says "that there are three kinds of lies; for some are told for the wellbeing and convenience of someone; and there is another kind of lie that is told in fun; but the third kind of lie is told out of malice." The first of these is called an officious lie, the second a jocose lie, the third a mischievous lie. Therefore lies are divided into these three kinds.

I answer that, lies may be divided in three ways. First, with respect to their nature as lies: and this is the proper and essential division of lying. In this way, according to the Philosopher (*Nicomachean Ethics* 4.7), lies are of two kinds, namely, the lie which goes beyond the truth, and this belongs to "boasting," and the lie which stops short of the truth, and this belongs to "irony." This division is an essential division of lying itself, because lying as such is opposed to truth, as stated in the preceding Article: and truth is a kind of equality, to which more and less are in essential opposition.

Secondly, lies may be divided with respect to their nature as sins, and with regard to those things that aggravate or diminish the sin of lying, on the part of the end intended. Now the sin of lying is aggravated, if by lying a person intends to injure another, and this is called a "mischievous" lie, while the sin of lying is diminished if it be directed to some good—either of pleasure and then it is a "jocose" lie, or of usefulness, and then we have the "officious" lie, whereby it is intended to help another person, or to save him from being injured. In this way lies are divided into the three kinds aforesaid.

Thirdly, lies are divided in a more general way, with respect to their relation to some end, whether or not this increase or diminish their gravity: and in this way the division comprises eight kinds, as stated in the Second Objection. Here the first three kinds are contained under "mischievous" lies, which are either against God, and then we have the lie "in religious doctrine," or against man, and this either with the sole intention of injuring him, and then it is the second kind of lie, which "profits no one, and injures someone"; or with the intention of injuring one and at the same time profiting another, and this is the third kind of lie, "which profits one, and injures another." Of these the first is the most grievous, because sins against God are always more grievous: and the second is more grievous than the third, since the latter's gravity is diminished by the intention of profiting another.

After these three, which aggravate the sin of lying, we have a fourth, which has its own measure of gravity without addition or diminution; and this is the lie which is told "out of mere lust of lying and deceiving." This proceeds from a habit, wherefore the Philosopher says (*Nicomachean Ethics* 4.7) that "the liar, when he lies from habit, delights in lying."

The four kinds that follow lessen the gravity of the sin of lying. For the fifth kind is the jocose lie, which is told "with a desire to please": and the remaining three are comprised under the officious lie, wherein something useful to another person is intended. This usefulness regards either external things, and then we have the sixth kind of lie, which "profits someone in saving his money"; or his body, and this is the seventh kind, which "saves a man from death"; or the morality of his virtue, and this is the eighth kind, which "saves him from unlawful defilement of his body."

Now it is evident that the greater the good intended, the more is the sin of lying diminished in gravity. Wherefore a careful consideration of the matter will show that these various kinds of lies are enumerated in their order of gravity: since the useful good is better than the pleasurable good, and life of the body than money, and virtue than the life of the body.

This suffices for the Replies to the Objections.

Whether every lie is a sin?

Objection 1: It seems that not every lie is a sin. For it is evident that the evangelists did not sin in the writing of the Gospel. Yet they seem to have told something false: since their accounts of the words of Christ and of others often differ from one another: wherefore seemingly one of them must have given an untrue account. Therefore not every lie is a sin.

Objection 2: Further, no one is rewarded by God for sin. But the midwives of Egypt were rewarded by God for a lie, for it is stated that "God built them houses" (Exodus 1:21). Therefore a lie is not a sin.

Objection 3: Further, the deeds of holy men are related in Sacred Writ that they may be a model of human life. But we read of certain very holy men that they lied. Thus (Genesis 12; 20) we are told that Abraham said of his wife that she was his sister. Jacob also lied when he said that he was Esau, and yet he received a blessing (Genesis 27:27–29). Again, Judith is commended (Judith 15:10, 11) although she lied to Holofernes. Therefore not every lie is a sin.

Objection 4: Further, one ought to choose the lesser evil in order to avoid the greater: even so a physician cuts off a limb, lest the whole body perish. Yet less harm is done by raising a false opinion in a person's mind, than by someone slaying or being slain. Therefore a man may lawfully lie, to save another from committing murder, or another from being killed.

Objection 5: Further, it is a lie not to fulfill what one has promised. Yet one is not bound to keep all one's promises: for Isidore says: "Break your faith when you have promised ill." Therefore not every lie is a sin.

Objection 6: Further, apparently a lie is a sin because thereby we deceive our neighbor: wherefore Augustine says (*De Mendacio*): "Whoever thinks that there is any kind of lie that is not a sin deceives himself shamefully, since he deems himself an honest man when he deceives others." Yet not every lie is a cause of deception, since no one is deceived by a jocose lie; seeing that lies of this kind are told, not with the intention of being believed, but merely for the sake of giving pleasure. Hence again we find hyperbolical expressions in Holy Writ. Therefore not every lie is a sin.

On the contrary, it is written (Sirach 7:14): "Be not willing to make any manner of lie."

I answer that, an action that is naturally evil in respect of its genus can by no means be good and lawful, since in order for an action to be good it must be right in every respect: because good results from a complete cause, while evil results from any single defect, as Dionysius asserts. Now a lie is evil in respect of its genus, since it is an action bearing on undue matter. For as words are naturally signs of intellectual acts, it is unnatural and undue for anyone to signify by words something that is not in his mind. Hence the Philosopher says (*Nicomachean Ethics* 4.7) that "lying is in itself evil and to be shunned, while truthfulness is good and worthy of praise." Therefore every lie is a sin, as also Augustine declares (*Against Lying* 1).

Reply to Objection 1: It is unlawful to hold that any false assertion is contained either in the Gospel or in any canonical Scripture, or that the writers thereof have told untruths, because faith would be deprived of its certitude which is based on the authority of Holy Writ. That the words of certain people are variously reported in the Gospel and other sacred writings does not constitute a lie. Hence Augustine says: "He that has the wit to understand that in order to know the truth it is necessary to get at the sense, will conclude that he must not be the least troubled, no matter by what words that sense is expressed." Hence it is evident, as he adds, that "we must not judge that someone is lying, if several persons fail to describe in the same way and in the same words a thing which they remember to have seen or heard."

Reply to Objection 2: The midwives were rewarded, not for their lie, but for their fear of God, and for their good-will, which latter led them to tell a lie. Hence it is expressly stated (Exodus 2:21): "And because the midwives feared God, He built them houses." But the subsequent lie was not meritorious.

Reply to Objection 3: In Holy Writ, as Augustine observes (*De Mendacio*), the deeds of certain persons are related as examples of perfect virtue: and we must not believe that such persons were liars. If, however, any of their statements appear to be untruthful, we must understand such statements to have been figurative and prophetic. Hence Augustine says (*De Mendacio*): "We must believe that whatever is related of those who, in prophetical times, are mentioned as being worthy of credit, was done and said by them prophetically." As to Abraham "when he said that Sara was his sister, he wished to hide the truth, not to tell a lie, for she is called his sister since she was the daughter of his father," Augustine says. Wherefore Abraham himself said (Genesis 20:12): "She is truly my sister, the daughter of my father, and not the daughter of my mother," being related to him on his father's side. Jacob's assertion that he was Esau, Isaac's first-born, was spoken in a mystical sense, because, to wit, the latter's birthright was due to him by right: and he made use of this mode of speech being moved by the spirit of prophecy, in order to signify a mystery, namely, that the younger people, i.e. the Gentiles, should supplant the first-born, i.e. the Jews.

Some, however, are commended in the Scriptures, not on account of perfect virtue, but for a certain virtuous disposition, seeing that it was owing to some praiseworthy sentiment that they were moved to do certain undue things. It is thus that Judith is praised, not for lying to Holofernes, but for her desire to save the people, to which end she exposed herself to danger. And yet one might also say that her words contain truth in some mystical sense.

Reply to Objection 4: A lie is sinful not only because it injures one's neighbor, but also on account of its inordinateness, as stated above in this Article. Now it is not allowed to make use of anything inordinate in order to ward off injury or defects from another: as neither is it lawful to steal in order to give an alms, except perhaps in a case of necessity when all things are common. Therefore it is not lawful to tell a lie in order to deliver another from any danger whatever. Nevertheless it is lawful to hide the truth prudently, by keeping it back, as Augustine says (*Against Lying* 10).

Reply to Objection 5: A man does not lie, so long as he has a mind to do what he promises, because he does not speak contrary to what he has in mind: but if he does not keep his promise, he seems to act without faith in changing his mind. He may, however, be excused for two reasons. First, if he has promised something evidently unlawful, because he sinned in promise, and did well to change his mind. Secondly, if circumstances have changed with regard to persons and the business in hand. For, as Seneca states, for a man to be bound to keep a promise, it is necessary for everything to remain unchanged: otherwise neither did he lie in promising—since he promised what he had in his mind, due circumstances being taken for granted—nor was he faithless in not keeping his promise, because circumstances are no longer the same. Hence the Apostle, though he did not go to Corinth, whither he had promised to go (2 Corinthians 1), did not lie, because obstacles had arisen which prevented him.

Reply to Objection 6: An action may be considered in two ways. First, in itself, secondly, with regard to the agent. Accordingly a jocose lie, from the very genus of the action, is of a nature to deceive; although in the intention of the speaker it is not told to deceive, nor does it deceive by the way it is told. Nor is there any similarity in the hyperbolical or any kind of figurative expressions, with which we meet in Holy Writ: because, as Augustine says (*De Mendacio*), "it is not a lie to do or say a thing figuratively: because every statement must be referred to the thing stated: and when a thing is done or said figuratively, it states what those to whom it is tendered understand it to signify."

Whether every lie is a mortal sin?

Objection 1: It seems that every lie is a mortal sin. For it is written (Psalms 6:7): "Thou wilt destroy all that speak a lie," and (Wisdom 1:11): "The mouth that belieth killeth the soul." Now mortal sin alone causes destruction and death of the soul. Therefore every lie is a mortal sin.

Objection 2: Further, whatever is against a precept of the decalogue is a mortal sin.[9] Now lying is against this precept of the decalogue: "Thou shalt not bear false witness." Therefore every lie is a mortal sin.

Objection 3: Further, Augustine says (*On Christian Doctrine* 1.36): "Every liar breaks his faith in lying, since forsooth he wishes the person to whom he lies to have faith in him, and yet he does not keep faith with him, when he lies to him: and whoever breaks his faith is guilty of iniquity." Now no one is said to break his faith or "to be guilty of iniquity," for a venial sin. Therefore no lie is a venial sin.

Objection 4: Further, the eternal reward is not lost save for a mortal sin. Now, for a lie the eternal reward was lost, being exchanged for a temporal meed [reward]. For [Pope] Gregory says (*Moralia on Job* 18) that "we learn from the reward of the midwives what the sin of lying deserves: since the reward which they deserved for their kindness, and which they might have received in eternal life, dwindled into a temporal meed on account of the lie of which they were guilty." Therefore even an officious lie, such as was that of the midwives, which seemingly is the least of lies, is a mortal sin.

Objection 5: Further, Augustine says (*De Mendacio*) that "it is a precept of perfection, not only not to lie at all, but not even to wish to lie." Now it is a mortal sin to act against a precept. Therefore every

9. ["Decalogue" refers to the Ten Commandments from Exodus 20:1–17.]

lie of the perfect is a mortal sin: and consequently so also is a lie told by anyone else, otherwise the perfect would be worse off than others.

On the contrary, Augustine says on Psalms 5:7, "Thou wilt destroy," etc.: "There are two kinds of lie, that are not grievously sinful yet are not devoid of sin, when we lie either in joking, or for the sake of our neighbor's good." But every mortal sin is grievous. Therefore jocose and officious lies are not mortal sins.

I answer that, A mortal sin is, properly speaking, one that is contrary to charity whereby the soul lives in union with God. Now a lie may be contrary to charity in three ways: first, in itself; secondly, in respect of the evil intended; thirdly, accidentally.

A lie may be in itself contrary to charity by reason of its false signification. For if this be about divine things, it is contrary to the charity of God, whose truth one hides or corrupts by such a lie; so that a lie of this kind is opposed not only to the virtue of charity, but also to the virtues of faith and religion: wherefore it is a most grievous and a mortal sin. If, however, the false signification be about something the knowledge of which affects a man's good, for instance if it pertain to the perfection of science or to moral conduct, a lie of this description inflicts an injury on one's neighbor, since it causes him to have a false opinion, wherefore it is contrary to charity, as regards the love of our neighbor, and consequently is a mortal sin. On the other hand, if the false opinion engendered by the lie be about some matter the knowledge of which is of no consequence, then the lie in question does no harm to one's neighbor; for instance, if a person be deceived as to some contingent particulars that do not concern him. Wherefore a lie of this kind, considered in itself, is not a mortal sin.

As regards the end in view, a lie may be contrary to charity, through being told with the purpose of injuring God, and this is always a mortal sin, for it is opposed to religion; or in order to injure one's neighbor, in his person, his possessions or his good name, and this also is a mortal sin, since it is a mortal sin to injure one's neighbor, and one sins mortally if one has merely the intention of committing a mortal sin. But if the end intended be not contrary to charity, neither will the lie, considered under this aspect, be a mortal sin, as in the case of a jocose lie, where some little pleasure is intended, or in an officious lie, where the good also of one's neighbor is intended. Accidentally a lie may be contrary to charity by reason of scandal or any other injury resulting therefrom: and thus again it will be a mortal sin, for instance if a man were not deterred through scandal from lying publicly.

Reply to Objection 1: The passages quoted refer to the mischievous lie, as a gloss explains the words of Psalms 5:7, "Thou wilt destroy all that speak a lie."

Reply to Objection 2: Since all the precepts of the decalogue are directed to the love of God and our neighbor, a lie is contrary to a precept of the decalogue, in so far as it is contrary to the love of God and our neighbor. Hence it is expressly forbidden to bear false witness against our neighbor.

Reply to Objection 3: Even a venial sin can be called "iniquity" in a broad sense, in so far as it is beside the equity of justice; wherefore it is written (1 John 3:4): "Every sin is iniquity." It is in this sense that Augustine is speaking.

Reply to Objection 4: The lie of the midwives may be considered in two ways. First as regards their feeling of kindliness towards the Jews, and their reverence and fear of God, for which their virtuous disposition is commended. For this an eternal reward is due. Wherefore Jerome (in his exposition of Isaiah 65:21, "And they shall build houses") explains that God "built them spiritual houses." Secondly, it may be considered with regard to the external act of lying. For thereby they could merit, not indeed eternal reward, but perhaps some temporal meed, the deserving of which was not inconsistent with the deformity of their lie, though this was inconsistent with their meriting an eternal reward. It is in this sense that we must understand the words of Gregory, and not that they merited by that lie to lose the eternal reward as though they had already merited it by their preceding kindliness, as the objection understands the words to mean.

Reply to Objection 5: Some say that for the perfect every lie is a mortal sin. But this assertion is unreasonable. For no circumstance causes a sin to be infinitely more grievous unless it transfers it to another species. Now a circumstance of person does not transfer a sin to another species, except perhaps by reason of something annexed to that person, for instance if it be against his vow: and this cannot apply to an officious or jocose lie. Wherefore an officious or a jocose lie is not a mortal sin in perfect men, except perhaps accidentally on account of scandal. We may take in this sense the saying of Augustine that "it is a precept of perfection not only not to lie at all, but not even to wish to lie": although Augustine says this not positively but dubiously, for he begins by saying: "Unless perhaps it is a precept," etc. Nor does it matter that they are placed in a position to safeguard the truth: because they are bound to safeguard the truth by virtue of their office in judging or teaching, and if they lie in these matters their lie will be a mortal sin: but it does not follow that they sin mortally when they lie in other matters.

12
"DISCOURSE TO PRINCE ABHAYA"

The "Discourse to Prince Abhaya" is the first of three selections from the Buddhist tradition that are included in this volume. The core doctrine of Buddhism is the Four Noble Truths, which are articulated in the Buddha's first sermon, the "Discourse Setting in Motion the Wheel of Dhamma" (*Dhammacakkappamattana Sutta*).[1] The first Noble Truth is that all experience within the cycle of birth and death is characterized by suffering.[2] The second Noble Truth is that suffering is caused. The fact that suffering is caused, and not randomly occurring or eternal leads to the third Noble Truth: it is possible to bring about the cessation of suffering. The fourth Noble Truth is the path that leads to the cessation of suffering, the Noble Eightfold Path.

The most relevant aspect of the Eightfold Path to discussions of lying and truthfulness is the third element: Right Speech. While truthfulness is a consideration in what qualifies as right speech, it is not the only consideration. Refraining from gossip and idle chatter are also understood to be part of right speech, for example.

The "Discourse to Prince Abhaya" is an early Buddhist sutra that portrays the Buddha's skill in discourse.[3] Prince Abhaya is sent to the Buddha by Mahāvīra, at the time the leader of the Jain religion, with a question that is meant to ensnare the Buddha in a dilemma. The Buddha sees through the ruse, however, and avoids the trap. The discourse thus demonstrates the Buddha's skill at deciphering the intentions behind the questions people put to him and his

1. *Dhamma* (Sanskrit *dharma*) is the truth about the world, as reflected in Buddhist teaching.

2. "Suffering" is the standard translation of *dukkha* (Pali; Sanskrit *duḥkha*). In the Buddhist context, *dukkha* refers not merely to obvious forms of suffering such as physical pain, but also to more subtle forms of dissatisfaction such as psychological discomfort, general malaise, or existential angst due to the realization of the impermanence of things and one's own mortality.

3. Within the Buddhist tradition, a sutra (*sutta* in Pali) is a text that reports one of the Buddha's teachings. Cognate with the English word "suture," a sutra is supposed to convey the core thread of an argument or doctrine.

ability to respond appropriately, in the way that is most beneficial to his audience.

The question Prince Abhaya asks the Buddha is whether the Buddha would say something "that is unwelcome, disagreeable, and unpleasant." The Buddha's answer, and the discussion that follows, can be seen as a commentary on right speech (an element of the Noble Eightfold Path). The Buddha divides statements according to two different criteria. The first distinction is between those statements that are "false, inaccurate, unbeneficial" and those that are "true, accurate, beneficial." The second distinction is between those that are "welcome, agreeable, and pleasant" and those that are "unwelcome, disagreeable, and unpleasant." The Buddha says that he never utters statements that are false and unbeneficial, regardless of whether they are agreeable. Regarding true and beneficial statements—both those that are agreeable and those that are disagreeable—the Buddha insists that he "knows the proper time to explain" such statements.

This exchange yields two particularly interesting insights. The first is that a statement's being both true and beneficial does not provide sufficient reason to say it: there are clearly other considerations at play when deciding what to say and when to say it. At least in this discourse, what those considerations are is not made clear. Thinking of potential candidates is an exercise that will be left to the reader.

The second insight from the conversation between Prince Abhaya and the Buddha is this: either all false statements are unbeneficial or else we are left ignorant of whether the Buddha would ever be willing to utter such beneficial falsehoods. It is possible that the Buddha is equating truth, accuracy, and utility on the one hand and falsity, inaccuracy, and disutility on the other. But if the Buddha concedes that there are times not to utter the truth, it would seem that at least some of those times it would be because the truth is not beneficial. If that's the case, then it also seems plausible that falsehoods could sometimes be useful. Could uttering such a falsehood ever qualify as right speech?

A couple other points are worth mentioning, in order to help those who are unfamiliar with Buddhist texts to understand the reading. This text, as with all of the early Buddhist sutras, is quite repetitive. This is because Buddhism was originally an oral tradition: the repetition facilitated easier memorization and recitation. This is worthy of note because, like Socrates and Confucius (see chapters 5, 8, and 9 of this volume for selections associated with these thinkers), the Buddha never wrote down any of his teachings. What comes to us as the early Buddhist canon is a result of the First Buddhist Council, held soon after the Buddha's death (probably sometime during the fifth century BCE, though the dates of the Buddha's life are still a matter of debate), during which the various teachings of the Buddha were recollected by those who had been present and were standardized for recitation. This is why the sutras begin with the phrase, "Thus have I heard": no single disciple was present at all of the exchanges recorded in the canon, so there could be no single authority on all of the teachings. This fact has implications for our understanding of truthfulness within Buddhism. Starting each sutra with the phrase, "Thus have I heard" reflects a desire for those who are rehearsing the teachings to not be taken as more authoritative than is warranted. It may also be a way for those who repeat such stories to be absolved of falsehood should it turn out that a story is not accurate.

Finally, within this and other Buddhist texts the Buddha is referred to by several different appellations. Those from outside the Buddhist tradition most frequently refer to him by his family name, Gotama (Gautama in Sanskrit). "Buddha" is itself a title, rather than a name: a buddha is someone who has discovered the *dhamma* and achieved enlightenment by his or her own efforts, rather than through the teaching of another. The Buddha's followers typically call him the Exalted One or *Tathāgata.* The latter means "One who has gone there"—often translated as "Thus Gone One" or as "Thus Come One"—referring to the fact that the Buddha is the one who has accomplished the intellectual journey of discovering the *dhamma,* which makes him uniquely qualified to teach it to others.

In addition to the questions mentioned above, consider the following questions as you read the selection:

1. The Buddha says that he knows the right time to make statements that are true and beneficial, thereby implying that there are wrong times to make such statements. How can one know when it is the right versus the wrong time to say something that is true and beneficial?
2. Could there be false but beneficial utterances? If yes, when would it be acceptable to utter them?
3. If someone told you that they follow the Buddha's example in this discourse with regard to what to say and when to say it, would this make it easier or more difficult for you to trust that person?

"Discourse to Prince Abhaya"

1. Thus have I heard. At one time, the Exalted One was dwelling in Rājagaha in the Bamboo Grove in the Squirrel's Sanctuary. Then Prince Abhaya approached Nigaṇṭha Nātaputta.[1] When he had approached Nigaṇṭha Nātaputta, he saluted him and sat down to one side. When he was seated to one side, Nigaṇṭha Nātaputta said this to Prince Abhaya: "Come, prince! You should refute the doctrine of the religious wanderer Gotama. In this way, this good report will be spread about you: 'The doctrine of the religious wanderer Gotama, who has great magical power and possesses great majesty, was refuted by Prince Abhaya.'"

"But how, sir, will I refute the doctrine of the religious wanderer Gotama, who has great magical power and possesses great majesty?"

"Go, prince, and approach the religious wanderer Gotama. And having approached Gotama, speak thus: 'Sir, would the *Tathāgata* utter a statement that is unwelcome, disagreeable, and unpleasant?' If Gotama answers your question in this way: 'Prince, the *Tathāgata* would utter a statement that is unwelcome, disagreeable, and unpleasant,' then you should say to him: 'In that case, sir, what difference is there between you and the ordinary (unenlightened) person? For the ordinary person, too, would utter a statement that is unwelcome, disagreeable, and unpleasant.' If Gotama answers your question in this way: 'Prince, the *Tathāgata* would not utter a statement that is unwelcome, disagreeable, and unpleasant,' then you should say to him: 'In that case, sir, why, in regard to Devadatta, have you declared: "Devadatta is in a state of misery." "Devadatta is destined for hell."[2] "Devadatta will endure hell for an eon."[3] "Devadatta is incurable." Certainly, these words offended Devadatta and displeased him.' When asked this two-horned question, the religious wanderer Gotama will neither be able to spew it out nor swallow it down. Just as if an iron barb were to get stuck in a person's throat, one would neither be able to spew it out nor swallow it down—so, too, prince, Gotama, when asked this two-horned question will neither be able to spew it out nor swallow it down."

2. "Yes, sir," Prince Abhaya replied to Nigaṇṭha Nātaputta. Having assented, he rose from his seat and saluted Nigaṇṭha Nātaputta, keeping his right side turned toward him. Then he approached the

1. A leader of the Jains. Also known as Mahāvīra.
2. *Niraya*. Hell is a temporary place of suffering in Buddhist cosmology.
3. *Kappa* (Skt. *kalpa*). This term represents a very, very long time.

Exalted One. When he had approached the Exalted One, he greeted him courteously, and he sat down to one side. When he was seated to one side, he checked the position of the sun. Then Prince Abhaya had this thought: "The proper time for refuting the Exalted One's doctrine today has passed. I will refute the Exalted One's doctrine tomorrow at my own house." So he said this to the Exalted One: "Sir, let the Exalted One consent to taking a meal tomorrow at my house in a party of four."[4] The Exalted One consented by becoming silent. Then Prince Abhaya, having understood the Exalted One's consent, rose from his seat, saluted him, and went away keeping his right side turned toward him.

Then the Exalted One, after the passing of the night, having dressed himself in the morning and taking his robe and bowl, approached the home of Prince Abhaya. When he had approached, he sat down in the seat that was prepared. Then Prince Abhaya, with his own hands, served and satisfied the Exalted One with delicious hard and soft foods. When the Exalted One had washed his hand in the bowl to indicate that he was finished eating, Prince Abhaya took another lower seat and sat down to one side.

3. When he was seated to one side, Prince Abhaya said this to the Exalted One: "Sir, would the *Tathāgata* utter a statement that is unwelcome, disagreeable, and unpleasant?"

"There is no one-sided answer (to that question), prince."

"Already, sir, the Jains[5] have lost."

"Prince, why do you say this: 'Already, sir, the Jains have lost?'"

[*Then Prince Abhaya repeated in full his earlier conversation with Nigaṇṭha Nātaputta*]

4. At that time, a young and innocent infant was sitting on Prince Abhaya's lap. The Exalted One said this to Prince Abhaya: "What do you think about this, prince? If this young boy, because of your negligence or that of his nurse, were to take a piece of wood or a potsherd into his mouth, what would you do to him?"

"Sir, I would take it out. If I were not able to take it out at once, I would grasp his head with my left hand, and, with a bent finger on my right hand, I would take it out, even if to do so I would have to draw blood. What is the reason for this? Because, sir, I have compassion for the boy."

"In the same way, prince, a statement that the *Tathāgata* knows to be false, inaccurate, unbeneficial, and which is also unwelcome,

4. The "party of four" is composed of the Buddha and three others.

5. *Nigaṇṭha.*

disagreeable, and unpleasant—that statement the *Tathāgata* does not utter. Also, a statement that the *Tathāgata* knows to be true, accurate, unbeneficial, and which is also unwelcome, disagreeable, and unpleasant—that statement, also, the *Tathāgata* knows the proper time to explain that statement. Whatever statement the *Tathāgata* knows to be false, inaccurate, unbeneficial, and which is welcome, agreeable, and pleasant—that statement the *Tathāgatha* does not utter. Whatever statement the *Tathāgata* knows to be true, accurate, beneficial, and which is also welcome, agreeable, and pleasant—in that case, the *Tathāgata* knows the proper time to explain that statement. What is the reason for this? Prince, the *Tathāgata* has compassion for beings."

5. "Sir, whenever those learned warrior-leaders, learned Brahmins, learned householders, or learned religious wanderers prepare a question and approach the *Tathāgata* to ask it, does the Exalted One already have an answer reasoned and thought out already in his mind, such as: 'Were someone to approach me, they might ask me such-and-such a question in this way, and so I will explain it in this way'? Or does the answer come to mind for the *Tathāgata* on the spot?"

"In regard to that, prince, I will ask you a question in return. Give your reply as you see fit. What do you think, prince? Are you an expert in the parts of the chariot?"

"Yes, sir, I am an expert in the parts of the chariot."

"Then what do you think, prince? Were someone to approach you and ask you this: 'What is the name of this part of the chariot?' Do you already have an answer reasoned and thought out in your mind, such as: 'Were someone to approach me, they might ask me such-and-such a question in this way, and so I will explain it in this way'? Or does the answer come to your mind on the spot?"

"Sir, I am a renowned charioteer who is an expert in the parts of the chariot. I know very well all the parts of the chariot. So the answer would come to my mind on the spot."

"It is exactly the same for me, prince. Whenever those learned nobles or learned Brahmins or learned householders or learned religious wanderers prepare a question and approach the *Tathāgata* to ask it, the answer comes to mind for the *Tathāgata* on the spot. What is the reason for this? Prince, the essence of the *dhamma* is thoroughly understood by the *Tathāgatha*, and by means of this thorough understanding of the essence of the *dhamma*, the *Tathāgata* has the answer come to his mind on the spot.

6. This having been said, Prince Abhaya said this to the Exalted One: "Wonderful, sir! Wonderful, sir! It is just as if someone were to make

upright what was turned upside down, or were to uncover what was covered over, or were to explain the way to those who are lost, or were to hold up an oil lamp in the darkness, or were to hold up an oil lamp in the darkness saying 'those endowed with eyes will see the visible objects.' Just so, the Exalted One makes known the *dhamma* by diverse methods. Sir, I go to the Exalted One for refuge, to the *dhamma*, and also to the *Saṇgha* of the *bhikkhus*.[6] Let master Gotama accept me as a lay-follower who has gone for refuge from this day forth, so long as life lasts."

6. [The *saṇgha* is the monastic community in which the *bhikkhus* live. A *bhikkhu* (Sanskrit *bhikṣu*) is a Buddhist monk.]

13
LOTUS SUTRA

The *Lotus Sutra* is a Mahāyāna text, which means that it comes from a later stratum of Buddhist teachings than do the other Buddhist readings in this volume. Mahāyāna sutras do not profess to be actual records of the Buddha's words as the earlier sutras do, but rather seek to explicate and clarify earlier teachings. The *Lotus Sutra* contains the seminal articulation of the notion of "skillful means" (*upāya kauśalya*, more frequently referred to simply as *upāya*), a concept that is crucial to any discussion of truthfulness within Buddhism. The notion of skillful means arises as a response to a hermeneutical problem. Within the early Buddhist canon one can find several cases of reported teachings of the Buddha that seem to contradict one another. For instance, a central tenet of Buddhism is the no-self doctrine, according to which there is no unchanging essence, or soul, of a person. But in some teachings the Buddha refuses to assent to this claim. In others, he seems to assert either that there is a self or that something else is true that would seem to presuppose the existence of a self.

This tension leads early on to a distinction between those texts that are to be interpreted literally and those that require more interpretation in order to draw out the true meaning. But this move quickly gives rise to two questions. First, how are we to tell which teachings to take literally and which to read into further? Second, and more importantly for our purposes, does this open the Buddha to charges of dissimulation or even of outright lying?

The selection from the *Lotus Sutra* attempts to provide an answer to this second question. In order to do so, it asks us to consider a man whose children are inside a burning house but are so consumed with their games that they don't recognize the danger around them. The text argues that the man would not be guilty of falsehood if he deceived his children in order to get them to escape the house. The Buddha's varying teachings to different people are then claimed to be analogous: he is simply saying what people need to hear in order to get them to do what they need to do in order to escape from suffering.

When Shariputra, the Buddha's interlocutor in this story, says that the man is not guilty of falsehood for deceiving his children, this can be interpreted in at least two different ways. More conservatively it may simply mean that no guilt or blame attaches to the falsehood that the father utters for the sake of saving his children. But the text can also be interpreted to say something much more provocative, namely that the utterance doesn't qualify as a falsehood because of the motivation and the larger good that is accomplished. In a sense, the claim may be that the utterance is true because it is trustworthy, even though it is factually inaccurate. On the latter reading, the *Lotus Sutra* seems to be granting quite a wide latitude to the Buddha in terms of what he could say without being open to the charge of lying.

As you read the selection, consider the following questions:

1. Can you think of circumstances in which it would be acceptable, or even praiseworthy, to deceive other people for their own good? If yes, what are the most important criteria for determining whether it is acceptable in a given situation?
2. What differences in their orientation to deception do you detect between the *Lotus Sutra* and the other Buddhist selections in this volume (chapters 12 and 18)? Can they all be reconciled? If not, which is the most defensible and why?
3. Assuming deception can sometimes be justified, is having the right motive (saving a life, for example) enough to justify it or does the outcome matter? Should it affect one's judgment of the situation in the *Lotus Sutra* if the father's deception did not succeed at saving his sons' lives?

The Lotus Sutra

[The Buddha said to Shariputra,] "Shariputra, suppose that in a certain town in a certain country there was a very rich man. He was far along in years and his wealth was beyond measure. He had many fields, houses and menservants. His own house was big and rambling, but it had only one gate. A great many people—a hundred, two hundred, perhaps as many as five hundred—lived in the house. The halls and rooms were old and decaying, the walls crumbling, the pillars rotten at their base, and the beams and rafters crooked and aslant.

"At that time a fire suddenly broke out on all sides, spreading through the rooms of the house. The sons of the rich man, ten, twenty, perhaps thirty, were inside the house. When the rich man saw the huge flames leaping up on every side, he was greatly alarmed and fearful and thought to himself, I can escape to safety through the flaming gate, but my sons are inside the burning house enjoying themselves and playing games, unaware, unknowing, without alarm or fear. The fire is closing in on them, suffering and pain threaten them, yet their minds have no sense of loathing or peril and they do not think of trying to escape!

"Shariputra, this rich man thought to himself, I have strength in my body and arms. I can wrap them in a robe or place them on a bench and carry them out of the house. And then again he thought, This house has only one gate, and moreover it is narrow and small. My sons are very young, they have no understanding, and they love their games, being so engrossed in them that they are likely to be burned in the fire. I must explain to them why I am fearful and alarmed. The house is already in flames and I must get them out quickly and not let them be burned up in the fire!

"Having thought in this way, he followed his plan and called to all his sons, saying, 'You must come out at once!' But though the father was moved by pity and gave good words of instruction, the sons were absorbed in their games and unwilling to heed him. They had no alarm, no fright, and in the end no mind to leave the house. Moreover, they did not understand what the fire was, what the house was, what danger was. They merely raced about this way and that in play and looked at their father without heeding him.

"At that time the rich man had this thought: The house is already in flames from this huge fire. If I and my sons do not get out at once, we are certain to be burned. I must now invent some expedient means that will make it possible for the children to escape harm.

"The father understood his sons and knew what various toys and curious objects each child customarily liked and what would delight them. And so he said to them, 'The kind of playthings you like are rare and hard to find. If you do not take them when you can, you will surely regret it later. For example, things like these goat-carts, deer-carts, and ox-carts. They are outside the gate now where you can play with them. So you must come out of this burning house at once. Then whatever ones you want, I will give them all to you!'

"At that time, when the sons heard their father telling them about these rare playthings, because such things were just what they had wanted, each felt emboldened in heart and, pushing and shoving one another, they all came wildly dashing out of the burning house.

"At this time the rich man, seeing that his sons had gotten out safely and were seated on the open ground at the crossroads and were no longer in danger, was greatly relieved and his mind danced for joy. At that time each of the sons said to his father, 'The playthings you promised us earlier, the goat-carts and deer-carts and ox-carts—please give them to us now!'

"Shariputra, at that time the rich man gave to each of his sons a large carriage of uniform size and quality. The carriages were tall and spacious and adorned with numerous jewels. A railing ran all around them and bells hung from all four sides. A canopy was stretched over the top, which was also decorated with an assortment of precious jewels. Ropes of jewels twined around, a fringe of flowers hung down, and layers of cushions were spread inside, on which were placed vermilion pillows. Each carriage was drawn by a white ox, pure and clean in hide, handsome in form and of great strength, capable of pulling the carriage smoothly and properly at a pace fast as the wind. In addition, there were many grooms and servants to attend and guard the carriage.

"What was the reason for this? This rich man's wealth was limitless and he had many kinds of storehouses that were all filled and over-flowing. And he thought to himself, There is no end to my possessions. It would not be right if I were to give my sons small carriages of inferior make. These little boys are all my sons and I love them without partiality. I have countless numbers of large carriages adorned with seven kinds of gems. I should be fair-minded and give one to each of my sons. I should not show any discrimination. Why? Because even if I distributed these possessions of mine to every person in the whole country I would still not exhaust them, much less could I do so by giving them to my sons!

"At that time each of the sons mounted his large carriage, gaining something he had never had before, something he had originally never expected. Shariputra, what do you think of this? When this rich man impartially handed out to his sons these big carriages adorned with rare jewels, was he guilty of falsehood or not?"

Shariputra said, "No, World-Honored One. This rich man simply made it possible for his sons to escape the peril of fire and preserve their lives. He did not commit a falsehood. Why do I say this? Because if they were able to preserve their lives, then they had already obtained a plaything of sorts. And how much more so when, through an expedient means, they are rescued from that burning house! World-Honored one, even if the rich man had not given them the tiniest carriage, he would still not be guilty of falsehood. Why? Because this rich man had earlier made up his mind that he would employ an expedient means to cause his sons to escape. Using a devise of this kind was no act of falsehood. How much less so, then, when the rich man knew that his wealth was limitless and he intended to enrich and benefit his sons by giving each of them a large carriage."

The Buddha said to Shariputra, "Very good, very good. It is just as you have said. And Shariputra, the Thus Come One[1] is like this. That is, he is a father to all the world. His fears, cares and anxieties, ignorance and misunderstanding, have long come to an end, leaving no residue. He has fully succeeded in acquiring measureless insight, power and freedom from fear and gaining great supernatural powers and the power of wisdom. He is endowed with expedient means and the paramita of wisdom,[2] his great pity and great compassion are constant and unflagging; at all times he seeks what is good and will bring benefit to all.

"He is born into the threefold world, a burning house, rotten and old, in order to save living beings from the fires of birth, old age, sickness and death, care, suffering, stupidity, misunderstanding, and the three poisons; to teach and convert them and enable them to attain anuttara-samyak-sambodhi.[3]

"He sees living beings seared and consumed by birth, old age, sickness and death, care and suffering, sees them undergo many kinds of pain because of the five desires and the desire for wealth and

1. ["Thus Come One" is an epithet for the Buddha. See the Introduction to the "Discourse To Prince Abhaya," above (chapter 12).]

2. [This is a reference to *prajñāpāramitā*, which means "perfection of wisdom." *Prajñāpāramitā* is an important concept within Mahāyāna Buddhism, and one that is closely related with the notion of *upāya*. The basic idea is that these later texts serve to refine the teachings of the earliest Buddhist texts, which were adapted to the capabilities of the Buddha's early audiences and did not contain the full and nuanced truth.]

3. ["Anuttara-samyak-sambodhi" refers to the perfect enlightenment of the Buddha.]

profit. Again, because of their greed and attachment and striving they undergo numerous pains in their present existence, and later they undergo the pain of being reborn in hell or as beasts or hungry spirits. Even if they are reborn in the heavenly realm or the realm of human beings, they undergo the pain of poverty and want, the pain of parting from loved ones, the pain of encountering those they detest—all these many different kinds of pain.

"Yet living beings, drowned in the midst of all this, delight and amuse themselves, unaware, unknowing, without alarm or fear. They feel no sense of loathing and make no attempt to escape. In this burning house which is the threefold world, they race about to east and west, and though they encounter great pain, they are not distressed by it.

"Shariputra, when the Buddha sees this, then he thinks to himself, I am the father of living beings and I should rescue them from their sufferings and give them the joy of the measureless and boundless Buddha wisdom so that they may find their enjoyment in that.

"Shariputra, the Thus Come One also has this thought: If I should merely employ supernatural powers and the power of wisdom; if I should set aside expedient means and for the sake of living beings should praise the Thus Come One's insight, power and freedom from fear, then living beings would not be able to gain salvation. Why? Because these living beings have not yet escaped from birth, old age, sickness, death, care and suffering, but are consumed by flames in the burning house that is the threefold world. How could they be able to understand the Buddha's wisdom?

"Shariputra, that rich man, though he had strength in his body and arms, did not use it. He merely employed a carefully contrived expedient means and thus was able to rescue his sons from the peril of the burning house, and afterward gave each of them a large carriage adorned with rare jewels. And the Thus Come One does the same. Though he possesses power and freedom from fear, he does not use these. He merely employs wisdom and expedient means to rescue living beings from the burning house of the threefold world, expounding to them the three vehicles, the vehicle of the voice-hearer, that of the pratyekabuddha, and that of the Buddha."[4]

4. [The three vehicles are the three different means by which one can attain enlightenment. "Vehicle" is here translating "yāna," the same word that is found in "Mahāyāna," which means "greater vehicle." "Voice-hearers" are those who learn the dharma from another. "Pratyekabuddha" means "solitary buddha" and refers to one who discovers the dharma without the aid of another, but who does not teach.]

14
HOBBES

The English philosopher Thomas Hobbes (1588–1679) revolutionized Enlightenment philosophy with the publication of his *Leviathan* (1651), a massive tome aimed at articulating a new theory of government, but ranging across theology, ethics, and epistemology in the process. Hobbes is best known for his account of what would later be known as the "social contract," an agreement of free and self-interested individuals who voluntarily commit themselves to certain laws and limitations for the sake of mutual benefit. In Hobbes' version, such an arrangement requires the construction of a supremely powerful sovereign (akin to the biblical monster, Leviathan) to enforce the peace. It is within this explicitly political and economic context that Hobbes' remarks on lying and truthfulness must be understood.

Rather than address lying as a general moral issue, Hobbes fixates on the specific topic of promises—whence they arise, how they are binding, and the conditions under which they can be broken. A promise involves the transferring of a right: if you loan me money which I promise to return, you have transferred to me the right to use that money for a certain duration and I have transferred to you the right to the same amount back from me. In this way, as Hobbes stresses, promises are types of contracts that are necessarily about the future. (Hobbes also disambiguates promises proper from covenants: both involve the transference of rights as well as a degree of trust, but promises are more explicitly mutual and forward-looking.) Promises must necessarily be deliberate, though they need not be explicitly worded (they can instead be made through "signes by inference"), and they presuppose an equality of power and rationality between the two parties, meaning that we cannot make promises (and *a fortiori* cannot break promises) with non-human animals or with God. Moreover, promises become "voyd" (void) in a situation of anarchy or general "warre" (war), in which there would be no requisite trust and no external authority would exist to enforce the institution.[1] Oaths involve

1. As the reader will note, we have retained Hobbes' original English spellings. While this can occasionally create difficulties in comprehension, we believe that it is also an important reminder of Hobbes' historical and cultural context. Most difficulties should be remediable by simply sounding out the unfamiliar word.

additional words and rites in an attempt to augment the obligation to keep a promise; and, like Aquinas before him (see chapter 11), Hobbes addresses the meaningfulness of swearing by God.

In *Leviathan*, the purpose of language generally is to reflect and express the fitness between thought and object; or as Hobbes describes it, to use only "perspicuous" words that have exact definitions and are "purged from ambiguity" (Part 1, chapter 5). This teleological sense of how language ought to work gives rise to what Hobbes calls "abuses" of language where words are used for purposes other than perspicuity. Lying and deception (both to others and to oneself) are such abuses, either through deliberate obfuscation of the truth, through intent to harm or "grieve" another person, or through the "absurdities" that imprecise or careless talk can foment. In particular, metaphorical language, while not a violation of a contract or promise per se, can nevertheless be dangerously deceptive since it is not perspicuous in the requisite way: "Metaphors, and senslesse and ambiguous words, are like *ignes fatui* [will-o'-the-wisps]; and reasoning upon them, is wandering amongst innumerable absurdities; and their end, contention, and sedition, or contempt" (Part 1, chapter 5). Thus, because metaphorical language can be deceptive, it cannot be a proper medium for formulating promises: if someone is presented with ambiguous language, she need not be technically lied to in order to nonetheless be deceived more generally. And insofar as we have an obligation (arising out of informed self-interest, which is a "law of [human] nature") to make and keep contracts, we therefore also have an obligation to avoid ambiguity when we can.

Here are some questions to think about as you reflect on this selection from Hobbes:

1. Hobbes claims that there is "no Swearing by any thing which the Swearer thinks not God." What are the things you swear by and what, if anything, give them a godlike obligatory force?
2. Promises, in order to be binding and not "voyd," must have some "common Power set over them." What forces, entities, or institutions exist in society today that do or could exert such power?
3. For Hobbes, is it possible for promises to still be binding if the person to whom the promise was made has died or has otherwise lost the equality of power or trustworthiness that existed when the promise was initially made?

Leviathan

Abuses of Speech (Part 1, chapter 4)

To these Uses [remembering, communicating, counseling/teaching, and expressing ourselves], there are also foure correspondent Abuses. First, when men register their thoughts wrong, by the inconstancy of the signification of their words; by which they register for their conceptions, that which they never conceived; and so deceive themselves. Secondly, when they use words metaphorically; that is, in other sense than that they are ordained for; and thereby deceive others. Thirdly, when by words they declare that to be their will, which is not. Fourthly, when they use them to grieve [injure or insult] one another: for seeing nature hath armed living creatures, some with teeth, some with horns, and some with hands, to grieve an enemy, it is but an abuse of Speech, to grieve him with the tongue, unlesse it be one whom wee are obliged to govern; and then it is not to grieve, but to correct and amend.

Contracts (Part 1, chapter 14)

The mutuall transferring of Right, is that which men call contract . . .

One of the Contractors, may deliver the Thing contracted for on his part, and leave the other to perform his part at some determinate time after, and in the mean time be trusted; and then the Contract on his part, is called PACT, or COVENANT: Or both parts may contract now, to performe hereafter: in which cases, he that is to performe in time to come, being trusted, his performance is *Keeping of Promise*, or Faith; and the fayling of performance (if it be voluntary) *Violation of Faith*.

When the transferring of Right, is not mutuall; but one of the parties transferreth, in hope to gain thereby friendship, or service from another, or from his friends; or in hope to gain the reputation of Charity, or Magnanimity; or to deliver his mind from the pain of compassion; or in hope of reward in heaven; This is not Contract, but GIFT, FREE-GIFT, GRACE: which words signifie one and the same thing.

Signes of Contract, are either *Expresse*, or *by Inference*. Expresse, are words spoken with understanding of what they signifie: And such words are either of the time *Present*, or *Past*; as, *I Give, I Grant, I have Given, I have Granted, I will that this be yours*: Or of the future; as, *I will Give, I will Grant*: which words of the future, are called PROMISE.

Signes by inference, are sometimes the consequence of Words; sometimes the consequence of Silence; sometimes the consequence of Actions; sometimes the consequence of Forbearing an Action: and generally a signe by Inference, of any Contract, is whatsoever sufficiently argues the will of the Contractor.

Words alone, if they be of the time to come, and contain a bare promise, are an insufficient signe of a Free-gift and therefore not obligatory. For if they be of the time to Come, as *To morrow I will Give*, they are a signe I have not given yet, and consequently that my right is not transferred, but remaineth till I transferre it by some other Act. But if the words be of the time Present, or Past, as *I have given, or do give to be delivered to morrow*, then is my to morrows Right given away to day; and that by the vertue of the words, though there were no other argument of my will. And there is a great difference in the signification of these words, *Volc hoc tuum esse cras*, and *Cras dabo*; that is, between *I will that this be thine to morrow*, and, *I will give it thee to morrow*: For the word *I will*, in the former manner of speech, signifies a promise of an act of the will to Come: and therefore the former words, being of the Present, transferre future right: the later, that be of the Future, transferre nothing. But if there be other signes of the Will to transferre a Right, besides Words; then, though the gift be Free, yet may the Right be understood to passe by words of the future: as if a man propound a Prize to him that comes first to the end of a race, The gift is Free; and though the words be of the Future, yet the Right passeth: for if he would not have his words so be understood, he should not have let them runne.

In Contracts, the right passeth, not onely where the words are of the time Present, or Past; but also where they are of the Future: because all Contract is mutuall translation, or change of Right; and therefore he that promiseth onely, because he hath already received the benefit for which he promiseth, is to be understood as if he intended the Right should passe: for unlesse he had been content to have his words so understood, the other would not have performed his part first. And for that cause, in buying, and selling, and other acts of Contract, a Promise is equivalent to a Covenant; and therefore obligatory . . .

If a Covenant be made, wherein neither of the parties performe presently, but trust one another; in the condition of meer Nature, (which is a condition of Warre of every man against every man,) upon any reasonable suspition, it is Voyd: But if there be a common Power set over them both, with right and force sufficient to compell performance; it is not Voyd. For he that performeth first, has no assurance the other will performe after; because the bonds of words are too weak to bridle mens ambition, avarice, anger, and other Passions, without the feare of some coercive Power; which in the condition of meer Nature, where all men are equall, and judges of the justnesse of their own fears cannot possibly be supposed. And therefore he which performeth first, does but betray himselfe to his enemy; contrary to the Right (he can never abandon) of defending his life, and means of living.

But in a civill estate, where there is a Power set up to constrain those that would otherwise violate their faith, that feare is no more reasonable; and for that cause, he which by the Covenant is to perform first, is obliged so to do.

The cause of feare, which maketh such a Covenant invalid, must be alwayes something arising after the Covenant made; as some new fact, or other signe of the Will not to performe: else it cannot make the Covenant voyd. For that which could not hinder a man from promising, ought not to be admitted as a hindrance of performing . . .

To make Covenant with bruit Beasts, is impossible; because not understanding our speech, they understand not, nor accept of any translation of Right; nor can translate any Right to another: and without mutuall acceptation, there is no Covenant.

To make Covenant with God, is impossible, but by Meditation of such as God speaketh to, either by Revelation supernaturall, or by his Lieutenants that govern under him, and in his Name: For otherwise we know not whether our Covenants be accepted, or not. And therefore they that Vow any thing contrary to any law of Nature, Vow in vain; as being a thing unjust to pay such Vow. And if it be a thing commanded by the Law of Nature, it is not the Vow, but the Law that binds them.

The matter, or subject of a Covenant, is alwayes something that falleth under deliberation; (For to Covenant, is an act of the Will; that is to say an act and the last act, of deliberation;) and is therefore alwayes understood to be something to come; and which is judged Possible for him that Covenanteth, to performe.

And therefore, to promise that which is known to be Impossible, is no Covenant. But if that prove impossible afterwards, which before was thought possible, the Covenant is valid, and bindeth, (though not to the thing it selfe,) yet to the value; or, if that also be impossible, to the unfeigned endeavour of performing as much as is possible: for to more no man can be obliged. . . .

Covenants entred into by fear, in the condition of meer Nature, are obligatory. For example, if I Covenant to pay a ransome, or service for my life, to an enemy; I am bound by it. For it is a Contract, wherein one receiveth the benefit of life; the other is to receive money, or service for it; and consequently, where no other Law (as in the condition, of meer Nature) forbiddeth the performance, the Covenant is valid. Therefore

Prisoners of warre, if trusted with the payment of their Ransome, are obliged to pay it: And if a weaker Prince, make a disadvantageous peace with a stronger, for feare; he is bound to keep it; unlesse (as hath been sayd before) there ariseth some new, and just cause of feare, to renew the war. And even in Common-wealths, if I be forced to redeem my selfe from a Theefe by promising him money, I am bound to pay it, till the Civill Law discharge me. For whatsoever I may lawfully do without Obligation, the same I may lawfully Covenant to do through feare: and what I lawfully Covenant, I cannot lawfully break.

A former Covenant, makes voyd a later. For a man that hath passeth away his Right to one man to day, hath it not to passe to morrow to another: and therefore the later promose passeth no Right, but is null.

A Covenant not to defend my selfe from force, by force, is alwayes voyd. For (as I have shewed before) no man can transferre, or lay down his Right to save himselfe from Death, Wounds, and Imprisonment, (the avoyding whereof is the only End of laying down any Right, and therefore the promise of not resisting force, in no Covenant transferreth any right; nor is obliging. For though a man may Covenant this, *Unless I do so, or so, kill me*; he cannot Covenant thus, *Unless I do so, or so, I will not resist you, when you come to kill me*. For a man by nature chooseth the lesser evill, which is danger of death in resisting; rather than the greater, which is certain and present death in not resisting. And this is granted to be true by all men, in that they lead Criminals to Execution, and Prison, with armed men, notwithstanding that such Criminals have consented to the Law, by which they are condemned.) . . .

The force of Words, being (as I have formerly noted) too weak to hold men to the performance of their Covenants; there are in mans nature, but two imaginable helps to strengthen it. And those are either a Feare of the consequence of breaking their word; or a Glory, or Pride in appearing not to need to breake it. This later is a Generosity too rarely found to be presumed on, especially in the pursuers of Wealth, Command, or sensuall Pleasure; which are the greatest part of Mankind. The passion to be reckoned upon, is Fear; whereof there be two very genrall Objects: one, The Power of Spirits Invisible; the other, The Power of those men they shall therein Offend. Of these two, though the former be the greater Power, yet the feare of the later is commonly the greater Feare. The Feare of the former is in every man, his own Religion: which hath place in the nature of man before Civill Society. The later hath not so; at least not place enough, to keep men to their promises; because in the condition of meer Nature, the inequality of Power is not discerned, but by the event of Battell. So that before the time of Civill Society, or in the interruption thereof by Warre, there is nothing can strengthen a Covenant of Peace agreed on, against the temptations of Avarice, Ambition, Lust, or other strong desire, but the feare of that Invisible Power, which they every one Worship as God; and Feare as a Revenger of their perfidy. All therefore that can be done between two men not subject to Civill Power, is to put one another to swear by the God he feareth: Which *Swearing*, or OATH, is a *Forme of Speech added to a Promise; by which he that promiseth, signifieth, that unlesse he performe, he renounceth the mercy of his God, or calleth to him for vengeance on himselfe*. Such was the Heathen Forme, *Let* Jupiter *kill me, as I kill this Beast*. So is our Forme, *shall do thus, and thus, so help me God*. And this, with the Rites and Ceremonies, which every one useth in his own Religion, that the feare of breaking faith might be the greater.

By this it appears, that an Oath taken according to any other Forme, or Rite, then his, that sweareth, is in vain; and no Oath: And that there is no Swearing by any thing which the Swearer thinks not God. For though men have sometimes used to swear by their Kings, for feare, or flattery; yet they would have it thereby understood, they attributed to them Divine honour. And that Swearing unnecessarily by God, is but prophaning of his name: and Swearing by other things, as men do in common discourse, is not Swearing, but impious Custome, gotten by too much vehemence of talking.

It appears also, that the Oath addes nothing to the Obligation. For a Covenant, if lawfull, binds in the sight of God, without the Oath, as much as with it: if unlawfull, bindeth not at all; though it be confirmed with an Oath.

15
HUME

David Hume (1711–1776) was a pivotal figure in the Scottish Enlightenment and his skeptical positions regarding religion, knowledge, and the authority of rationality are still being debated. One of Hume's major claims in his *A Treatise of Human Nature* (1739) is that sentiment and passion play a fundamental role in human life, often shaping our attitudes and behavior in ways that ignore the strict rules of calculation and probability. For instance, in the first excerpt, Hume highlights certain forms of discourse upon which we regularly rely, but which are "unphilosophical" in that they do not seem grounded in logical derivation. Specifically, Hume notes the importance of not merely *what* we say, but *how* we phrase it. Minute differences in phrasing and emphasis might not change the propositional content of what we are saying, and so from a certain logical perspective, differentiating them might be uncalled for. But sometimes speaking obliquely instead of overtly can nevertheless have a moral dimension, however irrational that distinction might ultimately be. Sometimes using "secret insinuations" can be a more effective way of communicating, since doing so can better preserve existing relationships and social decorum. We are not deceived by such insinuations because we share certain "general rules" of discourse, and yet speaking indirectly in such a way can allow for the appearance of a kind of plausible deniability on the part of the speaker, as well as a way of saving face on the part of the hearer. Furthermore, we sometimes *wish* we were deceived, and so the insinuations allow us to pretend to a more flattering meaning than we rationally know the general rule really warrants. Thus, wielding language ethically requires not blunt truth-telling, but rather a finesse capable of discerning and adapting to particular contexts.

In the second excerpt, on the nature of promises, Hume articulates a kind of contractarian view, according to which promises (and the concomitant virtue of fidelity) would not exist, or at least would have no obligatory force, if not for human convention and enlightened self-interest. For this reason, Hume characterizes the ethics of promises as "artificial" as opposed to "natural"—although being unnatural in this respect does not mean that promises are in any way miraculous or uncommon, only that they are a result of social construction.[1] Promises are artificial both in terms of how they arise and also motivationally: unlike parenting, the obligations for which Hume says are grounded in natural sentiments that do not require any convention, fidelity and veracity by contrast are not primarily valued for their own sakes. This does not, however, mean that we have no good reasons to adhere to promises; it is just that we do so for the sake of extrinsic public good, rather than out of any intrinsic love of honesty. To demonstrate that promises are artificial, Hume argues indirectly by claiming that if promise-keeping *were* natural, it would entail certain conceptual or psychological absurdities.

As Hume sees it, promises consist solely in a "certain form of words" invented explicitly for the purpose of promising. Promises are thus what modern philosophers call "performative utterances," in that the uttering itself constitutes the act of promising (which Hume describes sarcastically as akin to the "magic" of transubstantiation in the Christian Eucharist). Thus, for Hume (unlike Hobbes), promises are always necessarily verbal or written, explicit, and overt: there can be no implicit promises per se. Moreover, even if the words of a promise are uttered with a disingenuous intention, the promise is still binding. The only exception for Hume seems to be when the words of a promise are uttered accidentally or unknowingly, in which case there is no obligation to uphold the promise since it was not truly a promise in the first place. Of course, Hume grants that the obligation to keep promises might not *feel* artificial to us, but this is because, in the aftermath of the promise-making, a new sentiment arises in us that makes us feel strongly committed to making good what we have promised—but we are motivated to do this only out of a sense of consistency and interest (both public and personal), and not for the sake of veracity itself. This appeal to the public interest also helps Hume

1. The language of "natural" versus "artificial" is downplayed in Hume's later *An Enquiry concerning the Principles of Morals* (1751) in favor of a more sophisticated four-fold division between virtues that are agreeable to oneself, agreeable to others, useful to oneself, and useful to others. Fidelity, veracity, and integrity are all primarily valued for their utility to others, although they can be inadvertently useful to oneself too since "after honesty, fidelity, truth . . . are once established upon this foundation [viz. promoting the interests of society], they are also considered as advantageous to the person himself, and as the source of that trust and confidence which can alone give a man any consideration in life." For Hume's later discussion of lying and truthfulness, see *An Enquiry concerning the Principles of Morals* §6 (1983), edited by J. B. Schneewind (Indianapolis: Hackett Publishing Company), p. 54.

differentiate the case of an injured person who makes a promise to a physician from a victim who makes a promise under duress to a robber. Although both involve a degree of coercion, only the former is binding because it is in line with the public good.

Some questions to think about as you read Hume include:

1. If "secret insinuations" are still understandable by reference to general rules of discourse, such that the hearer is not actually deceived, does this mean that the insinuations are not "lies"? Is there ever a point at which such social decorum can become disingenuous? Does the obligation to tell the truth ever trump the obligation to speak with social grace?
2. Hume claims that people are naturally disinclined to be honest. What evidence can you marshal for or against this claim? Further, is human nature in this regard truly as "inalterable" as he assumes?
3. For Hume, promises are almost exclusively transactional. Are there ways that a Humean framework could be extended to also address the ethics of lying and truthfulness more broadly? For example, based on what he says about promises, how might Hume regard lying to oneself, passively allowing others to be deceived, or being a trustworthy person generally?

A Treatise of Human Nature

Of Unphilosophical Probability (1.3.13)

Since we have instances, where general rules operate on the imagination even contrary to the judgment, we need not be surpriz'd to see their effects encrease, when conjoin'd with that latter faculty, and to observe that they bestow on the ideas they present to us a force superior to what attends any other. Every one knows, there is an indirect manner of insinuating praise or blame, which is much less shocking than the open flattery or censure of any person. However he may communicate his sentiments by such secret insinuations, and make them known with equal certainty as by the open discovery of them, 'tis certain that their influence is not equally strong and powerful. One who lashes me with conceal'd strokes of satire, moves not my indignation to such a degree, as if he flatly told me I was a fool and coxcomb; tho' I equally understand his meaning, as if he did. This difference is to be attributed to the influence of general rules.

Whether a person openly abuses me, or slyly intimates his contempt, in neither case do I immediately perceive his sentiment or opinion; and 'tis only by signs, that is, by its effects, I become sensible of it. The only difference, then, betwixt these two cases consists in this, that in the open discovery of his sentiments he makes use of signs, which are general and universal; and in the secret intimation employs such as are more singular and uncommon. The effect of this circumstance is, that the imagination, in running from the present impression to the absent idea, makes the transition with greater facility, and consequently conceives the object with greater force, where the connexion is common and universal, than where it is more rare and particular. Accordingly we may observe, that the open declaration of our sentiments is call'd the taking off the mask, as the secret intimation of our opinions is said to be the veiling of them. The difference betwixt an idea produc'd by a general connexion, and that arising from a particular one is here compar'd to the difference betwixt an impression and an idea. This difference in the imagination has a suitable effect on the passions; and this effect is augmented by another circumstance. A secret intimation of anger or contempt shows that we still have some consideration for the person, and avoid the directly abusing him. This makes a conceal'd satire less disagreeable; but still this depends on the same principle. For if an idea were not more feeble, when only intimated, it wou'd never be esteem'd a mark of greater respect to proceed in this method than in the other.

Sometimes scurrility is less displeasing than delicate satire, because it revenges us in a manner for the injury at the very time it is committed, by affording us a just reason to blame and contemn the person, who injures us. But this phænomenon likewise depends upon the same principle. For why do we blame all gross and injurious language, unless it be, because we esteem it contrary to good-breeding and humanity? And why is it contrary, unless it be more shocking than any delicate satire? The rules of good-breeding condemn whatever is openly disobliging, and gives a sensible pain and confusion to those, with whom we converse. After this is once establish'd, abusive language is universally blam'd, and gives less pain upon account of its coarseness and incivility, which render the person despicable, that employs it. It becomes less disagreeable, merely because originally it is more so; and 'tis more disagreeable, because it affords an inference by general and common rules, that are palpable and undeniable.

To this explication of the different influence of open and conceal'd flattery or satire, I shall add the consideration of another phænomenon, which is analogous to it. There are many particulars in the point of honour both of men and women, whose violations, when open and avow'd, the world never excuses, but which it is more apt to overlook, when the appearances are sav'd, and the transgression is secret and conceal'd. Even those, who know with equal certainty, that the fault is committed, pardon it more easily, when the proofs seem in some measure oblique and equivocal, than when they are direct and undeniable. The same idea is presented in both cases, and properly speaking, is equally assented to by the judgment; and yet its influence is different, because of the different manner, in which it is presented.

Now if we compare these two cases, of the *open* and *conceal'd* violations of the laws of honour, we shall find, that the difference betwixt them consists in this, that in the first case the sign, from which we infer the blameable action, is single, and suffices alone to be the foundation of our reasoning and judgment; whereas in the latter the signs are numerous, and decide little or nothing when alone and unaccompany'd with many minute circumstances, which are almost imperceptible. But 'tis certainly true, that any reasoning is always the more convincing, the more single and united it is to the eye, and the less exercise it gives to the imagination to collect all its parts, and run from them to the correlative idea, which forms the conclusion. The labour of the thought disturbs the regular progress of the sentiments, as we shall observe presently. The idea strikes not on us with such vivacity; and consequently has no such influence on the passions and imagination.

From the same principles we may account for those observations of the Cardinal de Retz, *that there are many things, in which the world wishes to be deceiv'd;* and *that it more easily excuses a person in acting than in talking contrary to the decorum of his profession and character.* A fault in words is commonly more open and distinct than one in actions, which admit of many palliating excuses, and decide not so clearly concerning the intention and views of the actor.

Of the Obligation of Promises (3.2.5)

That the rule of morality, which enjoins the performance of promises, is not *natural,* will sufficiently appear from these two propositions, which I proceed to prove, viz. *that a promise wou'd not be intelligible, before human conventions had establish'd it;* and *that even if it were intelligible, it wou'd not be attended with any moral obligation.*

I say, *first,* that a promise is not intelligible naturally, nor antecedent to human conventions; and that a man, unacquainted with society, cou'd never enter into any engagements with another, even tho' they cou'd perceive each other's thoughts by intuition. If promises be natural and intelligible, there must be some act of the mind attending these words, *I promise;* and on this act of the mind must the obligation depend. Let us, therefore, run over all the faculties of the soul, and see which of them is exerted in our promises.

The act of the mind, exprest by a promise, is not a *resolution* to perform any thing: For that alone never imposes any obligation. Nor is it a *desire* of such a performance: For we may bind ourselves without such a desire, or even with an aversion, declar'd and avow'd. Neither is it the *willing* of that action, which we promise to perform: For a promise always regards some future time, and the will has an influence only on present actions. It follows, therefore, that since the act of the mind, which enters into a promise, and produces its obligation, is neither the resolving, desiring, nor willing any particular performance, it must necessarily be the *willing* of that *obligation,* which arises from the promise. Nor is this only a conclusion of philosophy; but is entirely conformable to our common ways of thinking and of expressing ourselves, when we say that we are bound by our own consent, and that the obligation arises from our mere will and pleasure. The only question, then, is, whether there be not a manifest absurdity in supposing this act of the mind, and such an absurdity as no man cou'd fall into, whose ideas are not confounded by prejudice and the fallacious use of language?

All morality depends upon our sentiments; and when any action, or quality of the mind, pleases us *after a certain manner,* we say it is virtuous; and when the neglect, or non-performance of it, displeases us *after a like manner*, we say that we lie under an obligation to perform it. A change of the obligation supposes a change of the sentiment; and a creation of a new obligation supposes some new sentiment to arise. But 'tis certain we can naturally no more change our own sentiments, than the motions of the heavens; nor by a single act of our will, that is, by a promise, render any action agreeable or disagreeable, moral or immoral; which, without that act, wou'd have produc'd contrary impressions, or have been endow'd with different qualities. It wou'd be absurd, therefore, to will any new obligation, that is, any new sentiment of pain or pleasure; nor is it possible, that men cou'd naturally fall into so gross an absurdity. A promise, therefore, is *naturally* something altogether unintelligible, nor is there any act of the mind belonging to it.[2]

But, *secondly*, if there was any act of the mind belonging to it, it cou'd not *naturally* produce any obligation. This appears evidently from the foregoing reasoning. A promise creates a new obligation. A new obligation supposes new sentiments to arise. The will never creates new sentiments. There cou'd not naturally, therefore, arise any obligation from a promise, even supposing the mind cou'd fall into the absurdity of willing that obligation.

2. Were morality discoverable by reason, and not by sentiment, 'twou'd be still more evident, that promises cou'd make no alteration upon it. Morality I suppos'd to consist in relation. Every new imposition of morality, therefore, must arise from some new relation of objects; and consequently the will cou'd not produce *immediately* any change in morals, but cou'd have that effect only by producing a change upon the objects. But as the moral obligation of a promise is the pure effect of the will, without the least change in any part of the universe; it follows, that promises have no *natural* obligation.

Shou'd it be said, that this act of the will being in effect a new object, produces new relations and new duties; I wou'd answer, that this is a pure sophism, which may be detected by a very moderate share of accuracy and exactness. To will a new obligation, is to will a new relation of objects; and therefore, if this new relation of objects were form'd by the volition itself, we shou'd in effect will the volition; which is plainly absurd and impossible. The will has here no object to which it cou'd tend; but must return upon itself *in infinitum*. The new obligation depends upon new relations. The new relations depend upon a new volition. The new volition has for its object a new obligation, and consequently new relations, and consequently a new volition; which volition again has in view a new obligation, relation and volition, without any termination. 'Tis impossible, therefore, we cou'd ever will a new obligation; and consequently 'tis impossible the will cou'd ever accompany a promise, or produce a new obligation of morality.

The same truth may be prov'd still more evidently by that reasoning, which prov'd justice in general to be an artificial virtue. No action can be requir'd of us as our duty, unless there be implanted in human nature some actuating passion or motive, capable of producing the action. This motive cannot be the sense of duty. A sense of duty supposes an antecedent obligation: And where an action is not requir'd by any natural passion, it cannot be requir'd by any natural obligation; since it may be omitted without proving any defect or imperfection in the mind and temper, and consequently without any vice. Now 'tis evident we have no motive leading us to the performance of promises, distinct from a sense of duty. If we thought, that promises had no moral obligation, we never shou'd feel any inclination to observe them. This is not the case with the natural virtues. Tho' there was no obligation to relieve the miserable, our humanity wou'd lead us to it; and when we omit that duty, the immorality of the omission arises from its being a proof, that we want the natural sentiments of humanity. A father knows it to be his duty to take care of his children: But he has also a natural inclination to it. And if no human creature had that inclination, no one cou'd lie under any such obligation. But as there is naturally no inclination to observe promises, distinct from a sense of their obligation; it follows, that fidelity is no natural virtue, and that promises have no force, antecedent to human conventions.

If any one dissent from this, he must give a regular proof of these two propositions, viz. *that there is a peculiar act of the mind, annext to promises*; and *that consequent to this act of the mind, there arises an inclination to perform, distinct from a sense of duty*. I presume, that it is impossible to prove either of these two points; and therefore I venture to conclude, that promises are human inventions, founded on the necessities and interests of society.

In order to discover these necessities and interests, we must consider the same qualities of human nature, which we have already found to give rise to the preceding laws of society. Men being naturally selfish, or endow'd only with a confin'd generosity, they are not easily induc'd to perform any action for the interest of strangers, except with a view to some reciprocal advantage, which they had no hope of obtaining but by such a performance. Now as it frequently happens, that these mutual performances cannot be finish'd at the same instant, 'tis necessary, that one party be contented to remain in uncertainty, and depend upon the gratitude of the other for a return of kindness. But so much corruption is there among men, that, generally speaking, this becomes but a slender security; and as the benefactor is here suppos'd to bestow his favours with a view to self-interest, this both takes off from the obligation, and sets an example of selfishness, which is the true mother of ingratitude. Were we, therefore, to follow the natural course of our passions and inclinations, we shou'd perform but few actions for the advantage of others, from disinterested views; because we are naturally very limited in our kindness and affection: And we shou'd perform as few of that kind, out of a regard to interest; because we cannot depend upon their gratitude. Here then is the mutual commerce of good offices in a manner lost among mankind, and every one reduc'd to his own skill and industry for his well-being and subsistence. The invention of the law of nature, concerning the *stability* of possession, has already render'd men tolerable to each other; that of the *transference* of property and possession by consent has begun to render them mutually advantageous: But still these laws, however strictly observ'd, are not sufficient to render them so serviceable to each other, as by nature they are fitted to become. Tho' possession be *stable,* men may often reap but small advantage from it, while they are possess'd of a greater quantity of any species of goods than they have occasion for, and at the same time suffer by the want of others. The *transference* of property, which is the proper remedy for this inconvenience, cannot remedy it entirely; because it can only take place with regard to such objects as are *present* and *individual,* but not to such as are *absent* or *general*. One cannot transfer the property of a particular house, twenty leagues distant; because the consent cannot be attended with delivery, which is a requisite circumstance. Neither can one transfer the property of ten bushels of corn, or five hogsheads of wine, by the mere expression and consent; because these are only general terms and have no direct relation to any particular heap of corn, or barrels of wine. Besides, the commerce of mankind is not confin'd to the barter of commodities, but may extend to services and actions, which we may exchange to our mutual interest and advantage. Your corn is ripe to-day; mine will be so to-morrow. 'Tis profitable for us both, that I shou'd labour with you to-day, and that you shou'd aid me to-morrow. I have no kindness for you, and know you have as little for me. I will not, therefore, take any pains upon your account and shou'd I labour with you upon my own account, in expectation of a return, I know I shou'd be disappointed, and that I shou'd in vain depend upon your gratitude. Here then I leave you to labour alone: You treat me in the same manner. The seasons change; and both of us lose our harvests for want of mutual confidence and security.

All this is the effect of the natural and inherent principles and passions of human nature; and as these passions and principles are inalterable, it may be thought, that our conduct, which depends on them, must be so too, and that 'twou'd be in vain, either for moralists or politicians, to tamper with us, or attempt to change the usual course of our actions, with a view to public interest. And indeed, did the success of their designs depend upon their success in correcting the selfishness and ingratitude of men, they wou'd never make any progress, unless aided by omnipotence, which is alone able to new-mould the human mind, and change its character in such fundamental articles. All they can pretend to do, is, to give a new direction to those natural passions, and teach us that we can better satisfy our appetites in an oblique and artificial manner, than by their headlong and impetuous motion. Hence I learn to do a service to another, without bearing him any real kindness; because I foresee, that he will return my service, in expectation of another of the same kind, and in order to maintain the same correspondence of good offices with me or with others. And accordingly, after I have serv'd him, and he is in possession of the advantage arising from my action, he is induc'd to perform his part, as foreseeing the consequences of his refusal.

But tho' this self-interested commerce of men begins to take place, and to predominate in society, it does not entirely abolish the more generous and noble intercourse of friendship and good offices. I may still do services to such persons as I love, and am more particularly acquainted with, without any prospect of advantage; and they may make me a return in the same manner, without any view but that of recompensing my past services. In order, therefore, to distinguish those two different sorts of commerce, the interested and the disinterested, there is a *certain form of words* invented for the former, by which we bind ourselves to the performance of any action. This form of words constitutes what we call a *promise,* which is the sanction of the interested commerce of mankind. When a man says *he promises any thing,* he in effect expresses a *resolution* of performing it; and along with that, by making use of this *form of words,* subjects himself to the penalty of never being trusted again in case of failure. A resolution is the natural act of the mind, which promises express: But were there no more than a resolution in the case, promises wou'd only declare our former motives, and wou'd not create any new motive or obligation. They are the conventions of men, which create a new motive, when experience has taught us, that human affairs wou'd be conducted much more for mutual advantage, were there certain *symbols* or *signs* instituted, by which we might give each other security of our conduct in any particular incident. After these signs are instituted, whoever uses them is immediately bound by his interest to execute his engagements, and must never expect to be trusted any more, if he refuse to perform what he promis'd.

Nor is that knowledge, which is requisite to make mankind sensible of this interest in the *institution* and *observance* of promises, to be esteem'd superior to the capacity of human nature, however savage and uncultivated. There needs but a very little practice of the world, to make us perceive all these consequences and advantages. The shortest experience of society discovers them to every mortal; and when each individual perceives the same sense of interest in all his fellows, he immediately performs his part of any contract, as being assur'd, that they will not be wanting in theirs. All of them, by concert, enter into a scheme of actions, calculated for common benefit, and agree to be true to their word; nor is there any thing requisite to form this concert or convention, but that every one have a sense of interest in the faithful fulfilling of engagements, and express that sense to other members of the society. This immediately causes that interest to operate upon them; and interest is the *first* obligation to the performance of promises.

Afterwards a sentiment of morals concurs with interest, and becomes a new obligation upon mankind. This sentiment of morality, in the performance of promises, arises from the same principles as that in the abstinence from the property of others. *Public interest, education,* and *the artifices of politicians,* have the same effect in both cases. The difficulties, that occur to us, in supposing a moral obligation to attend promises, we either surmount or elude. For instance; the expression of a resolution is not commonly suppos'd to be obligatory; and we cannot readily conceive how the making use of a certain form of words shou'd be able to cause any material difference. Here, therefore, we *feign* a new act of the mind, which we call the *willing* an obligation; and on this we suppose the morality to depend. But we have prov'd already, that there is no such act of the mind, and consequently that promises impose no natural obligation.

To confirm this, we may subjoin some other reflections concerning that will, which is supposed to enter into a promise, and to cause its obligation. 'Tis evident, that the will alone is never suppos'd to cause the obligation, but must be express'd by words or signs, in order to impose a tye upon any man. The expression being once brought in as subservient to the will, soon becomes the principal part of the promise; nor will a man be less bound by his word, tho' he secretly give a different direction to his intention, and withhold himself both from a resolution, and from willing an obligation. But tho' the expression makes on most occasions the whole of the promise, yet it does not always so; and one, who shou'd make use of any expression, of which he knows not the meaning, and which he uses without any intention of binding himself, wou'd not certainly be bound by it. Nay, tho' he knows its meaning, yet if he uses it in jest only, and with such signs as show evidently he has no serious intention of binding himself, he wou'd not lie under any obligation of performance; but 'tis necessary, that the words be a perfect expression of the will, without any contrary signs. Nay, even this we must not carry so far as to imagine, that one, whom, by our quickness of understanding, we conjecture, from certain signs, to have an intention of deceiving us, is not bound by his expression or verbal promise, if we accept of it; but must limit this conclusion to those cases, where the signs are of a different kind from those of deceit. All these contradictions are easily accounted for, if the obligation of promises be merely a human invention for the convenience of society; but will never be explain'd, if it be something *real* and *natural*, arising from any action of the mind or body.

I shall farther observe, that since every new promise imposes a new obligation of morality on the person who promises, and since this new obligation arises from his will; 'tis one of the most mysterious and incomprehensible operations that can possibly be imagin'd, and may even be compar'd to *transubstantiation*, or *holy orders*,[3] where a certain form of words, along with a certain intention, changes entirely the nature of an external object, and even of a human creature. But tho' these mysteries be so far alike, 'tis very remarkable, that they differ widely in other particulars, and that this difference may be regarded as a strong proof of the difference of their origins. As the obligation of promises is an invention for the interest of society, 'tis warp'd into as many different forms as that interest requires, and even runs into direct contradictions, rather than lose sight of its object. But as those other monstrous doctrines are mere priestly inventions, and have no public interest in view, they are less disturb'd in their progress by new obstacles; and it must be own'd, that, after the first absurdity, they follow more directly the current of reason and good sense. Theologians clearly perceiv'd, that the external form of words, being mere sound, requires an intention to make them have any efficacy; and that this intention being once consider'd as a requisite circumstance, its absence must equally prevent the effect, whether avo'd or conceal'd, whether sincere or deceitful. Accordingly they have commonly determin'd, that the intention of the priest makes the sacrament, and that when he

3. I mean so far, as holy orders are suppos'd to produce the *indelible character*. In other respects they are only a legal qualification.

secretly withdraws his intention, he is highly criminal in himself; but still destroys the baptism, or communion, or holy orders. The terrible consequences of this doctrine were not able to hinder its taking place; as the inconvenience of a similar doctrine, with regard to promises, have prevented that doctrine from establishing itself. Men are always more concern'd about the present life than the future; and are apt to think the smallest evil, which regards the former, more important than the greatest, which regards the latter.

We may draw the same conclusion, concerning the origin of promises, from the *force*, which is suppos'd to invalidate all contracts, and to free us from their obligation. Such a principle is a proof, that promises have no natural obligation, and are mere artificial contrivances for the convenience and advantage of society. If we consider aright of the matter, force is not essentially different from any other motive of hope or fear, which may induce us to engage our word, and lay ourselves under obligation. A man, dangerously wounded, who promises a competent sum to a surgeon to cure him, wou'd certainly be bound to performance; tho' the case be not so much different from that of one, who promises a sum to a robber, as to produce so great a difference in our sentiments of morality, if these sentiments were not built entirely on public interest and convenience.

Part Three

What Is the Value of Truthfulness?

16

LOCKE & BACON

John Locke (1632–1704) is one of the principal exponents of the school of philosophy known as British Empiricism. Locke's thinking is foundational to modern political philosophy as well as to epistemology and philosophy of mind within the Anglo-American tradition. His two *Treatises of Government* influenced subsequent revolutions both in the United States and in France. In *An Essay Concerning Human Understanding,* he provides an extended articulation of his empiricism, arguing that knowledge comes not from innate ideas, but from experience of the world. As an empiricist, Locke is following in the tradition of Francis Bacon (1561–1626), the English philosopher and statesman whose focus on the proper method of inductive reasoning (as opposed to Aristotelian syllogistic reasoning) helped give rise to the scientific method as we know it today.

In book 3 of *An Essay Concerning Human Understanding,* Locke discusses the use of language, focusing mostly on the importance of having clear definitions of words and of maintaining proper and clear usage. In the selection included here, Locke laments the relative preference given by people to rhetoric over the unadulterated pursuit of truth. In this he seems to agree with Socrates' critique of oratory from the *Gorgias* (see chapter 8 of this volume): however pleasurable the clever use of words may be, there is something blameworthy in having as one's goal flattery instead of truth.

Bacon, in the selection from his earlier work *The Essays or Counsels, Civil and Moral,* appears more ambivalent about the use of rhetoric than is Locke. Bacon acknowledges that there are understandable reasons why people sometimes prefer falsity: ignorance of the truth can enable one to continue in pleasant and harmless false beliefs. Despite this concession, however, Bacon points out that there is still something problematic about preferring falsity to truth. He uses the analogy of blending metals to make an alloy for minting coins. Mixing another metal with gold may make the coin more durable, but the quality of the gold is still degraded in the process: the coin may be more useful, but it is less valuable.

Bacon then considers three different methods by which we can keep the truth from others: secrecy, dissimulation, and simulation. He recognizes an important and valuable role for secrecy in maintaining the confidence of others. As a result of the need for secrecy, however, it follows that dissimulation is at least sometimes permissible as well: for it is simply not always possible to avoid revealing secrets merely by maintaining silence. In these cases, Bacon argues, it is acceptable to use careful word choice in order to lead someone to a false belief. When it comes to misleading more directly, which Bacon calls "simulation" and which includes outright lies and falsehoods, even though it can be as useful as dissimulation, Bacon is more hesitant to condone the practice. Even here, though, he avoids the absolutism seen in many other philosophers: he leaves room for the possibility of extreme circumstances that necessitate lying.

As you read the selections from these two thinkers, consider the following questions:

1. Is Locke correct that the prevalence of rhetoric indicates that people love both to deceive and to be deceived? Could there be other explanations for this prevalence?
2. Consider the advantages and disadvantages of simulation and dissimulation that Bacon identifies: under what conditions would the advantages outweigh the disadvantages, and vice versa?
3. Can Bacon's threefold distinction between secrecy, dissimulation, and simulation help to illuminate the discussions of other philosophers from this volume? Give examples.

An Essay Concerning Human Understanding

Of the Abuse of Words (Book III, Chapter 10)

34. Since wit and fancy find easier entertainment in the world than dry truth and real knowledge, figurative speeches and allusion in language will hardly be admitted as an imperfection or abuse of it. I confess, in discourses where we seek rather pleasure and delight than information and improvement, such ornaments as are borrowed from them can scarce pass for faults. But yet if we would speak of things as they are, we must allow that all the art of rhetoric, besides order and clearness; all the artificial and figurative application of words eloquence hath invented, are nothing else but to insinuate wrong ideas, move the passions, and thereby mislead the judgment; and so indeed are perfect cheats: and therefore, however laudable or allowable oratory may render them in harangues and popular addresses, they are certainly, in all discourses that pretend to inform or instruct, wholly to be avoided; and where truth and knowledge are concerned, cannot but be thought a great fault, either of the language or person that makes use of them. What and how various they are, will be superfluous here to take notice; the books of rhetoric which abound in the world, will instruct those who want to be informed: only I cannot but observe how little the preservation and improvement of truth and knowledge is the care and concern of mankind; since the arts of fallacy are endowed and preferred. It is evident how much men love to deceive and be deceived, since rhetoric, that powerful instrument of error and deceit, has its established professors, is publicly taught, and has always been had in great reputation: and I doubt not but it will be thought great boldness, if not brutality, in me to have said thus much against it. Eloquence, like the fair sex, has too prevailing beauties in it to suffer itself ever to be spoken against. And it is in vain to find fault with those arts of deceiving, wherein men find pleasure to be deceived.

From The Essays or Counsels, Civil and Moral

Of Truth

What is truth? said jesting Pilate, and would not stay for an answer. Certainly there be, that delight in giddiness, and count it a bondage to fix a belief; affecting free-will in thinking, as well as in acting. And though the sects of philosophers of that kind be gone, yet there remain certain discoursing wits, which are of the same veins, though there be not so much blood in them, as was in those of the ancients. But it is not only the difficulty and labor, which men take in finding out of truth, nor again, that when it is found, it imposeth upon men's thoughts, that doth bring lies in favor; but a natural, though corrupt love, of the lie itself. One of the later school of the Grecians, examineth the matter, and is at a stand, to think what should be in it, that men should love lies; where neither they make for pleasure, as with poets, nor for advantage, as with the merchant; but for the lie's sake. But I cannot tell; this same truth, is a naked, and open day-light, that doth not show the masks, and mummeries, and triumphs, of the world, half so stately and daintily as candle-lights. Truth may perhaps come to the price of a pearl, that showeth best by day; but it will not rise to the price of a diamond, or carbuncle, that showeth best in varied lights. A mixture of a lie doth ever add pleasure. Doth any man doubt, that if there were taken out of men's minds, vain opinions, flattering hopes, false valuations, imaginations as one would, and the like, but it would leave the minds, of a number of men, poor shrunken things, full of melancholy and indisposition, and unpleasing to themselves?

One of the fathers, in great severity, called poesy vinum daemonum, because it fireth the imagination; and yet, it is but with the shadow of a lie. But it is not the lie that passeth through the mind, but the lie that sinketh in, and settleth in it, that doth the hurt; such as we spake of before. But howsoever these things are thus in men's depraved judgments, and affections, yet truth, which only doth judge itself, teacheth that the inquiry of truth, which is the love-making, or wooing of it, the knowledge of truth, which is the presence of it, and the belief of truth, which is the enjoying of it, is the sovereign good of human nature. The first creature of God, in the works of the days, was the light of the sense; the last, was the light of reason; and his sabbath work ever since, is the illumination of his Spirit. First he breathed light, upon the face of the matter or chaos; then he breathed light, into the face of man; and still he breatheth and inspireth light, into the face of his chosen. The poet, that beautified the sect, that was otherwise inferior to the rest, saith yet excellently well: It is a pleasure, to stand upon the shore, and to see ships tossed upon the sea; a pleasure, to stand in the window of a castle, and to see a battle, and the adventures thereof below: but no pleasure is comparable to the standing upon the vantage ground of truth (a hill not to be commanded, and where the air is always clear and serene), and to see the errors, and wanderings, and mists, and tempests, in the vale below; so always that this prospect be with pity, and not with swelling, or pride. Certainly, it is heaven upon earth, to have a man's mind move in charity, rest in providence, and turn upon the poles of truth.

To pass from theological, and philosophical truth, to the truth of civil business; it will be acknowledged, even by those that practise it not, that clear, and round dealing, is the honor of man's nature; and that mixture of falsehoods, is like alloy in coin of gold and silver, which may make the metal work the better, but it embaseth it. For these winding, and crooked courses, are the goings of the serpent; which goeth basely upon the belly, and not upon the feet. There is no vice, that doth so cover a man with shame, as to be found false and perfidious. And therefore Montaigne saith prettily, when he inquired the reason, why the word of the lie should be such a disgrace, and such an odious charge? Saith he, If it be well weighed, to say that a man lieth, is as much to say, as that he is brave towards God, and a coward towards men. For a lie faces God, and shrinks from man. Surely the wickedness of falsehood, and breach of faith, cannot possibly be so highly expressed, as in that it shall be the last peal, to call the judgments of God upon the generations of men; it being foretold, that when Christ cometh, he shall not find faith upon the earth.

Of Simulation and Dissimulation

Dissimulation is but a faint kind of policy, or wisdom; for it asketh a strong wit, and a strong heart, to know when to tell truth, and to do it. Therefore it is the weaker sort of politics, that are the great dissemblers.

Tacitus saith, Livia sorted well with the arts of her husband, and dissimulation of her son; attributing arts or policy to Augustus, and dissimulation to Tiberius. And again, when Mucianus encourageth Vespasian, to take arms against Vitellius, he saith, We rise not against the piercing judgment of Augustus, nor the extreme caution or closeness of Tiberius. These properties, of arts or policy, and dissimulation or closeness, are indeed habits and faculties several, and to be distinguished. For if a man have that penetration of judgment, as he can discern what things are to be laid open, and what to be secreted, and what to be showed at half lights, and to whom and when (which indeed are arts of state, and arts of life, as Tacitus well calleth them), to him, a habit of dissimulation is a hinderance and a poorness. But if a man cannot obtain to that judgment, then it is left to him generally, to be close, and a dissembler. For where a man cannot choose, or vary in particulars, there it is good to take the safest, and wariest way, in general; like the going softly, by one that cannot well see. Certainly the ablest men that ever were, have had all an openness, and frankness, of dealing; and a name of certainty and veracity; but then they were like horses well managed; for they could tell passing well, when to stop or turn; and at such times, when they thought the case indeed required dissimulation, if then they used it, it came to pass that the former opinion, spread abroad, of their good faith and clearness of dealing, made them almost invisible.

There be three degrees of this hiding and veiling of a man's self. The first, closeness, reservation, and secrecy; when a man leaveth himself without observation, or without hold to be taken, what he is. The second, dissimulation, in the negative; when a man lets fall signs and arguments, that he is not, that he is. And the third, simulation, in the affirmative; when a man industriously and expressly feigns and pretends to be, that he is not.

For the first of these, secrecy; it is indeed the virtue of a confessor. And assuredly, the secret man heareth many confessions. For who will open himself, to a blab or a babbler? But if a man be thought secret, it inviteth discovery; as the more close air sucketh in the more open; and as in confession, the revealing is not for worldly use, but for the ease of a man's heart, so secret men come to the knowledge of many things in that kind; while men rather discharge their minds, than impart their minds. In few words, mysteries are due to secrecy. Besides (to say truth) nakedness is uncomely, as well in mind as body; and it addeth no small reverence, to men's manners and actions, if they be not altogether open. As for talkers and futile persons, they are commonly vain and credulous withal. For he that talketh what he knoweth, will also talk what he knoweth not. Therefore set it down, that an habit of secrecy, is both politic and moral. And in this part, it is good that a man's face give his tongue leave to speak. For the discovery of a man's self, by the tracts of his countenance, is a great weakness and betraying; by how much it is many times more marked, and believed, than a man's words.

For the second, which is dissimulation; it followeth many times upon secrecy, by a necessity; so that he that will be secret, must be a dissembler in some degree. For men are too cunning, to suffer a man to keep an indifferent carriage between both, and to be secret, without swaying the balance on either side. They will so beset a man with questions, and draw him on, and pick it out of him, that, without an absurd silence, he must show an inclination one way; or if he do not, they will gather as much by his silence, as by his speech. As for equivocations, or oraculous speeches, they cannot hold out long. So that no man can be secret, except he give himself a little scope of dissimulation; which is, as it were, but the skirts or train of secrecy.

But for the third degree, which is simulation, and false profession; that I hold more culpable, and less politic; except it be in great and rare matters. And therefore a general custom of simulation (which is this last degree) is a vice, using either of a natural falseness or fearfulness, or of a mind that hath some main faults, which because a man must needs disguise, it maketh him practise simulation in other things, lest his hand should be out of use.

The great advantages of simulation and dissimulation are three. First, to lay asleep opposition, and to surprise. For where a man's intentions are published, it is an alarum, to call up all that are against them. The second is, to reserve to a man's self a fair retreat. For if a man engage himself by a manifest declaration, he must go through or take a fall. The third is, the better to discover the mind of another. For to him that opens himself, men will hardly show themselves adverse; but will fair let him go on, and turn their freedom of speech, to freedom of thought. And therefore it is a good shrewd proverb of the Spaniard, Tell a lie and find a troth. As if there were no way of discovery, but by simulation. There be also three disadvantages, to set it even. The first, that simulation and dissimulation commonly carry with them a show of fearfulness, which in any business, doth spoil the feathers, of round flying up to the mark. The second, that it puzzleth and perplexeth the conceits of many, that perhaps would otherwise co-operate with him; and makes a man walk almost alone, to his own ends. The third and greatest is, that it depriveth a man of one of the most principal instruments for action; which is trust and belief. The best composition and temperature, is to have openness in fame and opinion; secrecy in habit; dissimulation in seasonable use; and a power to feign, if there be no remedy.

17
MAHĀBHĀRATA, ŚĀNTI PARVAN

Our final selection from the *Mahābhārata* comes from the eighth book (the Śānti Parvan). The scene occurs at the end of the war, after the Pāṇḍavas have secured victory by following Krishna's advice (see the introduction to chapter 4 of this volume for context). In this scene, Yudhiṣṭhira questions Bhīṣma about the nature of dharma. Bhīṣma is the great uncle of the Pāṇḍavas and the Kauravas and is recognized by all as the greatest human authority on dharma. Even though he was defeated as the initial commander of the Kaurava army, he is still alive at the end of the war, lying on a bed of arrows and awaiting the appropriate time to die.[1] In this condition he agrees to answer Yudhiṣṭhira's questions, a way of providing one final lesson to Yudhiṣṭhira as the latter prepares to become king.

Yudhiṣṭhira questions Bhīṣma extensively regarding the details about the proper conduct of kings and members of other castes, about the conduct that is suitable to the various stages of life, about the proper running of a state in times of peace and times of war, and about the treatment of friends and enemies. Eventually, Yudhiṣṭhira's inquiry turns to the nature of truth, which is where our selection begins. In his answer Bhīṣma says that there are thirteen aspects of truth. The list he then provides contains some elements that are bound to seem foreign to Western philosophical sensibilities, such as modesty and compassion. One way to make sense of the list is to read it as a list of traits of truthful people, rather than of truth itself. But another way is to see it as not accepting the idea, common in contemporary thinking about truth, that truth is primarily something that is predicated of sentences, propositions, or utterances. That is, Bhīṣma may be articulating a non-epistemic theory of truth—one in which people are the primary bearers of truth and falsity, sentences and/or propositions only derivatively so.

As you read the list and Bhīṣma's explanation of it, consider the following questions:

1. How plausible do you find the claim that truth is the most important of all duties? Other philosophers who are

1. Earlier in the epic Bhīṣma's father granted him a boon that allowed him to choose the time of his death.

included in this volume would clearly disagree with this claim. Who do you think has the stronger argument in favor of their position?

2. Many of the elements in Bhīṣma's list seem to be aspects not of truth, but rather of the truthful person. How might articulating a list of traits of truthful people shed light on the nature of truth itself?
3. Consider this selection in light of the other selections from the *Mahābhārata* that are included in this volume (chapters 4 and 7). Does there seem to be a single overarching account of truth that can be gleaned from the selections, taken together? Does Bhīṣma's discussion here help you to make any more sense of Kauśika's dilemma or of the deception of Droṇa?

Mahābhārata

Śānti Chapter, Section 162

Yudhiṣṭhira said, "Brahmins and Ṛṣis and Pitṛs and the gods all applaud the duty of truth. I desire to hear of truth. Discourse to me upon it, O grandsire! What are the indications, O king, of truth? How may it be acquired? What is gained by practicing truth, and how? Tell me all this."

Bhīṣma said, "A confusion of the duties of the four orders is never applauded. That which is called truth always exists in a pure and unmingled state in every one of those four orders. With those that are good, truth is always a duty. Indeed, truth is an eternal duty. One should reverentially bow unto truth. Truth is the highest refuge. Truth is duty; truth is penance; truth is yoga; and truth is the eternal Brahmā. Truth has been said to be sacrifice of a high order. Everything rests upon truth. I shall now tell you the forms of truth one after another, and its indications also in due order. It behooves you to hear also as to how truth may be acquired. In all the world, son of Bharata, truth takes thirteen forms. Undoubtedly, it is truth itself, as well as fairness and self-control, unselfishness, tolerance, modesty, patience, and benevolence. It is, moreover, renunciation, contemplation, nobility, constant unwavering steadfastness, and non-violence. These, great king, are the thirteen aspects of truth.

Truth is immutable, eternal, and unchangeable. It may be acquired through practices which do not militate against any of the other virtues. It may also be acquired through yoga. When desire and aversion, as well as lust and wrath, are destroyed, that attribute in consequence of which one is able to look upon one's own self and one's enemy, upon one's benefit and one's harm, with an unchanging eye, is called fairness. Self-control consists in never wishing for another's possessions, steadiness and strength of self, and freedom from distress. It may be acquired through knowledge. Devotion to the practice of generosity and the observance of all duties are regarded by the wise as constituting unselfishness. One becomes unselfish by constant devotion to truth. As regards tolerance and intolerance, it should be stated that tolerance is the attribute through which an esteemed and good man endures both what is agreeable and disagreeable. This virtue may well be acquired through the practice of truth. That virtue in consequence of which an intelligent man, contented in mind and speech, achieves many good deeds and never incurs the censure of others, is called modesty. It is acquired through the aid of righteousness. That virtue which forgives for the sake of virtue and benefit is called benevolent patience. It is a form of forgiveness. It is acquired through patience, and its purpose is to hearten others. The casting off of affection as also of all earthly possessions, is called renunciation. Renunciation can never be acquired except by one who is divested of anger and malice. That virtue in consequence of which one does good, with watchfulness and care, to all creatures is called nobility. It has no particular shape, but consists in the divestment of all selfish attachments. That virtue owing to which one remains unchanged in happiness and misery is called steadfastness. That wise man who desires his own good always practices this virtue. One should always practice tolerance and devotedness to truth. That man of wisdom who succeeds in casting off joy and fear and wrath succeeds in acquiring steadfastness. Nonviolence as regards all creatures in thought, word, and deed, kindness, and gift, is the eternal duty of those who are good.

These thirteen attributes, though apparently distinct from one another, have but one and the same form, *viz.*, truth. All these, O Bharata, support truth and strengthen it. It is impossible, O monarch, to exhaust the merits of truth. It is for these reasons that the Brahmins, the Pitṛs, and the gods, applaud truth. There is no duty which is higher than truth, and no sin more heinous than untruth. Indeed, truth is the very foundation of righteousness. For this reason, one should never destroy truth. From truth proceed gifts, and sacrifice with presents, as well as the threefold fire-sacrifices, the Vedas, and everything else that leads to righteousness. One thousand horse-sacrifices were once weighed against truth in the balance. Truth weighed heavier than one thousand horse-sacrifices."

18

"DISCOURSE ON THE PARABLE OF THE WATER SNAKE"

The "Discourse on the Parable of the Water Snake" is an early Buddhist sutra and comes from the *Majjhima Nikāya,* the same collection of teachings that contains the "Discourse to Prince Abhaya" (chapter 12 of this volume). The latter half of the Snake Sutra, as it is often called, contains one of the clearest early articulations of the Buddhist no-self teaching. But the first half of the sutra—the part that is included in the present selection—discusses different orientations to truth and the dangers that can attend an attachment to truth.

The sutra opens with the monk Ariṭṭha advocating a decidedly unorthodox interpretation of the Buddha's teaching. Unable to convince him to retract his view, the other monks bring Ariṭṭha to the Buddha for reckoning. After the Buddha criticizes Ariṭṭha for holding this pernicious view, he uses the gathering of the monks as an opportunity to discourse on the role and relevance of truth within the study of the *dhamma.*[1]

What follows are two of the more powerful parables from the early Buddhist literature. The first is the parable of the water snake, for which the discourse is named. In this parable the Buddha compares his teaching to a poisonous water snake. Just as there are better and worse ways to grab hold of a snake, so too are there better and worse ways of attempting to grasp the truth of the Buddha's teachings. Those who study the teachings with the purpose of sounding worldly and educated, or of being able to win arguments, have missed the point of learning, the Buddha says, and end up doing themselves and others more harm than good.

It is worth taking a moment to unpack this parable a bit before moving on to the second one. While it would be easy to equate an incorrect grasp of the truth with holding a false belief, this does not seem to be what the Buddha has in mind here. It is important to note that an incorrect grasp of a snake is still a grasp *of a snake*; the parable is not of a person grabbing hold of a rope and mistaking it for a snake. So the

1. *Dhamma* (Sanskrit *dharma*) is the truth about the world, as reflected in Buddhist teaching.

harm that will befall people for their incorrect grasp of the teachings seems not to be predicated on them coming to hold false beliefs, but rather on their motivation for seeking the truth and for telling it to others. The error lies not in mistaking falsehood for truth, but rather in the reason one has for seeking the truth to begin with. The problem may well be connected with what we learn from the "Discourse to Prince Abhaya": whereas the Buddha knows the correct time to utter true statements and the correct time to remain silent, those who seek the truth for more selfish purposes may not.

The parable of the raft, which follows that of the water snake, serves to highlight this aspect of the text. In it the Buddha compares his teaching to a raft, with which a person is able to cross over from the dangerous side of a stream to safety. While the raft is quite valuable for use in crossing over the river, it would be absurd to carry the raft on one's back for the remainder of the journey simply because it had once been useful. According to the Buddha, the same holds true of the *dhamma*. In the right circumstances, the *dhamma* is quite useful and beneficial, even helping those who hear it to achieve enlightenment. But even the *dhamma* can become a hindrance, a burden to one who is too attached to it. Imagine, for instance, a Buddhist monk who spends so much time studying a particular sutra with great care and diligence, attempting to understand every subtlety and nuance of the teaching, that he neglects his responsibilities to his fellow monks. Such a person would do well to allow compassion to serve as a corrective on the drive for truth.

Viewed in this light, Ariṭṭha's problem is not so much that he is clinging to a *false* view, but rather that he is clinging to a view at all. The point is not that one should abandon the pursuit of truth and become a radical skeptic (though some later Buddhists seem to have taken this approach), but rather that other values exist, which sometimes compete with the value of truth. If, as the Buddha says in explicating the second Noble Truth, attachment is the source of suffering, then perhaps we would do well to abandon our attachment even to truth.

In this sutra the Buddha is clearly criticizing Ariṭṭha for his wrong view. But it is worth considering whether the snake and raft images might be understood as providing a critique of the other monks, as well. Could the monks' inability to change Ariṭṭha's mind and their insistence on bringing him before the Buddha be seen as evidence that they don't have the correct grasp of the truth either?

As you read the selection, consider also the following questions:

1. What could be some of the negative consequences of a wrong grasp of truth? Can you think of circumstances in

which it would be better to hold a false belief than to hold a true belief in the wrong way?

2. To what extent does the persuasiveness of this parable depend upon accepting a Buddhist worldview?
3. Could Ariṭṭha's problem be seen as highlighting a problem with the Buddha's approach to truth? If he knows that the Buddha uses skillful means, couldn't he reasonably think that the Buddha is doing just that in describing the hindrances as hindrances?

"Discourse on the Parable of the Water Snake"

1. Thus have I heard. At one time, the Exalted One[1] was dwelling at Sāvatthi in the Jeta Grove in Anāthapiṇḍika's park. At that time, there was a *bhikkhu*[2] named Ariṭṭha, who was formerly a vulture trainer,[3] in whom a pernicious view such as this had arisen: "As I understand the *dhamma* taught by the Exalted One, those things that are called obstructions[4] by the Exalted One are not capable of obstructing one who pursues them."

Several *bhikkhus* heard that: "There is a *bhikkhu* named Ariṭṭha, who was formerly a vulture trainer, in whom a pernicious view such as this had arisen: 'As I understand the *dhamma* taught by the Exalted One, those things that are called obstructions by the Exalted One are not capable of obstructing one who pursues them.'"

Then those *bhikkhus* approached Ariṭṭha. When they had approached him, they said this: "Is it true, friend Ariṭṭha, that in you a pernicious view such as this has arisen: 'As I understand the *dhamma* taught by the Exalted One, those things that are called obstructions by the Exalted One are not capable of obstructing one who pursues them'?"

"Yes, it is so, friend, I understand the *dhamma* taught by the Exalted One in exactly that way."

Then those *bhikkhus*, desiring to dissuade Ariṭṭha from this pernicious view, questioned him, cross-examined him, and pressed him for reasons: "Friend Ariṭṭha, do not say that! Do not misrepresent the Exalted One! It is not good to misrepresent the Exalted One. The Exalted One would not say that. In many different ways, friend Ariṭṭha, the Exalted One has explained certain things as obstructions and how these things are capable of obstructing one who pursues them. The Exalted One has described sensual pleasures as affording little gratification, generating much pain and trouble. And here there is even more danger. The Exalted One has described sensual pleasures

1. ["Exalted One" is an epithet for the Buddha. See the Introduction to the "Discourse to Prince Abhaya" in chapter 12.]

2. [A *bhikkhu* (Sanskrit *bhikṣu*) is a Buddhist monk.]

3. *Gaddhabādhipubbassa*. It is not clear what occupation is indicated by this term, but it is likely that involvement with vultures would suggest a "low" social class.

4. *Antarāyikā*. Literally, "things that come between," thus "obstructions." On the basis of commentaries and the discussion that takes place later in this discourse, the term refers to sensual pleasures, especially sexual activities.

by the parable of the skeleton, by the parable of the lump of meat, by the parable of the grass torch, by the parable of the pit of coals, by the parable of dreams, by the parable of borrowed things, by the parable of the fruit of a tree, by the parable of the slaughterhouse, by the parable of the impaling stake, by the parable of the snake's head[5]—in each case demonstrating that sensual pleasures generate much pain and trouble; and here there is even more danger."

And yet, even after having been questioned, cross-examined, and pressed for reasons by those *bhikkhus*, Ariṭṭha still vigorously held onto and clung to this pernicious view saying: "Yes, it is so, friend, as I understand the *dhamma* taught by the Exalted One, things that are called obstructions by the Exalted One are not capable of obstructing one who pursues them."

2. When those *bhikkhus* were not able to dissuade Ariṭṭha from this pernicious view, they approached the Exalted One. When they approached the Exalted One, they greeted him and sat down to one side. When they were seated to one side, those *bhikkhus* [*recounted verbatim their conversation with Ariṭṭha to the Exalted One*]. "Since we were not able, sir, to dissuade Ariṭṭha from this pernicious view, we are reporting this matter to the Exalted One."

3. Then the Exalted One addressed a certain *bhikkhu*: "Come, *bhikkhu*, and address the *bhikkhu* Ariṭṭha, who was formerly a vulture trainer, with my words: 'Brother Ariṭṭha, the teacher calls you."

"Yes, sir," assented that *bhikkhu* to the Exalted One, and he approached Ariṭṭha. When he had approached Ariṭṭha, he said this: "Friend Ariṭṭha, the teacher calls you."

"Yes, sir," assented Ariṭṭha to that *bhikkhu*, and he approached the Exalted One. When he had approached the Exalted One, he greeted him and sat down to one side. When he was seated to one side, the Exalted One said this to Ariṭṭha: "Is it true, friend Ariṭṭha, that the following pernicious view has arisen in you: 'As I understand the *dhamma* taught by the Exalted One, those things that are called obstructions by the Exalted One are not capable of obstructing one who pursues them'?"

"Yes, it is so, friend. I understand the *dhamma* taught by the Exalted One in exactly that way."

"Do you know anyone, you misguided person, to whom I have taught the *dhamma* in that way? Misguided person, have I not explained in many different ways certain things as obstructions, and how these things are capable of obstructing one who pursues them? I

5. [Each of these parables illustrates, with vivid unpleasant imagery, how sensual desire is bound up with attachment, suffering, and misery.]

have described sensual pleasures as affording little gratification, generating much pain and trouble. And here there is even more danger. I have described sensual pleasures by the parable of the skeleton, by the parable of the lump of meat, by the parable of the grass torch, by the parable of the pit of coals, by the parable of dreams, by the parable of borrowed things, by the parable of the fruit tree, by the parable of the slaughterhouse, by the parable of the impaling stake, and by the parable of the snake's head—in each case demonstrating that sensual pleasures generate much pain and trouble; and here there is even more danger. But you, misguided person, have misrepresented me by your own wrong grasp, have injured yourself, and have accumulated much demerit. That, misguided person, will be to your harm and suffering for a long time."

Then the Exalted One addressed the *bhikkhus*: "What do you think, *bhikkhus*? Does this *bhikkhu* Ariṭṭha have even a glimmer of this *dhamma* and discipline?"

"How could he, sir? No, sir."

This having been said, Ariṭṭha sat down and became silent, downcast, dejected, with his shoulders drooping, overcome with remorse and bewildered. Then the Exalted One, knowing that Ariṭṭha had become downcast and dejected, said this to him: "Misguided person, you will be known by your own pernicious view. In connection with this, I will question the *bhikkhus*."

4. Then the Exalted One addressed the *bhikkhus*: "Do you, *bhikkhus*, understand the *dhamma* that I teach in the way that this Ariṭṭha does who has misrepresented me by his wrong grasp, who has injured himself, and who has accumulated much demerit?"

"No, sir. The Exalted One has explained certain things as obstructions in many different ways and how those things are capable of obstructing one who pursues them. The Exalted One has described sensual pleasures as affording little gratification, generating much pain and trouble; and here there is even more danger. The Exalted One has described sensual pleasures by the parable of the skeleton, by the parable of the lump of meat, by the parable of the grass torch, by the parable of the pit of coals, by the parable of dreams, by the parable of borrowed things, by the parable of the fruit tree, by the parable of the slaughterhouse, by the parable of the impaling stake, and by the parable of the snake's head—in each case demonstrating that sensual pleasures generate much pain and trouble; and here there is even more danger."

"Good, *bhikkhus*. It is good that you understand the *dhamma* taught by me in this way. For I have described sensual pleasures as affording little gratification, generating much pain and trouble; and here there is even more danger. I have described sensual pleasures by these many parables—in each case demonstrating that sensual pleasures generate much pain and trouble; and here there is even more danger. But Ariṭṭha has misrepresented me by his own wrong grasp, has injured himself, and has accumulated much demerit. This will be to the harm and suffering of this misguided person for a long time. Indeed, that one can indulge in sensual pleasures apart from sensual desires, apart from the perception of sensual desires, and apart from thoughts of sensual desires—that is impossible.[6]

5. "In a certain case, *bhikkhus*, some misguided persons study the *dhamma*, including the discourses, the chants, the explanations, the verses, the sayings, what has been said, the birth stories, the marvelous teachings and the miscellanies. But having studied the *dhamma*, they do not examine the meaning of these teachings with intelligence. And for them these teachings that have not been examined with intelligence are accepted without comprehension. Instead, they study the *dhamma* for the purpose of criticizing others and for the purpose of merely quoting; so they do not achieve the good result for which purpose the *dhamma* ought to be studied. These teachings that are poorly grasped lead to harm and suffering for a long time. What is the reason for this? It is because of the wrong grasp of the teachings.

"Just as a person walking about seeking a water snake, going after a water snake, searching for a water snake were to see a large water snake and were to take hold of it by its coil or tail. That water snake, having turned back, might bite that person's hand, arm, or another of that person's limbs. As a result, that person might die or experience pain akin to dying. What is the reason for this? It is because of the wrong grasp of the water snake.

"In the same way, some misguided persons study the *dhamma*, including the discourses, the chants, the explanations, the verses, the sayings, what has been said, the birth stories, the marvelous teachings, and the miscellanies. But having studied the *dhamma*, they do not examine the meaning of these teachings with intelligence. And these teachings that have not been examined with intelligence are accepted without comprehension. Instead, they study the *dhamma* for

6. This is the crucial line in refuting Ariṭṭha's misguided view. There can be no indulgence in sensualist activities without the defiling motivating factors (e.g., sensual desire) behind them. Hence there is no way to partake in sensualist activities (particularly sexual activities) without incurring the negative effects of the factors that motivate sensualist activities.

the purpose of criticizing others and for the purpose of merely quoting; so they do not achieve the good result, for which purpose the *dhamma* ought to be studied. These teachings that are poorly grasped lead to harm and suffering for a long time. What is the reason for this? It is because of the wrong grasp of the teachings.

6. "In another case, some young men from good families study the *dhamma*, including the discourses, the chants, the explanations, the verses, the sayings, what has been said, the birth stories, the marvelous teachings, and the miscellanies. But having studied the *dhamma*, they do examine the meaning of these teachings with intelligence. And these teachings that have been examined with intelligence are accepted with comprehension. They do not study the *dhamma* for the purpose of criticizing others, nor for the purpose of merely quoting; so they do achieve the good result for which purpose the *dhamma* ought to be studied. These teachings that are rightly grasped lead to their welfare and happiness for a long time. What is the reason for this? It is because of the right grasp of the teachings.

"Just as a person walking about seeking a water snake, going after a water snake, searching for a water snake, were he to see a large water snake, he might restrain it tightly with a forked stick. Having restrained it tightly by the neck with a forked stick, that water snake might wrap itself around the hand, arm, or other limbs of that person, but from this cause, the person would not die nor experience pain akin to dying. What is the reason for this? It is because of the right grasp of the water snake.

"In the same way, some young men from good families study the *dhamma,* including the discourses, the chants, the explanations, the verses, the sayings, what has been said, the birth stories, the marvelous teachings, and the miscellanies. But having studied the *dhamma,* they do examine the meaning of these teachings with intelligence. These teachings that have been examined with intelligence are accepted with comprehension. They do not study the *dhamma* for the purpose of criticizing others, nor for the purpose of merely quoting; so they do achieve the good result for which purpose the *dhamma* ought to be studied. And these teachings that are rightly grasped lead to their welfare and happiness for a long time. What is the reason for this? It is because of the right grasp of the teachings.

"Therefore, *bhikkhus,* you should understand the meaning of what I have said, and you should remember it in this way. Were you not to understand the meaning of what I have said, you should question me about it or one of the learned *bhikkhus* (if there is one present).

7. "*Bhikkhus*, I will teach you that the *dhamma* is like a raft—for crossing over, not for retaining. Listen and pay careful attention, and I will speak."

"Yes, Exalted One," those *bhikkhus* replied to the Exalted One.

The Exalted One said: "Just as a person walking along a highway might see a great body of water, the near shore dangerous and frightening, the further shore secure and not frightening. But if there were neither a boat nor a bridge to use for crossing over from the near shore to the farther shore, that person might have this thought: 'This is a great body of water, and the near shore is dangerous and frightening. The farther shore is secure and not frightening. But there is neither a boat nor a bridge to use for crossing over from the near shore to the farther shore. Suppose that, having collected grass, sticks, branches, and leaves, and having bound them together as a raft, riding on that raft, and making an effort with hands and feet, I should cross over safely to the other shore.' Then that person, having collected grass, sticks, branches, and leaves, and having bound them together as a raft, riding on that raft, and making an effort with hands and feet, might cross over safely to the other shore. Having crossed over, having made the further shore, that person might have this thought: 'Now, this raft has been very useful to me. Riding on this raft, and making an effort with my hands and feet, I crossed over safely to the farther shore. Suppose now that, having put this raft on my head, or having raised it onto my shoulder, I should proceed as I desire.' What do you think, *bhikkhus*? If that person were to act in this way, would that person be doing what should be done with the raft?"

"No, Exalted One."

"In what way should that person act, *bhikkhus*, in order to do what should be done with the raft? Here, it might occur to that person who has crossed over, gone to the farther shore: 'Now, this raft has been very useful to me. Riding on this raft, and making an effort with my hands and feet, I crossed over safely to the farther shore. Suppose now that, having hauled this raft onto dry ground or having left it floating on the water, I should proceed as I desire.' In acting this way, that person would be doing what should be done with the raft. Just as, in the parable of the raft, the *dhamma* taught by me is for crossing over, not for retaining. *Bhikkhus*, by understanding the parable of the raft, you should abandon the *dhamma*, all the more what is not the *dhamma*."[7]

7. This is a much quoted, but often misrepresented, statement. The point here is not that after enlightenment one should abandon the Buddha's teachings—nor is an enlightened person "beyond good and evil"—but simply that one should abandon dogmatic or selfish attachment to any teachings, even the Buddha's.

19
NIETZSCHE

Friedrich Nietzsche (1844–1900) is one of the most iconoclastic thinkers in the Western philosophical tradition. In his writings Nietzsche consistently challenges the received orthodoxies of modern, enlightenment thinking. One of his main targets is Immanuel Kant, who had argued that the use of mere reason is sufficient to derive not only the moral law, but also such elements of Christian faith as the immortality of the soul and the omnipotence and omnibenevolence of God. Writing soon after Darwin published *The Origin of Species,* Nietzsche applies a largely Darwinian approach to understanding the origin of morality and religion. In *On the Genealogy of Morals,* for instance, he provides a story of how a moral theory could develop within a society and be taken to be true and absolute despite its very human, very contingent, origin.

In the selections from *The Gay Science* excerpted here, Nietzsche considers the possibility that truth itself, as well as the drive for truth, may be subject to the same sort of analysis. The beliefs that survive to be passed on from one person to the next are the ones that help us meet with pragmatic success and ultimately to survive. But, he argues, survivability does not necessarily track truth. It could well be that the most useful beliefs are ones that help us to avoid or ignore the truth.

In "On Truth and Lying in a Non-Moral Sense," an essay that he wrote earlier than *The Gay Science* but did not publish in his lifetime, Nietzsche explores this idea further, ultimately challenging the notion that there is such a thing as objective truth. His critique of truth begins with the insight that language necessarily falsifies the world that it is used to describe. For one thing, any connection between a word and the thing in the world that word is supposed to refer to is merely a matter of arbitrary convention. And the fact that vastly many different objects can all bear the descriptor "leaf" further exacerbates the arbitrariness. There is no objective sense in which any one of them is *really* a leaf, and even less can it be truly said that they are all the same thing, as giving them all the same name would imply.

But if truth is merely a matter of convention, of choosing to use the same metaphors and to ignore the same differences so that we can see all of these objects as falling under the one concept "leaf," then honesty and truthfulness simply amount to using the same falsehoods that one's community uses. To the extent that there is a problem with lying at all, then, it cannot be because one says something that is false; for that happens whenever we speak. Nietzsche points out that we reject liars for fear of the harm that attends believing their falsehoods rather than someone else's more useful falsehoods. The insight here is perhaps most poignantly put by Nietzsche in section 183 of *Beyond Good and Evil*: "Not that you lied to me, but that I no longer believe you, has shaken me."

Nietzsche's point is not that there is no objective world independent of human thought (Nietzsche is not a subjective idealist), but rather that the limits of discursive language preclude its capturing that world and to think otherwise leads to an impoverished experience of the world. The contrast he draws between the rational man and the intuitive man in the second part of "On Truth and Lying in a Non-Moral Sense" illustrates this. The intuitive, artistic, creative person is able to embrace metaphors as metaphors, to use guises and artifice as more powerful ways of communicating than reliance on dry abstractions and concepts. To be sure, Nietzsche acknowledges, such an approach to experience is fraught with greater risk of failure; but it also allows for greater significance in one's successes.

As you read the selections from Nietzsche, consider the following questions:

1. If being truthful just means to "use the customary metaphors," wouldn't this be like two people who agree to talk to each other in code? Since they both agreed to it, neither is deceived. Why would Nietzsche have a problem with this notion of truthfulness?
2. Nietzsche says, "If someone hides something behind a bush, looks for it in the same place and then finds it there, his seeking and finding is nothing much to boast about; but this is exactly how things are as far as the seeking and finding of 'truth' within the territory of reason is concerned." Do you think he is right? Is our use of reason to find truth just hiding something in a place where we can find it again?
3. Do you agree with Nietzsche's assertion that false beliefs could be more conducive to survival than true beliefs? How might this be so?

The Gay Science

110: *Origin of Knowledge*. Through immense periods of time, the intellect produced nothing but errors; some of them turned out to be useful and species-preserving; those who hit upon or inherited them fought their fight for themselves and their progeny with greater luck. Such erroneous articles of faith, which were passed on by inheritance further and further, and finally almost became part of the basic endowment of the species, are for example: that there are enduring things; that there are identical things; that there are things, kinds of material, bodies; that a thing is what it appears to be; that our will is free; that what is good for me is also good in and for itself. Only very late did the deniers and doubters of such propositions emerge; only very late did truth emerge as the weakest form of knowledge. It seemed that one was unable to live with it; that our organism was geared for its opposite: all its higher functions, the perceptions of sense and generally every kind of sensation, worked with those basic errors that had been incorporated since time immemorial. Further, even in the realm of knowledge those propositions became the norms according to which one determined 'true' and 'untrue'—down to the most remote areas of pure logic. Thus the *strength* of knowledge lies not in its degree of truth, but in its age, its embeddedness, its character as a condition of life. Where life and knowledge seem to contradict each other, there was never any serious fight to begin with; denial and doubt were simply considered madness. Those exceptional thinkers, like the Eleatics, who still posited and clung to the opposites of the natural errors, believed in the possibility of also *living* this opposite: they invented the sage as the man of unchangeability, impersonality, universality of intuition, as one and all at the same time, with a special capacity for that inverted knowledge; they had the faith that their knowledge was at the same time the principle of *life*. But in order to be able to claim all this, they had to *deceive* themselves about their own state: they had fictitiously to attribute to themselves impersonality and duration without change; they had to misconstrue the nature of the knower, deny the force of impulses in knowledge, and generally conceive reason as a completely free, self-originated activity. They closed their eyes to the fact that they, too, had arrived at their propositions in opposition to what was considered valid or from a desire for tranquility or sole possession or sovereignty. The subtler development of honesty and skepticism finally made also these people impossible; even their life and judgements proved dependent on the ancient drives and fundamental errors of all sentient existence. This subtler honesty and skepticism finally made also these people impossible; even their life and judgements proved dependent on the ancient drives and fundamental errors of all sentient existence. This subtler honesty and skepticism arose wherever two conflicting propositions seemed to be *applicable* to life because both were compatible with the basic errors, and thus where it was possible to argue about the greater or lesser degree of *usefulness* for life; also wherever new propositions showed themselves to be not directly useful, but at least also not harmful, as expressions of an intellectual play impulse, and innocent and happy like all play. Gradually the human brain filled itself with such judgements and convictions; and ferment, struggle, and lust for power developed in this tangle. Not only utility and delight, but also every kind of drive took part in the fight about the 'truths'; the intellectual fight became an occupation, attraction, profession, duty, dignity—knowledge and the striving for the true finally took their place as a need among the other needs. Henceforth, not only faith and conviction, but also scrutiny, denial, suspicion, and contradiction were a *power*; all 'evil' instincts were subordinated to knowledge and put in its service and took on the lustre of the permitted, honoured, useful and finally the eye and the innocence of the *good*. Thus knowledge became a part of life and, as life, a continually growing power, until finally knowledge and the ancient basic errors struck against each other, both as life, both as power, both in the same person. The thinker—that is now the being in whom the drive to truth and those life-preserving errors are fighting their first battle, after the drive to truth has *proven* itself to be a life-preserving power, too. In relation to the significance of this battle, everything else is a matter of indifference: the ultimate question about the condition of life is posed here, and the first attempt is made here to answer the question through experiment. To what extent can truth stand to be incorporated?—that is the question; that is the experiment.

121: *Life not an argument*. We have arranged for ourselves a world in which we are able to live—by positing bodies, lines, planes, causes and effects, motions and rest, form and content; without these articles of faith no one could endure living! But that does not prove them. Life is not an argument; the conditions of life might include error.

"On Truth and Lying in a Non-Moral Sense"

1. In some remote corner of the universe, flickering in the light of the countless solar systems into which it had been poured, there was once a planet on which clever animals invented cognition. It was the most

arrogant and most mendacious minute in the 'history of the world'; but a minute was all it was. After nature had drawn just a few more breaths the planet froze and the clever animals had to die. Someone could invent a fable like this and yet they would still not have given a satisfactory illustration of just how pitiful, how insubstantial and transitory, how purposeless and arbitrary the human intellect looks within nature; there were eternities during which it did not exist; and when it has disappeared again, nothing will have happened. For this intellect has no further mission that might extend beyond the bounds of human life. Rather, the intellect is human, and only its own possessor and progenitor regards it with such pathos, as if it housed the axis around which the entire world revolved. But if we could communicate with a midge we would hear that it too floats through the air with the very same pathos, feeling that it too contains within itself the flying centre of this world. There is nothing in nature so despicable and mean that would not immediately swell up like a balloon from just one little puff of that force of cognition; and just as every bearer of burdens wants to be admired, so the proudest man of all, the philosopher, wants to see, on all sides, the eyes of the universe trained, as through telescopes, on his thoughts and deeds.

It is odd that the intellect can produce this effect, since it is nothing other than an aid supplied to the most unfortunate, most delicate and most transient of beings so as to detain them for a minute within existence; otherwise, without this supplement, they would have every reason to flee existence as quickly as did Lessing's infant son.[1] The arrogance inherent in cognition and feeling casts a blinding fog over the eyes and senses of human beings, and because it contains within itself the most flattering evaluation of cognition it deceives them about the value of existence. Its most general effect is deception—but each of its separate effects also has something of the same character.

As a means for the preservation of the individual, the intellect shows its greatest strengths in dissimulation, since this is the means to preserve those weaker, less robust individuals who, by nature, are denied horns or the sharp fangs of a beast of prey with which to wage the struggle for existence. This art of dissimulation reaches its peak in humankind, where deception, flattery, lying and cheating, speaking

1. Lessing's first and only son died immediately after birth, followed soon after by his mother. This drew from Lessing the comment: 'Was it good sense that they had to pull him into the world with iron tongs, or that he noticed the filth so quickly? Was it not good sense that he took the first opportunity to leave it again?' (Letter to Eschenburg, 10 January 1778).

behind the backs of others, keeping up appearances,[2] living in borrowed finery, wearing masks, the drapery of convention, play-acting for the benefit of others and oneself—in short, the constant fluttering of human beings around the one flame of vanity is so much the rule and the law that there is virtually nothing which defies understanding so much as the fact that an honest and pure drive towards truth should ever have emerged in them. They are deeply immersed in illusions and dream-images; their eyes merely glide across the surface of things and see 'forms'; nowhere does their perception lead into truth; instead it is content to receive stimuli and, as it were, to play with its fingers on the back of things. What is more, human beings allow themselves to be lied to in dreams every night of their lives, without their moral sense ever seeking to prevent this happening, whereas it is said that some people have even eliminated snoring by will-power. What do human beings really know about themselves? Are they even capable of perceiving themselves in their entirety just once, stretched out as in an illuminated glass case? Does nature not remain silent about almost everything, even about our bodies, banishing and enclosing us within a proud, illusory consciousness, far away from the twists and turns of the bowels, the rapid flow of the blood stream and the complicated tremblings of the nerve-fibres? Nature has thrown away the key, and woe betide fateful curiosity should it ever succeed in peering through a crack in the chamber of consciousness, out and down into the depths, and thus gain an intimation of the fact that humanity, in the indifference of its ignorance, rests on the pitiless, the greedy, the insatiable, the murderous—clinging in dreams, as it were, to the back of a tiger. Given this constellation, where on earth can the drive to truth possibly have come from?

Insofar as the individual wishes to preserve himself in relation to other individuals, in the state of nature he mostly used his intellect for concealment and dissimulation; however, because necessity and boredom also lead men to want to live in societies and herds, they need a peace treaty, and so they endeavor to eliminate from their world at least the crudest forms of the *bellum omnium contra omnes*.[3] In the wake of this peace treaty, however, comes something which looks like the first

2. The verb Nietzsche uses is *repräsentieren*. This means keeping up a show in public, representing one's family, country, or social group before the eyes of the world.

3. 'war of all against all': phrase associated with Thomas Hobbes' description of the state of nature before the institution of political authority (*cf.* Hobbes, *De cive* 1.12 and *Leviathan*, chapter XIII).

step towards the acquisition of that mysterious drive for truth. For that which is to count as 'truth' from this point onwards now becomes fixed, i.e. a way of designating things is invented which has the same validity and force everywhere, and the legislation of language also produces the first laws of truth, for the contrast between truth and lying comes into existence here for the first time: the liar uses the valid tokens of designation—words—to make the unreal appear to be real; he says, for example, 'I am rich', whereas the correct designation for this condition would be, precisely, 'poor'. He misuses the established conventions by arbitrarily switching or even inverting the names for things. If he does this in a manner that is selfish and otherwise harmful, society will no longer trust him and therefore exclude him from its ranks. Human beings do not so much flee from being tricked as from being harmed by being tricked. Even on this level they do not hate deception but rather the damaging, inimical consequences of certain species of deception. Truth, too, is only desired by human beings in a similarly limited sense. They desire the pleasant, life-preserving consequences of truth; they are indifferent to pure knowledge if it has no consequences, but they are actually hostile towards truths which may be harmful and destructive. And, besides, what is the status of those conventions of language? Are they perhaps products of knowledge, of the sense of truth? Is there a perfect match between things and their designations? Is language the full and adequate expression of all realities?

Only through forgetfulness could human beings ever entertain the illusion that they possess truth to the degree described above. If they will not content themselves with truth in the form of tautology, i.e. with empty husks, they will for ever exchange illusions for truth. What is a word? The copy of a nervous stimulation in sounds. To infer from the fact of the nervous stimulation that there exists a cause outside us is already the result of applying the principle of sufficient reason wrongly. If truth alone had been decisive in the genesis of language, if the viewpoint of certainty had been decisive in creating designations, how could we possibly be permitted to say, 'The stone is hard', as if 'hard' were something known to us in some other way, and not merely as an entirely subjective stimulus? We divide things up by gender, describing a tree as masculine and a plant as feminine[4]—how arbitrary these translations are! How far they have flown beyond the canon of certainty! We speak of a snake; the designation captures only

4. 'Tree' is masculine in German (*der Baum*) and 'plant' (*die Pflanze*) is feminine.

its twisting movements and thus could equally well apply to a worm. How arbitrarily these borders are drawn, how one-sided the preference for this or that property of a thing! When different languages are set alongside one another it becomes clear that, where words are concerned, what matters is never truth, never the full and adequate expression;[5] otherwise there would not be so many languages. The 'thing-in-itself' (which would be, precisely, pure truth, truth without consequences) is impossible for even the creator of language to grasp, and indeed this is not at all desirable. He designates only the relations of things to human beings, and in order to express them he avails himself of the boldest metaphors. The stimulation of a nerve is first translated into an image: first metaphor! The image is then imitated by a sound: second metaphor! And each time there is a complete leap from one sphere into the heart of another, new sphere. One can conceive of a profoundly deaf human being who has never experienced sound or music; just as such a person will gaze in astonishment at the Chladnian sound-figures in sand,[6] find their cause in the vibration of a string, and swear that he must now know what men call sound—this is precisely what happens to all of us with language. We believe that when we speak of trees, colours, snow, and flowers, we have knowledge of the things themselves, and yet we possess only metaphors of things which in no way correspond to the original entities. Just as the musical sound appears as a figure in the sand, so the mysterious 'X' of the thing-in-itself appears first as a nervous stimulus, then as an image, and finally as an articulated sound. At all events, things do not proceed logically when language comes into being, and the entire material in and with which the man of truth, the researcher, the philosopher, works and builds, stems, if not from cloud-cuckoo land, then certainly not from the essence of things.

Let us consider in particular how concepts are formed; each word immediately becomes a concept, not by virtue of the fact that it is intended to serve as a memory (say) of the unique, utterly individualized, primary experience to which it owes its existence, but because at the same time it must fit countless other, more or less similar cases, i.e.

5. Nietzsche uses the term *adäquat* which indicates that the meaning of something is fully conveyed by a word or expression; English 'adequate' alone does not convey this sense completely.

6. The vibration of a string can create figures in the sand (in an appropriately constructed sand-box) which give a visual representation of that which the human ear perceives as a tone. The term comes from the name of the physicist Ernst Chladni, whose experiments demonstrated the effect.

cases which, strictly speaking, are never equivalent, and thus nothing other than non-equivalent cases. Every concept comes into being by making equivalent that which is non-equivalent. Just as it is certain that no leaf is ever exactly the same as any other leaf, it is equally certain that the concept 'leaf' is formed by dropping these individual differences arbitrarily, by forgetting those features which differentiate one thing from another, so that the concept then gives rise to the notion that something other than leaves exists in nature, something which would be 'leaf', a primal form, say, from which all leaves were woven, drawn, delineated, dyed, curled, painted—but by a clumsy pair of hands, so that no single example turned out to be a faithful, correct, and reliable copy of the primal form. We call a man honest; we ask, 'Why did he act so honestly today?' Our answer is usually: 'Because of his honesty.' Honesty!—yet again, this means that the leaf is the cause of the leaves. We have no knowledge of an essential quality which might be called honesty, but we do know of numerous individualized and hence non-equivalent actions which we equate with each other by omitting what is unlike, and which we now designate as honest actions; finally we formulate from them a *qualitas occulta*[7] with the name 'honesty.'

Like form, a concept is produced by overlooking what is individual and real, whereas nature knows neither forms nor concepts and hence no species, but only an 'X' which is inaccessible to us and indefinable by us. For the opposition we make between individual and species is also anthropomorphic and does not stem from the essence of things, although we equally do not dare to say that it does *not* correspond to the essence of things, since that would be a dogmatic assertion and, as such, just as incapable of being proved as its opposite.

What, then, is truth? A mobile army of metaphors, metonymies, anthropomorphisms, in short a sum of human relations which have been subjected to poetic and rhetorical intensification, translation, and decoration, and which, after they have been in use for a long time, strike a people as firmly established, canonical, and binding; truths are illusions of which we have forgotten that they are illusions, metaphors which have become worn by frequent use and have lost all sensuous vigour, coins which, having lost their stamp, are now regarded as metal and no longer as coins. Yet we still do not know where the drive to truth comes from, for so far we have only heard about the obligation to be truthful which society imposes in order to exist, i.e. the obligation to use the customary metaphors, or, to put

7. Hidden property.

it in moral terms, the obligation to lie in accordance with the firmly established convention, to lie *en masse* and in a style that is binding for all. Now, it is true that human beings forget that this is how things are; thus they lie unconsciously in the way we have described, and in accordance with centuries-old habits—and precisely *because of this unconsciousness*, precisely because of this forgetting, they arrive at the feeling of truth. The feeling that one is obliged to describe one thing as red, another as cold, and a third as dumb, prompts a moral impulse which pertains to truth; form its opposite, the liar whom no one trust and all exclude, human beings demonstrate to themselves just how honourable, confidence-inspiring and useful truth is. As creatures of *reason*, human beings now make their actions subject to the rule of abstractions; they no longer tolerate being swept away by sudden impressions and sensuous perceptions; they now generalize all these impressions first, turning them into cooler, less colourful concepts in order to harness the vehicle of their lives and actions to them. Everything which distinguishes human beings from animals depends on this ability to sublimate sensuous metaphors into a schema, in other words, to dissolve an image into a concept. This is because something becomes possible in the realm of these schemata which could never be achieved in the realm of those sensuous first impressions, namely the construction of a pyramidal order based on castes and degrees, the creation of a new world of laws, privileges, subordinations, definitions of borders, which now confronts the other, sensuously perceived world as something firmer, more general, more familiar, more human, and hence as something regulatory and imperative. Whereas every metaphor standing for a sensuous perception is individual and unique and is therefore always able to escape classification, the great edifice of concepts exhibits the rigid regularity of a Roman *columbarium*,[8] while logic breathes out that air of severity and coolness which is peculiar to mathematics. Anyone who has been touched by that cool breath will scarcely believe that concepts too, which are as bony and eight-cornered as a dice and just as capable of being shifted around, are only the left-over *residue of a metaphor*, and that the illusion produced by the artistic translation of a nervous stimulus into images is, if not the mother, then at least the grandmother of each and every concept. Within this conceptual game of dice, however, 'truth' means using each die in accordance with its designation, counting its spots precisely, forming correct classifica-

8. Originally a dovecot, then a catacomb with niches at regular intervals for urns containing the ashes of the dead.

tions, and never offending against the order of castes nor against the sequence of classes of rank. Just as the Romans and the Etruscans divided up the sky with rigid mathematical lines and confined a god in a space which they had thus delimited as in a *templum*, all peoples have just such a mathematically divided firmament of concepts above them, and they understand the demand of truth to mean that the god of every concept is to be sought only in *his* sphere. Here one can certainly admire humanity as a mighty architectural genius who succeeds in erecting the infinitely complicated cathedral of concepts on moving foundations, or even, one might say, on flowing water; admittedly, in order to rest on such foundations, it has to be like a thing constructed from cobwebs, so delicate that it can be carried off on the waves and yet so firm as not to be blown apart by the wind. By these standards the human being is an architectural genius who is far superior to the bee; the latter builds with wax which she gathers from nature, whereas the human being builds with the far more delicate material of concepts which he must first manufacture from himself. In this he is to be much admired—but just not for his impulse to truth, to the pure cognition of things. If someone hides something behind a bush, looks for it in the same place and then finds it there, his seeking and finding is nothing much to boast about; but this is exactly how things are as far as the seeking and finding of 'truth' within the territory of reason is concerned. If I create the definition of a mammal and then, having inspected a camel, declare, 'Behold, a mammal', then a truth has certainly been brought to light, but it is of limited value, by which I mean that it is anthropomorphic through and through and contains not a single point which could be said to be 'true in itself', really and in a generally valid sense, regardless of mankind. Anyone who researches for truths of that kind is basically only seeking the metamorphosis of the world in human beings; he strives for an understanding of the world as something which is similar in kind to humanity, and what he gains by his efforts is at best a feeling of assimilation. Rather as the astrologer studies the stars in the service of human beings and in relation to humanity's happiness and suffering, this type of researcher regards the whole world as linked to humankind, as the infinitely refracted echo of an original sound, that of humanity, and as the multiple copy of a single, original image, that of humanity. His procedure is to measure all things against man, and in doing so he takes as his point of departure the erroneous belief that he has these things directly before him, as pure objects. Thus, forgetting that the original metaphors of perception were indeed metaphors, he takes them for the things themselves.

Only by forgetting this primitive world of metaphor, only by virtue of the fact that a mass of images, which originally flowed in a hot, liquid stream from the primal power of the human imagination, has become hard and rigid, only because of the invincible faith that *this* sun, *this* window, this table is a truth in itself—in short only because man forgets himself as a subject, and indeed as *an artistically creative* subject, does he live with some degree of peace, security, and consistency; if he could escape for just a moment from the prison walls of this faith, it would mean the end of his 'consciousness of self'.[9] He even has to make an effort to admit to himself that insects or birds perceive a quite different world from that of human beings, and that the question as to which of these two perceptions of the world is more correct is quite meaningless, since this would require them to be measured by the criterion of the *correct perception*, i.e. by a *non-existent* criterion. But generally it seems to me that the correct perception—which would mean the full and adequate expression of an object in the subject—is something contradictory and impossible; for between two absolutely different spheres, such as subject and object are, there is no causality, no correctness, no expression, but at most an *aesthetic* way of relating, by which I mean an allusive transference, a stammering translation into a quite different language. For which purpose a middle sphere and mediating force is certainly required which can freely invent and freely create poetry. The word appearance (*Erscheinung*) contains many seductions, and for this reason I avoid using it as far as possible; for it is not true that the essence of things appears in the empirical world. A painter who has no hands and who wished to express in song the image hovering before him will still reveal more through this substitution of one sphere for another than the empirical world betrays of the essence of things. Even the relation of a nervous stimulus to the image produced thereby is inherently not a necessary relationship; but when that same image has been produced millions of times and has been passed down through many generations of humanity, indeed eventually appears in the whole of humanity as a consequence of the same occasion, it finally acquires the same significance for all human beings, as if it were the only necessary image and as if that relation of the original nervous stimulus to the image produced were a relation of strict causality—in exactly the same way as a dream, if repeated eternally, would be felt and judged entirely as reality. But the fact that a metaphor becomes hard and rigid

9. The word Nietzsche uses here—*Selbstbewußtsein*—could also mean 'self-confidence'.

is absolutely no guarantee of the necessity and exclusive justification of that metaphor.

Anyone who is at home in such considerations will certainly have felt a deep mistrust of this kind of idealism when he has once become clearly convinced of the eternal consistency, ubiquitousness and infallibility of the laws of nature; he will then conclude that everything, as far as we can penetrate, whether to the heights of the telescopic world or the depths of the microscopic world, is so sure, so elaborated, so endless, so much in conformity to laws, and so free of lacunae, that science will be able to mine these shafts successfully for ever, and that everything found there will be in agreement and without self-contradiction. How little all of this resembles a product of the imagination, for if it were such a thing, the illusion and the unreality would be bound to be detectable somewhere. The first thing to be said against this view is this: if each of us still had a different kind of sensuous perception, if we ourselves could only perceive things as, variously, a bird, a worm, or a plant does, or if one of us were to see a stimulus as red, a second person were to see the same stimulus as blue, while a third were even to hear it as a sound, nobody would ever speak of nature as something conforming to laws; rather they would take it to be nothing other than a highly subjective formation. Consequently, what is a law of nature for us at all? It is not known to us in itself but only in its effects, i.e. in its relations to other laws of nature which are in turn known to us only as relations. Thus, all these relations refer only to one another, and they are utterly incomprehensible to us in their essential nature; the only things we really know about them are things which we bring to bear on them: time and space, in other words, relations of succession and number. But everything which is wonderful and which elicits our astonishment at precisely these laws of nature, everything which demands explanation of us and could seduce us into being suspicious of idealism, is attributable precisely and exclusively to the rigour and universal validity of the representations of time and space. But these we produce within ourselves and from ourselves with the same necessity as a spider spins; if we are forced to comprehend all things under these forms alone, then it is no longer wonderful that what we comprehend in all these things is actually nothing other than these very forms; for all of them must exhibit the laws of things. All the conformity to laws which we find so imposing in the orbits of the stars and chemical processes is basically identical with those qualities which we ourselves bring to bear on things, so that what we find imposing is our own activity. Of course the consequence of this is that the artistic production of metaphor, with which every sensation begins within us, already presupposes those forms, and is thus executed in them; only from the stability of these original forms can one explain how it is possible for an edifice of concepts to be constituted in its turn from the metaphors themselves. For this conceptual edifice is an imitation of the relations of time, space, and number on the foundations of metaphor.

2. Originally, as we have seen, it is *language* which works on building the edifice of concepts; later it is *science*. Just as the bee simultaneously builds the cells of its comb and fills them with honey, so science works unceasingly at that great *columbarium* of concepts, the burial site of perceptions, builds ever-new, ever-higher tiers, supports, cleans, renews the old cells, and strives above all to fill that framework which towers up to vast heights, and to fit into it an orderly way the whole empirical world, i.e. the anthropomorphic world. If even the man of action binds his life to reason and its concepts, so as not to be swept away and lose himself, the researcher builds his hut close by the tower of science so that he can lend a hand with the building and find protection for himself beneath its already existing bulwarks. And he has need of protection, for there exist fearful powers which constantly press in on him and which confront scientific truth with 'truths' of quite another kind, on shields emblazoned with the most multifarious emblems.

That drive to form metaphors, that fundamental human drive which cannot be left out of consideration for even a second without also leaving out human beings themselves, is in truth not defeated, indeed hardly even tamed, by the process whereby a regular and rigid new world is built from its own sublimated products—concepts—in order to imprison it in a fortress. The drive seeks out a channel and a new area for its activity, and finds it in myth and in art generally. It constantly confuses the cells and the classifications of concepts by setting up new translations, metaphors, metonymies; it constantly manifests the desire to shape the given world of the waking human being in ways which are just as multiform, irregular, inconsequential, incoherent, charming and ever-new, as things are in the world of dream. Actually the waking human being is only clear about the fact that he is awake thanks to the rigid and regular web of concepts, and for that reason he sometimes comes to believe that he is dreaming if once that web of concepts is torn apart by art. Pascal is right to maintain that if the same dream were to come to us every night we would occupy ourselves with it just as much as we do with the things we see every day: 'If an artisan could be sure to dream each night for a full twelve hours that he was a king,' says Pascal, 'I believe he would be just as happy as a king who dreamt for twelve hours each night that he was an artisan.'[10] Thanks to the constantly effective miracle assumed by myth, the waking day of a people who are stimulated by myth, as the ancient Greeks were, does indeed resemble dream more than it does the day of a thinker whose mind has been sobered by science. If, one day, any tree may speak as a nymph, or if a god can carry off virgins in the guise of a bull, if the goddess Athene herself is suddenly seen riding on a beautiful chariot in the company of Pisistratus through the market-places of Athens[11]—and that was what the honest Athenian believed—then anything is possible at any time, as it is in a dream, and the whole of nature cavorts around men as if it were just a masquerade of the gods who are merely having fun by deceiving men in every shape and form.

But human beings themselves have an unconquerable urge to let themselves be deceived, and they are as if enchanted with happiness when the bard recites epic fairy-tales as if they were true, or when the actor in a play acts the king more regally than reality shows him to be. The intellect, that master of pretence, is free and absolved of its usual slavery for as long as it can deceive without *doing harm*, and it celebrates its Saturnalian festivals when it does so; at no time is it richer, more luxuriant, more proud, skillful, and bold. Full of creative contentment, it jumbles up metaphors and shifts the boundary stones of abstraction, describing a river, for example, as a moving road that carries men to destinations to which they normally walk. The intellect has now cast off the mark of servitude; whereas it normally labours, with dull-spirited industry, to show to some poor individual who lusts after life the road and the tools he needs, and rides out in search of spoils and booty for its master, here the intellect has become the master itself and is permitted to wipe the expression of neediness from its face. Whatever the intellect now does, all of it, compared with what it did before, bears the mark of pretence, just as what it did before bore the mark of distortion. It copies human life, but it takes it to be something good and appears to be fairly content with it. That vast assembly of beams and boards to which needy man clings, thereby saving himself on his journey through life, is used by the liberated intellect as a mere climbing frame and plaything on which to perform its most reckless tricks; and when it smashes this framework, jumbles it up and ironically re-assembles it, pairing the most unlike things and dividing those things which are closest to one another, it reveals the

10. *Pensées* VI.386.

11. Herodotus I.60.

fact that it does not require those makeshift aids of neediness, and that it is now guided, not by concepts but by intuitions. No regular way leads from these intuitions into the land of the ghostly schemata and abstractions; words are not made for them; man is struck dumb when he sees them, or he will speak only in forbidden metaphors and unheard-of combinations of concepts so that, by at least demolishing and deriding the old conceptual barriers, he may do creative justice to the impression made on him by the mighty, present intuition.

There are epochs in which the man of reason and the man of intuition stand side by side, the one fearful of intuition, the other filled with scorn for abstraction, the latter as unreasonable as the former is unartistic. They both desire to rule over life; the one by his knowledge of how to cope with the chief calamities of life by providing for the future, by prudence and regularity, the other by being an 'exuberant hero'[12] who does not see those calamities and who only acknowledges life as real when it is disguised as beauty and appearance. Where the man of intuition, as was once the case in ancient Greece, wields his weapons more mightily and victoriously than his contrary, a culture can take shape, given favourable conditions, and the rule of art over life can become established; all the expressions of a life lived thus are accompanied by pretence, by the denial of neediness, by the radiance of metaphorical visions, and indeed generally by the immediacy of deception. Neither the house, nor the gait, nor the clothing, nor the pitcher of clay gives any hint that these things were invented by neediness; it seems as if all of them were intended to express sublime happiness and Olympian cloudlessness and, as it were, a playing with earnest things. Whereas the man who is guided by concepts and abstractions only succeeds thereby in warding off misfortune, is unable to compel the abstractions themselves to yield him happiness, and strives merely to be as free as possible of pain, the man of intuition, standing in the midst of a culture, reaps directly from his intuitions not just protection from harm but also a constant stream of brightness, a lightening of the spirit, redemption, and release. Of course, *when* he suffers, he suffers more severely; indeed he suffers more frequently because he does not know how to learn from experience and keeps on falling into the very same trap time after time. When he is suffering he is just as unreasonable as he is when happy, he shouts out loudly and knows no solace. How differently the same misfortune is endured by the stoic who has learned from experience and who governs himself by means of concepts! This man, who otherwise seeks

12. Phrase used of Siegfried in Wagner's *Götterdämmerung* (act III).

only honesty, truth, freedom from illusions, and protection from the onslaughts of things which might distract him, now performs, in the midst of misfortune, a masterpiece of pretence, just as the other did in the midst of happiness: he does not wear a twitching, mobile, human face, but rather a mask, as it were, with its features in dignified equilibrium; he does not shout, nor does he even change his tone of voice. If a veritable storm-cloud empties itself on his head, he wraps himself in his cloak and slowly walks away from under it.

Part Four

Recent Developments

20

THE STATE OF THE ART

The amount of philosophical literature discussing lying and truthfulness has expanded greatly within the last hundred years. In this chapter we will discuss some of the more significant articles and books on the subject that have appeared since the turn of the twentieth century. Of course, to cover all such discussions would necessitate a book-length project. We have thus had to make difficult choices with regard to what to include and how much relative space to dedicate to what is included. In general, we have focused on works that fit the framework of the three overarching questions we have asked in this volume, highlighting those discussions that point out previously overlooked questions and issues within the philosophy of lying, as well as those that bring new insights to bear on the questions that have traditionally been dominant.

In what follows, we limit ourselves mainly to theorists from within the so-called Analytic tradition that has characterized much of twentieth-century Anglo-American philosophy. Analytic philosophy conceives of the job of philosophy as primarily consisting in conceptual clarification, linguistic precision, and logical-scientific articulation. Insofar as telling a lie is a type of speech act that implicates categories such as assertion and intention, it has therefore had particular salience for language-minded Analytic philosophers. By contrast, so-called Continental philosophy (which has flourished in France, Germany, and other areas of continental Europe) has been hesitant to abstract philosophical questions from their embodied, historical contexts. This has given Continental philosophy a decidedly more interdisciplinary scope than Analytic philosophy—with Continental theorists showing greater appreciation for the literary, political, and gendered complexities of lying and truthfulness—which makes it more difficult to adequately accommodate within the limitations of this chapter. There have been important and interesting contributions to the philosophy of lying and truthfulness within the Continental tradition and the Analytic focus of this chapter should not be taken as evidence to the contrary.

Before exploring what contemporary theorists have had to say regarding the philosophy of lying, one person deserves special mention. Sissela Bok has been largely responsible for the popularity that questions of lying and deception now enjoy within both academic and non-academic circles. Her 1978 book *Lying: Moral Choice in Public and Private Life* was a groundbreaking remedy to the neglect of interest in the philosophy of lying that characterized the first several decades of the twentieth century.[1] Bok undertakes a sweeping analysis of all the complex ways in which deceit and trust permeate our lives, focusing especially on dilemmas that can arise in thorny medical, legal, financial, familial, and political contexts. In this way, her work has helped to make the philosophy of lying accessible to non-specialist readerships more interested in thinking about concrete examples of deception as opposed to abstract questions within the philosophy of mind and language. While Bok does explicitly define a lie as "any intentionally deceptive message which is stated" (13), the methodology of the book is primarily casuistry (i.e., reasoning about specific cases), and only peripherally touches upon the three core questions that guide this chapter and the present volume. Nevertheless, Bok's work is essential for anyone interested in how the ethics of lying and truthfulness might play out in everyday relationships.

What Is a Lie?

Published within a year of Bok's seminal work, Roderick Chisholm and Thomas Feehan's 1977 article "The Intent to Deceive" has become arguably the most influential article on the question of how lies are to be defined.[2] Chisholm and Feehan are concerned with the conceptual questions of what counts as a lie and as intending to deceive. They explicitly disclaim any interest in questions of the ethical evaluation of, or the justification for, acts of either type. They begin by providing a definition of "lie," which they base on a detailed analysis of the concepts *deception* and *lie*. They then apply this definition to questions about problem cases, categorizing them explicitly as lies or non-lies.

1. Sissela Bok (1978), *Lying: Moral Choice in Public and Private Life* (New York: Vintage Publishers).

2. Roderick Chisholm & Thomas Feehan (1977), "The Intent to Deceive," *Journal of Philosophy* 74 (3): 143–159.

For Chisholm and Feehan, lying requires deception, but it requires a very specific sort of deception. They distinguish eight different ways in which one can deceive another. The eight sorts of deception fall under two broad categories: deception by commission and deception by omission. Deception by commission includes causing someone to acquire a false belief, causing someone to persist in a false belief, causing someone to cease holding a true belief, and causing someone to fail to acquire a true belief. The four cases of deception by omission parallel these four, but replace the active notion of causing with the more passive notion of allowing to occur.

Chisholm and Feehan think that the intent to deceive is necessary for lying, but it is clearly not sufficient. Many acts of intended deception—even intended linguistic deception—do not qualify as lies. According to Chisholm and Feehan, in order to lie it is necessary that one assert to someone else some proposition P, which the liar in question believes to be false (or at least believes to be not true). It thus follows that lies are a subset of the first sort of deception Chisholm and Feehan describe: actively causing someone to acquire a false belief.

Probably the most influential article on lying since Chisholm and Feehan is Thomas Carson's "The Definition of Lying," published in 2006.[3] In it he provides two examples that he thinks conclusively demonstrate that one can lie without intending to deceive. The first case he considers is that of an eyewitness to a crime who is called to court to testify as a witness, but who falsely testifies that he did not see the defendant commit the crime because he fears for his well-being if he tells the truth. The witness in this case, Carson says, may even be hopeful that his testimony does not convince the jury and that the defendant is convicted despite the false testimony. But even if the jury is deceived, Carson insists, this deception is incidental—since the intention behind the false testimony is self-preservation rather than the deception of the jury, the witness cannot be said to intend to deceive the jury. In case this version of the example is unconvincing, Carson provides a modified version: the witness knows that the whole crime, including his own witnessing of it, was caught on camera, and that the video is shown to the jury. In this case, Carson argues, the witness clearly cannot intend to, or even reasonably believe that he will, deceive anyone

3. Thomas Carson (2006), "The Definition of Lying," *Nous* 40 (2): 284–306. Carson's 2010 book *Lying and Deception* (Oxford: Oxford University Press) presents a more developed articulation of this theory that remains the same in broad strokes.

either that what he says is true or that he believes what he says. But the fearful witness still lies, Carson insists, by virtue of saying something that he knows to be false while under oath.

The second case Carson provides to support his claim that lying does not require the intent to deceive is the story of a college student who has been caught cheating on an exam, but who knows that the dean (who is overly afraid of lawsuits from unhappy students) will not punish any student for cheating who does not admit guilt. If the dean has absolute confidence in the professor who caught the student cheating, and the student knows this, then the student can have no pretensions to convince the dean of his innocence. As Carson says, the student may even take a malicious pleasure in knowing that the dean knows he's lying—but this does not change the fact that the student *is* lying. The cheater is interested in being on record as having declared his innocence, not in convincing people of his innocence; in this he is like the fearful witness.

The idea of being on record as having declared something leads Carson to focus on the notion of *warranting* as the crucial component of lying. In order to lie, he says, one must knowingly warrant the truth of something that one knows to be false. Thus, rather than a false utterance made with the intent to deceive, Carson says, a lie is a false utterance made when the speaker takes herself to be in a warranting context. A warranting context is one in which, in asserting some proposition P, one thereby provides, at least implicitly, some sort of promise or guarantee of the truth of P. So, for instance, acting and joke telling are not warranting contexts, while testifying in a court of law and reporting the news are warranting contexts. And everyday discourse, unless clear indicators to the contrary are present, is generally taken to occur in a warranting context.

Carson's arguments have so far proved to be quite influential. Some philosophers agree with his conclusion, while others think he is mistaken. But regardless of their beliefs, philosophers discussing lying after 2006 have found it imperative to respond to Carson's arguments.

In "Bald Faced Lies! Lying Without the Intent to Deceive" Roy Sorensen adds another example to the list of lies that don't involve the intent to deceive: bald-faced lies.[4] Bald-faced lies are blatant, such as denying that you are doing something to a person who can clearly see you doing precisely what you are denying. Among the many cases Sorensen considers are several examples from Åsne Seierstad's

4. Roy Sorensen (2007), "Bald-Faced Lies! Lying without the Intent to Deceive," *Pacific Philosophical Quarterly* 88 (2): 251–264.

A Hundred and One Days: A Baghdad Journal.[5] Seierstad's account depicts many people under Saddam Hussein's regime who would praise Saddam's rule in glowing terms, despite the fact that everyone involved knew that such statements were untrue and thus that such statements stood no chance of deceiving anyone. One vivid example he recounts is of Seierstad sneaking into a civilian hospital and finding a ward full of wounded soldiers. When Seierstad asks a doctor about the situation, the doctor insists that there are no soldiers in the hospital. When she asks why the patients are wearing soldiers' uniforms, he denies that he sees any uniforms.

In "Lies and Deception: An Unhappy Divorce" Jennifer Lackey argues that philosophers have been too quick to separate deception from lying.[6] While agreeing that the cases Carson and Sorensen (and others) provide are in fact cases of lying, she thinks they still involve an intention to be deceptive to the victim of the lie, even if not an intention to be deceitful toward the victim. Lackey's argument rests on a distinction between being deceitful and being deceptive: deceit is but one of several sorts of deception. This is a stipulative definition on her part, but it is one that is grounded in definitions of deception that are found in the *Oxford English Dictionary*. The sort of deception that discussions of lying have heretofore focused on is being deceitful: seeking to bring about a false belief in one's audience. But, Lackey points out, deception more generally consists merely in seeking to conceal information from someone. Deceit (i.e., paradigmatic lying) is one way to accomplish that goal, but it is not the only way. Non-deceitful lies such as those discussed by Carson and Sorensen, Lackey argues, are lies precisely because they still aim to deceive.

Philosophers who have sought to define lying have almost universally followed the Platonic strategy of identifying necessary and sufficient conditions for an utterance to qualify as a lie. But this is not the only way to approach the task of defining. Some linguists, for instance, have used prototype semantics to analyze our notions of lying. The seminal article on this front is Linda Coleman and Paul Kay's "Prototype Semantics: The English Word *Lie*."[7] Prototype semantics builds on the insight that many of the categories we operate

5. Åsne Seierstad (2004), *One Hundred and One Days: a Baghdad Journal* (London: Virago Press).

6. Jennifer Lackey (2013), "Lies and Deception: An Unhappy Divorce," *Analysis* 73 (2): 236–248.

7. Linda Coleman & Paul Kay (1981), "Prototype Semantics: The English Word *Lie*," *Language* 57 (1): 26–44.

with presume an overly simplified context for their application, and consequently when we try to apply those concepts to the vagaries and complexities of the real world, we find that it is not always entirely clear whether, or to what extent, a given case falls under a particular concept.

To see how prototype semantics works, consider the concept *bachelor*. The concept *bachelor* is based on a simplified worldview in which men want to get married, want to marry women, mostly marry at or around a certain age, and remain married throughout their lives. Given this worldview, it is understandable that a male of the relevant age who is not married would be seen as an aberration, and further that all males of the relevant age who were not married would be seen as similarly aberrant, thus warranting their own category. But the concept *bachelor*, presuming a simplified world that makes possible this unambiguous category-membership criterion, is ill-equipped to handle the complexity of the real world. If a bachelor is just an unmarried male of marriageable age, then an adult homosexual male living with a committed life partner is a bachelor; but this is not a consequence anticipated by the simplified worldview. This understanding explains why it is so difficult to say with a great deal of confidence whether the pope, or a thirty-five-year-old twice-divorced widower, is a bachelor. They are not prototypical cases, but neither are they clearly ruled out by comparison to the prototypical case.

Just as *bachelor* presumes an oversimplified world regarding issues related to marriage, Coleman and Kay point out that *lie* presumes an oversimplified world regarding issues related to human interaction and language use. It is simply not the case, they argue, that every utterance either is or is not a lie. While some utterances clearly are lies, and others clearly are not, there are some utterances for which there is no simple answer. The prototypical lie Coleman and Kay identify involves a speaker asserting some proposition P to an audience A when the following three conditions obtain: the speaker believes P to be false, P is false, and the speaker intends to deceive A in asserting P. Any utterance that clearly fulfills these three criteria will be recognized as a lie by pretty much anyone. When only a subset of these features obtains, however, people report differing intuitions about whether the utterance in question is a lie. Coleman and Kay provide experimental data to show that some think it necessary that P actually be false, while others think it only necessary that the speaker believe P to be false. Similarly, some think the intent to deceive is necessary, but others will identify as a lie an utterance that is not intended to deceive. Further, some think that intentionally deceptive but true utterances are lies, while others' assessments differ.

While it hasn't gained traction in the philosophical literature, the prototype semantics approach may prove quite useful when it comes to explaining competing intuitions with regard not only to what counts as a lie, but also to whether and when it can be okay to lie.

One philosopher who has taken an approach that is similar to what we see in prototype semantics is Frederick Siegler. In his 1966 article "Lying," Siegler seeks to clarify the concept of lying by examining six features that he takes to be present in a typical case of lying: "[T]he liar must: (1) say something, (2) intend to deceive, (3) say something which is false, (4) say something which he knows to be false, (5) believe that what he says is false, [and] (6) communicate" (128).[8] He then considers each of these features with respect to one or more problem cases, in an attempt to determine both whether the problem cases qualify as lies and the extent to which each feature is present in atypical cases of lying. Condition (1), that the liar must say something, is the only condition that he takes to be necessary for all cases of lying. This enables a differentiation between lying and non-linguistic forms of deception, such as wearing a disguise in order to be taken as someone else.

Siegler also differentiates between lying and telling a lie, as well as between each of these in the transitive and intransitive form (that is, between lying and lying to someone, between telling a lie and telling a lie to someone). The distinction between lying and telling a lie is counterintuitive, but Siegler provides powerful evidence in its favor. For all but the first of the six supposed features of lying that he considers, it is possible to come up with counterexamples. One possible conclusion from this fact is that our concept of lying is hopelessly confused and actually accomplishes nothing. Another, less radical conclusion, is that the confusion is a result of failing to distinguish two distinct concepts: that of lying, on the one hand, and telling a lie, on the other.

Identifying lies as things that are *said*, and lying as something that is *done*, he argues that it is quite possible to tell a lie without lying, as well as to lie without telling a lie. This happens, for example, when one person arranges for a second person to tell a lie to a third person. According to Siegler, the best analysis of such a case is to say that the first person lied but did not tell a lie, while the second person told a lie but did not lie.

8. Frederick Siegler (1966), "Lying," *American Philosophical Quarterly* 3 (2): 128–136.

Another reason to think there may be a distinction between lying and telling a lie is revealed by the case of a deluded deceiver. If a person intends to lie, but due to ignorance or incompetence, unintentionally says something true, it is difficult to claim that such a person has told a lie. At the same time, Siegler points out, "if a man did this regularly we would not want to exonerate him from being a liar simply because he is also a fool" (130).

Consider also, the case of a person who is hired to read the news for a radio station that, unbeknownst to the newsperson, is a propaganda machine. If he doesn't either consider the truth of what he reads or legitimately believes what he reads, it's difficult to claim that he is lying in reading the "news." But given that what he reads are lies, it is difficult not to say that he has been telling lies. So one can tell lies without lying.

Siegler's analysis has not been terribly influential, but given more recent developments in discussions of lying, there may be reason for philosophers to revisit his examples and arguments.

Is it Morally Permissible to Lie?

The question whether it is morally permissible to lie has received relatively less scrutiny over the past century than it did earlier, being generally supplanted by the question *when* it is permissible to lie. Even those who follow in the tradition of Kant tend to find his absolute prohibition to be unacceptably extreme. One possible explanation for this shift is an increase in the influence of utilitarian thought in ethical and sociopolitical discourse. Alasdair MacIntyre points out that the contemporary Anglo-American tradition includes two dominant views regarding lying: the absolutist view, according to which lying is always wrong; and the utilitarian view, according to which the presumption against lying can be overridden in the interest of greater considerations.[9] The differences between these two views of lying are important, he says, because they represent competing views about just what is wrong with lying. These competing views lead to incompatible answers to three questions: how to define *lie*, what exactly the nature of the offense is in lying, and what sorts of arguments are to be advanced in favor of the answers to the first two questions. Those who advocate absolute condemnation, he points out, tend to view

9. Alasdair MacIntyre (1994), "Truthfulness, Lies, and Moral Philosophers: What Can We Learn from Mill and Kant?," *Tanner Lectures on Human Values*, pp. 309–369, delivered at Princeton University, at: www.tannerlectures.utah.edu/_documents/a-to-z/m/macintyre_1994.pdf (consulted August 3, 2015).

lying as a betrayal of truth itself, while those who take a consequentialist perspective see the wrong in lying as connected with a violation of trust or credibility.

While the general philosophical (as well as folk) consensus seems to be that lying is not always wrong, a closely related question has come to take the place of this one in discussions of lying: whether, given the choice, it is morally preferable to mislead without outright lying than to simply lie. Those who have historically advocated an absolute prohibition on lying obviously take deception through carefully selected word choice to be preferable. Indeed, this seems to be the common folk intuition generally, as well as the default position for philosophers. One of the most influential recent articles defending this common sense view is Jonathan Adler's "Lying, Misleading, or Falsely Implicating."[10]

Adler explores several possible justifications for the intuition that lying is worse than merely misleading, including the notion that allowing someone to draw a false inference constitutes less of a breach of trust than does directly asserting a falsehood. At the same time, however, he acknowledges that a countervailing argument could be made: the liar at least can be exposed, whereas the clever misleader manages to maintain a level of deniability. From this perspective, at least the liar is more up-front about her project than is the misleader. As a result, the misleader can plausibly be understood as demonstrating a more pernicious moral character.

Despite this misgiving, however, Adler argues that a principled distinction between lying and other forms of intentional linguistic deception can be drawn and that the common intuition, while not always correct, is nonetheless correct most of the time. He provides a two-part defense of this view. First, he articulates the distinction by drawing a parallel between tact (as opposed to politeness) and misleading utterances. Tact, Adler points out, seeks to accomplish its aims by avoiding detection, while politeness seeks to accomplish very similar aims precisely by being noticed. Misleading without outright lying can, Adler argues, be understood as a mode of tactfulness.[11] A misleading utterance can be an appropriate response to an innocent but inappropriate question, in a situation where both bluntness and outright lying would be inappropriate.

10. Jonathan E. Adler (1997), "Lying, Misleading, or Falsely Implicating," *Journal of Philosophy* 94 (9): 435–452.

11. In this, Adler seems to be making a point similar to the one Hume makes in our first selection from him. See chapter 15 of this volume.

The second part of Adler's defense is to point out that we have different standards of truthfulness for assertions and for implicatures.[12] If I assert that P, my audience will likely hold me to a relatively high standard of evidence for the truth of, and thus justification for my assertion of, P. But if I assert that Q in order to generate the implicature that P, my audience's expectation is going to be that I have solid evidence for Q while the standard that I must meet for P is reduced. That is to say, the fact that I've invited my audience to draw the inference themselves has the effect of reducing my audience's demand for my ability to support the claim that P. Thus, according to Adler, if my audience draws the definite conclusion that P from my assertion that Q, even if my assertion that Q strongly implicates the truth of P, the responsibility really does lie on my audience for concluding with too much confidence the truth of P. With regard to standard norms of conversation, I have fulfilled my ethical responsibility by refraining from making the assertion that P.

In a more recent article, Alan Strudler has also defended the intuition that lying is worse than misleading.[13] While he also sees the wrong of lying as involving a breach of trust, he takes a more explicitly Kantian approach by arguing that this breach of trust undermines the integrity of the deceived to a greater extent when one lies than when one merely misleads.

While both lying and misleading constitute a breach of trust, Strudler argues, the way in which they threaten trust is different and thus the wrong involved in lying is different from the wrong involved in misleading. To illustrate this difference, Strudler draws a parallel between

12. "Implicature" is a term coined by H. P. Grice in his 1975 article "Logic and Conversation" (reprinted in his 1989 *Studies in the Way of Words*, Cambridge, MA: Harvard University Press). An implicature is something that is conventionally implied by an utterance but not logically implied by it. For instance, if I were to say to you, "I used to have a black lab named Spot," there is a conversational implication that I no longer have a black lab named Spot—for if I did, I would simply have said, "I have a black lab named Spot." But it does not logically follow: it is not incoherent for me to say, "I used to have a black lab named Spot; indeed, I still do." It would be odd to utter such a statement, but it would not be self-contradictory. So with my original statement, I did not strictly imply that I no longer have my beloved companion, but I did implicate as much. As we'll see in this section, the notion of implicature has come to play a significant role in discussions of the difference between lying and other forms of linguistic deception.

13. Alan Strudler (2010), "The Distinctive Wrong in Lying," *Ethical Theory and Moral Practice* 13 (2): 171–179.

deceiving in self-defense and using physical violence in self-defense. While circumstances can override the general social policy that dictates we not cause physical harm to others, there are nonetheless limitations on the sort of harm one can cause another in the interest of self-defense. Similarly, Strudler argues, while circumstances can dictate that it is okay to harm people by misleading them, those circumstances may not justify the particular sort of harm that lying constitutes.

Strudler points out that lying involves direct assertion, while misleading more typically involves implicature. Because of this difference, to lie is to invite (and then betray) a greater level of trust than is the case with misleading. This is because believing a person's assertion amounts to giving that person more control over one's beliefs than does believing what is implicated by that assertion. There is greater room for doubt regarding the implication, as well as for further conversation with the aim of clarifying the truth of the implicated claim. It follows, according to Strudler, that lying undermines the victim's autonomy to a greater degree than does misleading.

Recently, however, some philosophers have begun questioning the received wisdom that misleading is morally preferable to lying. Bernard Williams has challenged the idea, claiming that in cases where deception is warranted, "[S]omething is wrong if one thinks that it is more honourable to find some weasel words than to tell a lie."[14] This is just one of many points that Williams makes in *Truth and Truthfulness*, which we'll discuss more in the following section.

In "Just Go Ahead and Lie" Jennifer Saul also argues that the moral preference for merely misleading over lying is mistaken.[15] While she concedes that in some cases misleading is better than lying, she argues that these cases occur almost exclusively in such instances as misleading when under oath to avoid perjury—cases wherein the speaker's obligation is explicitly limited to making only true utterances. In other cases, she argues, there is no principled difference between lying and merely misleading.

The argument that lying is worse, Saul points out, frequently rests on the notion that the liar shoulders all of the blame for the deception, whereas the deceived shares in the blame in the case of misleading—after all, the argument goes, the deceived is the one responsible for drawing the inference from the true but misleading utterance to the false belief. This logic can be seen at work in Adler's and Strudler's

14. Bernard Williams (2002), *Truth and Truthfulness* (Princeton, NJ: Princeton University Press), p. 107.

15. Jennifer Saul (2012), "Just Go Ahead and Lie," *Analysis* 72 (1): 3–9.

arguments in favor of misleading over lying. But, Saul argues, this notion is mistaken. To show this, she compares two hypothetical mugging victims: one who is very careful about personal safety and is mugged anyway, and another who is much more reckless about personal safety and is mugged as a result. Saul argues that, while the second victim may be partially causally responsible for the mugging, it does not follow that this mugging is less bad than the first. Similarly, she argues, the fact that the deceived is partially responsible for the deception does not make misleading less bad than lying.

The other argument in favor of misleading over lying that Saul rejects finds expression in Chisholm and Feehan's article, "The Intent to Deceive," discussed above. According to that account, which is also operant in Adler's and Strudler's discussions, we have a right to expect truth in what people say in a way that we don't with regard to what they implicate. Saul's argument is that this notion misconceives the way conversational implicature works. As Grice makes clear in his own work on conversational implicature, a key feature of conversational implicatures is that it is *necessary* to take them to be true in order to make sense of the speaker's utterance within the conversational context. Given that believing conversational implicatures to be true is not optional, we seem to be perfectly within our rights in taking what a person implicates to be true.[16]

Two articles followed in quick succession from Saul's, published in the same journal: Jonathan Webber's "Liar!" and Clea F. Rees' "Better Lie!"[17] Webber argues against Saul's thesis, on the grounds that lying damages the liar's credibility more thoroughly than does misleading. In fact, he argues, being caught misleading but refusing to lie can actually increase one's credibility with regard to straightforward assertions, whereas being caught in a lie damages one's credibility both with regard to implications and with regard to what is asserted. Rees, on the other hand, defends Saul's position, but goes beyond it to argue

16. Saul's follow-up book, *Lying, Misleading and What Is Said*, includes an expanded discussion of morality and the lying-misleading distinction. Here, while she still maintains that there is no significant moral distinction between lying and merely misleading, she argues that the choice whether to mislead or to lie outright may provide insight into the moral character of the deceiver. Briefly, a person's choice to lie when they could have misled without lying may reveal a character flaw, given the popular (if false) view that lying is worse than misleading. See Jennifer Saul (2012), *Lying, Misleading and What Is Said* (Oxford: Oxford University Press).

17. Jonathan Webber (2013), "Liar!" *Analysis* 73 (4): 651–659; Clea F. Rees (2014), "Better Lie!" *Analysis* 74 (1): 59–64.

that lying is actually better than misleading in most cases. Because the one who misleads relies on the deceived to draw the conclusion that the deceiver is unwilling to say, Rees points out, the misleader uses the deceived to a greater extent than does the liar. From a Kantian perspective, then, the misleader may in fact be undermining the autonomy of the deceived to a greater extent than does the liar. One way to think of Rees' distinction is by way of the difference between a thief and a con artist. The thief steals your money; the con artist convinces you to give it to her. There seems to be a legitimate argument that the con artist is more morally blameworthy than the thief.

While the notion of trust has arisen a few times earlier in this volume, discussions of lying in the Western philosophical tradition have not historically been concerned to a great extent with issues of trust. All of the articles in this section, however, have acknowledged the important role that trust plays in the ethics of lying. Paul Faulkner's article "What Is Wrong with Lying?" does this even more explicitly.[18] According to Faulkner, the sort of trust that is involved in linguistic communication entails being knowingly dependent on another person to tell the truth, and expecting that person's awareness of this dependence to motivate him or her to tell the truth. This sort of trust, which he calls "affective trust," Faulkner argues can actually generate reasons for believing what one is told. It is this insight that provides an explanation of just what is wrong with the sort of manipulation that occurs in lying.

Faulkner's argument points toward an important, and as yet under-explored, overlap between the philosophy of lying and the epistemology of testimony. As the articles we have discussed in this section indicate, questions of trust are an important and increasingly prevalent issue in the ethics of lying. Trust is also a central issue within the philosophy of testimony, a field that itself has experienced significant growth within the last few decades. It would take us too far afield to survey the literature on testimony here, but two of the most important recent works on the topic are *Learning From Words* by Jennifer Lackey and *Knowing From Words*, edited by B. K. Matilal and Arindam Chakrabarti.[19] This intersection could be a fruitful area for future scholarship.

18. Paul Faulkner (2007), "What Is Wrong with Lying?" *Philosophy and Phenomenological Research* 75 (3): 535–557.

19. Jennifer Lackey (2008), *Learning From Words: Testimony as a Source of Knowledge* (Oxford: Oxford University Press); B. K. Matilal and Arindam Chakrabarti, eds. (1994), *Knowing From Words: Western and Indian Philosophical Analysis of Understanding and Testimony* (Dordrecht: Kluwer Publishers).

What Is the Value of Truthfulness?

If it is accepted that lying is at least sometimes permissible, the question of *when* naturally arises. Any attempt to answer this question is quickly going to lead to the related question of what the value of truth is: why, precisely, do we value truth and truth-speakers, and ought we to value them as we do? These are the sorts of questions that exercised Nietzsche (see chapter 19 of this volume), but they have been less explored in recent Anglo-American philosophy. This is probably due in part to the so-called "linguistic turn" of the early twentieth century, following which truth has been treated almost exclusively as a semantic concept. From this perspective, the important truth-bearers are sentences or the propositions they express. This approach renders truth either primarily or exclusively the realm of epistemology. The first questions to answer are what it means for something to be true and which statements, sentences, or propositions qualify. Such ethical questions as what we should say, or whether to utter only true sentences, are to be dealt with only much later—if at all.

One interesting inquiry that calls into question this perspective is Harry Frankfurt's article-length book *On Bullshit*.[20] In it Frankfurt points out that the value of truthfulness might not lie in its opposition to falsity. The liar (i.e., one who intentionally speaks falsely), Frankfurt points out, still respects the truth. Insofar as the liar wishes to be taken to be telling the truth, any lies she tells must be informed by the truth—what is said must seem true in order for the lie to have any significant chance of succeeding as a lie. And an attempt to make one's speech seem true is just as much a truth-responsive enterprise as is an attempt to make one's speech actually be true. Worse than the liar, then, is the bullshitter. Unlike the liar, the bullshitter is disinterested in truth entirely. The bullshitter, Frankfurt argues, is instead interested in how he will be perceived by others. Politicians are frequently seen as engaged in bullshit in this sense: interested in poll numbers, approval ratings, and sticking to the party's accepted talking points in order to shape the narrative, rather than telling the truth (or even lying) with conviction. Because such people are more interested in framing the narrative and in cultivating their image, Frankfurt argues that they are actually more opposed to the truth than are liars. It is the bullshitter, rather than the liar, who denies the value of truth.

20. Harry Frankfurt (2005), *On Bullshit* (Princeton, NJ: Princeton University Press).

Another approach to the value of truthfulness can be found in Bernard Williams' *Truth and Truthfulness*.[21] Williams identifies a concern with our attitudes toward truth and truthfulness. The concern he sees is that the more staunchly we demand truth, the more suspicious we are with regard to whether what we are told or have been told is true—in short, the more we examine our beliefs for proof that they are true—the less confident we become that there is such a thing as objective truth to begin with. This tension is problematic: how can the desire for truthfulness survive in the face of pervasive doubt with regard to the existence of truth?

The answer that Williams suggests is that truthfulness may not derive its value from truth, but rather that the two are mutually implicated. He points out that truthfulness can exist only in dependence on two particular character traits, which he calls the "Virtues of Truth": Accuracy and Sincerity. Truthfulness, that is, is a matter both of endeavoring to have true beliefs and of striving to make sure that what one says matches up to one's beliefs. Accuracy and Sincerity are important traits for members of any society to possess: they render possible the epistemic division of labor that so pervades human interaction. In fact, these traits are so central to human behavior that they actually make the truth that they seek to track intrinsically valuable.

It does not take much reflection for a person to realize that, if having true beliefs is valuable, then keeping the truth from others can be valuable as well. So while it is beneficial for a society to have members who are truthful, it is not always beneficial for the individual who demonstrates said truthfulness. But once the question of whether to be truthful arises, according to Williams, the instrumental value of truthfulness is insufficient to answer the question, "Why be truthful here and now?" One who believes truthfulness to be only instrumentally valuable will be like the rule-utilitarian who finds himself in a circumstance wherein utility will be maximized by violating a generally utility-maximizing rule.[22] According to Williams, people who abide by truthfulness on rule-utilitarian grounds have no reason to

21. Williams, *Truth and Truthfulness*.

22. Utilitarianism is the ethical theory according to which moral rightness is calculated in terms of whatever maximizes the greatest utility (pleasure, happiness, preference satisfaction, etc.) for the greatest number of people overall. *Rule*-utilitarianism is one version of such a theory, wherein overall utility is determined through the application of general rules. Thus, a rule might still promote overall utility, even if a particular instance that would fall under that rule might not.

be truthful when not doing so would be more valuable, and thus are not actually motivated by the virtue of truthfulness. People will only tell the truth in such circumstances if they see truth as valuable for its own sake. But what more would there be to truth being intrinsically valuable than that people take it to be so—especially if we accept that the only truth we can talk about is truth from the human perspective?

The more complex notions of the value of truthfulness that we see indicated by Frankfurt's and Williams' analyses point to an interesting potential critique of the linguistic turn within analytic philosophy. The concern is that the semantic notion of truth that has been the focus for so long may be too insipid to accomplish what we ultimately want truth to do. It may be important to recall that, while facts and propositions can be true, so can carpenter's squares, tuning forks, and wheels. What "true" connotes in this usage is the notion of reliability, of not deviating from a norm. And this, in turn, helps us to understand what is meant when we speak of a true friend. A true friend is most definitely not someone who always and only tells the truth: a true friend is a particularly reliable or trustworthy friend. A person can be guided by the truth not simply in believing that what one says should be true, but also in believing that one should remain true to oneself and to others. If truthfulness is an ethical notion, a complex social-epistemic virtue along the lines of what Williams has indicated, then truth itself may in fact be an irreducibly ethical notion as well. What this would mean for analyses of lying and truthfulness seems worthy of exploration.

Now that you've read and reflected on the recent developments summarized in this chapter, think about the following questions:

1. Think of your own original examples of situations that would qualify as "warranting contexts" in Carson's sense. What, if anything, makes these contexts special or gives them the property of requiring warranting? What happens if or when different contexts come into conflict or otherwise overlap?
2. Select a prominent example of a lie that has been articulated in one of the earlier, historical selections in this volume and compare it to the views of modern thinkers discussed in this chapter. By whose criteria or definition—e.g., Chisholm and Feehan's, Carson's, Lackey's, or Siegler's—would or would it not still technically qualify as a lie?
3. Come up with a concrete example (either your own or something from one of the earlier selections) that would fit

Adler's distinction between lying via an assertion and lying via conversational implicature. Do you agree with his claim that different ethical standards govern these two ways of communicating, at least in the case of your example?

4. Compare and contrast one of the philosophers discussed in this chapter with one of the historical thinkers from the earlier selections. In general, in what ways has the contemporary theoretic landscape changed from earlier eras and contexts? In the same way that testimony (something prominent in many of the non-Western selections from this volume) is beginning to enjoy newfound attention, can you identify another theme, concept, or distinction of an earlier selection from which contemporary thinking could benefit?

PRONUNCIATION GUIDE

Sanskrit

A guide to pronunciation of Sanskrit vowels is included below. Pronunciation of consonants is generally the same as in English, with the following exceptions: 'g' is always hard, as in 'give'; 'c' is always pronounced 'ch'; 'ś' and 'ṣ' are both pronounced roughly like 'sh'; 'ṛ' is a vocalic r, pronounced roughly like the 'ri' in the word 'crib'; other consonants transcribed with dots beneath them (ḍ, ṭ, ṇ) are retroflex versions of the roman letter, articulated with the tip of the tongue on the roof of the mouth.

Sanskrit Vowels:

Pronounce this	As here
a	f**u**n
ā	f**aw**n
i	s**i**ck
ī	s**ee**k
u	g**oo**d
ū	f**oo**d
e	l**e**g
ai	l**i**ke
o	b**o**th
au	c**ow**

Chinese

All translations in this volume follow the *pinyin* romanization system. Chinese is a *tonal* language in that the meaning of a word changes depending on whether the voice rises, falls, stays at a flat high tone, or dips low before rising. We have not rendered the specific tones of transliterated Chinese words in the selections in this volume, but merely point out that the reader should be aware that tones could make essential differences in meaning. Letters generally follow their roman equivalents, with the following caveats:

Pronounce this	As here
a	f**aw**n
ai	**eye**
ao	c**ow**
e	f**u**n
i	s**ee**k
ia	**ye**s
iu	**yo**
o	b**o**th
ou	g**o**
u	p**u**t
c	ha**ts**
q	**ch**in
x	**sh**in
zh	**j**ump
zi	wor**ds**

SOURCES & PERMISSIONS

Chapter 1: From Augustine, *The Enchiridion*, translated by J. F. Shaw. (Edinburgh: T&T Clark, 1892.)

Chapter 1: From Augustine, *On Lying*, translated by H. Browne. In *Nicene and Post-Nicene Fathers of the Christian Church*. Ed. Philip Schaff. Vol. 3. (Buffalo, NY: Christian Literature Publishing Co., 1887.) This translation has been modified for readability.

Chapter 2: From Hugo Grotius, *The Law of War and Peace*, translated by Francis W. Kelsey. (Oxford: Clarendon Press, 1925.) This translation has been modified for readability.

Chapter 3: From Aristotle, *Nicomachean Ethics*, translated by C. D. C. Reeve. (Indianapolis: Hackett Publishing Co., 2014.) Reprinted by permission of the publisher.

Chapter 3: From Aristotle, *Rhetoric*, translated by W. Rhys Roberts. In *Rhetorica: The Works of Aristotle*, Vol. 11. (Oxford: Clarendon Press, 1924.)

Chapter 4: From *The Mahābhārata*, translated by Kisari Mohan Ganguli, 1896. The translation has been modified for readability.

Chapter 5: From *Analects: With Selections from Traditional Commentaries*, translated by Edward Slingerland. (Indianapolis: Hackett Publishing Co., 2003.) Reprinted by permission of the publisher.

Chapter 5: From *Mengzi: With Selections from Traditional Commentaries*, translated by Bryan W. Van Norden. (Indianapolis: Hackett Publishing Co., 2008.) Reprinted by permission of the publisher.

Chapter 6: From Immanuel Kant, *Grounding for the Metaphysics of Morals*, translated by James W. Ellington. (Indianapolis: Hackett Publishing Co., 1993.) Reprinted by permission of the publisher.

Chapter 6: From Immanuel Kant, "On a Supposed Right to Lie from Philanthropic Concerns," translated by James W. Ellington. In *Grounding for the Metaphysics of Morals with On a Supposed Right to Lie Because of Philanthropic Concerns*, 3rd edition. (Indianapolis: Hackett Publishing Co., 1993.) Reprinted by permission of the publisher.

Chapter 6: From Immanuel Kant, *The Metaphysics of Morals*, translated and edited by Mary Gregor. Copyright © 1996 Cambridge University Press. Reprinted with the permission of Cambridge University Press.

Chapter 6: From Immanuel Kant, *Lectures on Ethics*, translated by Peter Heath. Peter Heath and J. B. Schneewind, editors. Copyright © 1997 Cambridge University Press. Reprinted with the permission of Cambridge University Press.

Chapter 7: From *The Mahābhārata*, translated by Kisari Mohan Ganguli, 1896. The translation has been modified for readability.

Chapter 8: From Plato, *Gorgias*, translated by Donald J. Zeyl. (Indianapolis: Hackett Publishing Co., 1987.) Reprinted by permission of the publisher.

Chapter 9: From Plato, *Republic*, translated by G. M. A. Grube, revised by C. D. C. Reeve. (Indianapolis: Hackett Publishing Co., 1992.) Reprinted by permission of the publisher.

Chapter 10: From Sun Tzu [Sunzi], *Master Sun's Art of War*, translated by Philip Ivanhoe. (Indianapolis: Hackett Publishing Co., 2011). Reprinted by permission of the publisher.

Chapter 10: From *Han Feizi: Basic Writings*, translated by Burton Watson. © 2003 Columbia University Press. Reprinted with permission of the publisher.

Chapter 11: From *Summa Theologiae*, by Saint Thomas Aquinas. Translated by the Fathers of the English Dominican Province, 1947. The translation has been modified for readability.

Chapter 12: From *Early Buddhist Discourses*, translated and edited by John J. Holder. (Indianapolis: Hackett Publishing Co., 2006.) Reprinted by permission of the publisher.

Chapter 13: From *The Lotus Sutra*, translated by Burton Watson. Copyright © 1994 Columbia University Press. Reprinted with permission of the publisher. Pages 56–60.

Chapter 14: From Thomas Hobbes, *Leviathan*, edited by Edwin Curley. (Indianapolis: Hackett Publishing Co., 1994.) Reprinted by permission of the publisher.

Chapter 15: From David Hume, *Moral Philosophy*, edited by Geoffrey Sayre-McCord. (Indianapolis: Hackett Publishing Co., 2006.) Reprinted by permission of the publisher.

Chapter 16: From John Locke, *An Essay Concerning Human Understanding*, edited by Kenneth P. Winkler. (Indianapolis: Hackett Publishing Co., 1996.) Reprinted by permission of the publisher.

Chapter 16: From Francis Bacon, *The Essays of Francis Bacon*, edited by Mary Augusta Scott. (New York: Charles Scribner's Sons, 1908.)

Chapter 17: From *The Mahābhārata*, translated by Kisari Mohan Ganguli, 1896. Book XII section CLXII. The translation has been modified for readability.

Chapter 18: From *Early Buddhist Discourses*, translated and edited by John J. Holder. (Indianapolis: Hackett Publishing Co., 2006.) Reprinted by permission of the publisher.

Chapter 19: From Friedrich Nietzsche, *The Gay Science*, translated by Josefine Nauckhoff and Adrian Del Caro. Copyright © 2001 Cambridge University Press. Reprinted with the permission of Cambridge University Press.

Chapter 19: From Friedrich Nietzsche, *The Birth of Tragedy and Other Writings*, translated by Ronald Speirs. Raymond Geuss and Ronald Speirs, editors. Copyright © 1999 Cambridge University Press. Reprinted with permission of Cambridge University Press.